The Uncrowned King

Jan Lindrum

The Uncrowned King

Jan Lindrum

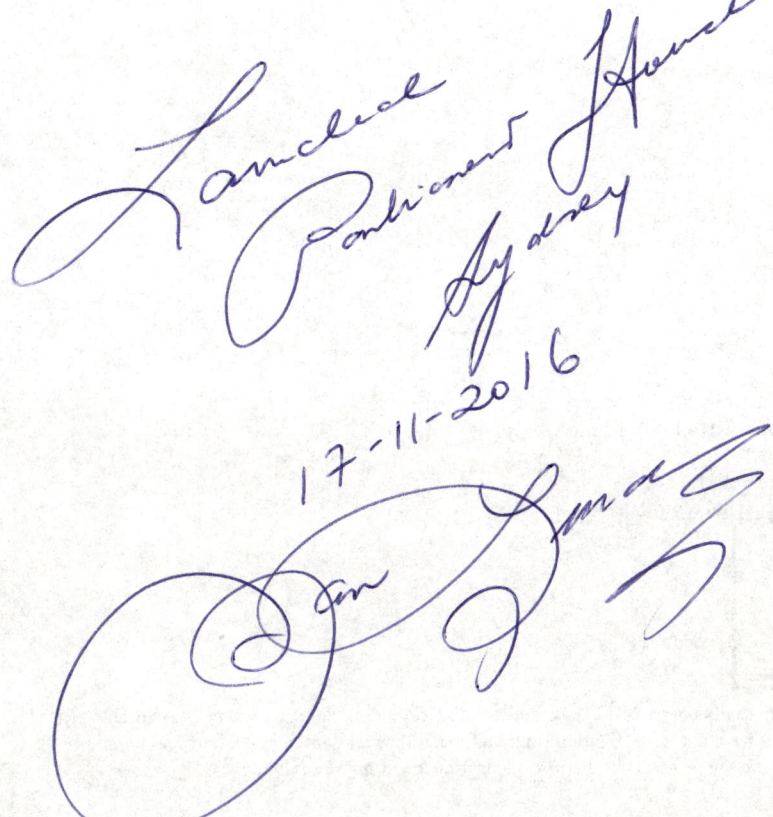

The Uncrowned King

Copyright © 2016 Janne (Jan) Clara Lindrum

All rights reserved under conditions described in the Copyright Act 1968 of Australia. No part of this book may be reproduced, stored, or transmitted by any means - whether auditory, graphic, mechanical, or electronic - without written permission of both publisher and author, except in the case of brief excerpts used in critical articles and reviews. Unauthorized reproduction of any part of this work is illegal and is punishable by law. Under the Copyright Act of 1968 It is a fair dealing to make a reproduction for the purposes of research or study, of one or more articles on the same subject in a periodical publication, or, in the case of any other work, of a reasonable portion of a work. In the case of a published work in hardcopy form that is not less than 10 pages and is not an artistic work, 10% of the number of pages, or one chapter, is a reasonable portion.

National Library of Australia Cataloguing-in-Publication Entry

    Creator: Janne (Jan) Clara Lindrum

    Title: The Uncrowned King

    Genre: Biography

    Country of Authorship: Australia

    Publisher: Primrose Hall Publishing Group

    ISBN: 978-1-326-80911-9 (Hard Cover)

    ISBN: 978-1-326-81685-8 (Soft Cover)

First Published in 2016
by the Primrose Hall Publishing Group
London (UK)
Sydney (Australia)
www.primrosehall.com

Every effort has been made to trace and acknowledge copyright. However, should any infringement have occurred, the publisher and the author tenders their apology and invite the copyright owner to contact them so the infringement may be remedied.

Dedication

I dedicate *The Uncrowned King* to my grandmother Clara (Violet) Lindrum; my father Horace Lindrum; my mother Joy Lindrum (born White), whose tireless efforts in preserving the Lindrum record made this story possible; my incredible children Michael, Robert and Samantha; my sister Tammy, my beautiful grandchildren Matthew James and Summer Cate; and my husband Robert. Without their love and support this work would not have been possible.

Also, to the good souls in the acknowledgements who journeyed with me on this pilgrimage and to the men and women in the engine-room of nations across the globe who, through thick and thin, keep our world spinning even when the sphere is struck on its retarded side.

God bless you all

TM

The Uncrowned King is my first story. It is an intensely human story If there is a message in this story, it is simple. We are passengers on a bullet train travelling in the same direction in a world that was, once upon a time, a veritable paradise.

Jan

The legendary Lindrums who conquered the world of snooker

Jan Lindrum combines a daughter's affection with a scholar's detachment in writing about her famous father Horace Lindrum, a leading member of the world's most remarkable family of snooker and billiards champions.

The Uncrowned King depicts other renowned Lindrums, including Frederick and Walter, and tells of the generations of expert Lindrum billiardists who preceded them, first in Germany and then in Australia.

There were, of course, not only the men who played the games but the capable and loyal Lindrum women who managed, organised, planned, supported and kept the whole demanding show on the road for many decades. As well, they ran the world-famous Lindrum's billiard rooms in Melbourne and Sydney, where the sport's elite gathered and competed.

We read about the arcane world of professional snooker, which calls for the highest levels of self-discipline, skill, strategy, endurance and artistry. Added for flavour is a dash of showmanship as Horace performed the dazzling trick shots that delighted audiences.

The author has preserved for present and future readers a significant slice of sporting history that transcends the limits of sport. She gives readers new insights into the social history of the nation in the early 20th century, between the wars and after 1945.

Ms Lindrum introduces us to colourful Australian characters and a way of life that can seem simpler, clearer and more distinctive than our much more diffuse and cosmopolitan contemporary mode. Through many photographs, illustrations and memorabilia, the book evokes a nostalgic twinge for a time that has passed.

In this absorbing tale, meticulous research and imaginative writing bring to vivid life a fascinating family whose wizardry with the cue is not likely to be seen again.

John Carrick, editor

Author's Reflection

The Uncrowned King
by
Janne Clara Lindrum

I grew up in the swinging sixties watching Johnny O'Keefe's "Sing, Sing, Sing", the Mickey Mouse Club and, later, the horror of the Vietnam War.

In those and subsequent chapters of my life I was completely oblivious to the story standing, waiting for me on the doorstep. I can't describe the awakening to you for the experience was and continues to be a painful one. It wasn't simply a matter of some bell going off in my head. It was more like a giant Cyclops ramming my cerebral cortex with a ruddy big club. My life was nearly gone and I hadn't started my life's work.

So much to do.

So little time to do it.

To tell my father's story was never going to be an easy task. I had to 'trace the river back to its countless sources, in order to capture the secret of all the contradictions, all the eddies that make up a single being'[1] and I had to be prepared for the "unexpected".

In the beginning I thought: "Once I complete the Epilogue, *The Uncrowned King* will be finished." I have come to the realisation, through the process of writing this intensely human story, that my journey has only just started.

There is a lot more to be written into history.

---

[1] Francois Mauriac, *Vie de Jean Racine* (The life of Jean Racine)

Contents

DEDICATION	5
THE LEGENDARY LINDRUMS WHO CONQUERED THE WORLD OF SNOOKER	7
AUTHOR'S REFLECTION	8
PROLOGUE	10
1. IN THE FOOTSTEPS OF THE OTHER	18
2 HORACE'S STAR IN THE ASCENDANT	34
3 CLARA'S STORY	53
4 THE REAL MCCOY	79
5 EVERYTHING'S GOING TO BE BONZA!	108
6 JOY'S JOURNEY	122
7 IT'S ALL IN THE STARS…	142
8 THE EYES HAVE IT…	155
9 TWO SIDES OF THE SAME PENNY	185
EPILOGUE	233
AUTHOR'S BIOGRAPHY	241
ACKNOWLEDGEMENTS	242

Prologue

A 1998 article in *The Australian Financial Review* reported: "Billiard legend inspires theme for new chain: Mr David Marriner will launch a chain of boutique hotels and resorts around the country, named after world champion Australian billiards legend Walter Lindrum...the Lindrum hotel chain will incorporate six to eight hotels and eco-tourism lodges."[2]

The media release, one of several releases issued by a private company,[3] related specifically to the proposed redevelopment of the News Limited building at 26 Flinders Street at the corner of Spring Street, Melbourne, opposite the pathway down to the Melbourne Cricket Ground.

My mother and I were taken aback that someone would try to use the Lindrum family name and history on a commercial development without consultation with the family or their consent. We were concerned about an apparent attempt to sever links in a family chain through the focus on a solitary champion, and the conspicuous silence about the achievements of the Lindrum family as a whole.

I was and remain the registered owner of most of the intellectual property protecting the Lindrum name. The only trademark I had not yet registered was the hotel mark.

During the Christmas–December–January holiday break, when most legal offices are closed the developer lodged an application to IP Australia for the trademark in the hotel class. When I became aware that the application had been lodged, I tried to contact the developer but he refused to speak to me. I was eventually able to speak with the developer's project manager and, sometime later, with the developer's solicitor, Ian Callinan. I flew to Melbourne to meet Mr Callinan at the law firm Freehills. He was acting for the developer on intellectual property matters. My effort was met with arrogance and disdain and it was obvious that the developer was going to proceed without regard to our feelings. At no time did Mr Callinan disclose to me that his firm acted for Cbus [4] or that Cbus was involved in the matter. On the contrary, he led me to believe that Staged Developments Pty Limited was the owner of the land on which the Lindrum Hotel was to be developed.

The original Lindrum's billiard room in Melbourne (1921–1973) was in Flinders Lane; it closed prior to my father's death in 1974, due to demolition of the premises, touted as making way for progress.

At my father's funeral wake, my second cousin Irene (Dolly) May Ellis (born Dunn)[5] requested permission to use the Lindrum name to re-establish a Lindrum billiard room because her husband, a ship's engineer, was drinking heavily and she wanted to get him off the ships. My mother gave her consent. Dolly ran Lindrum's in the News Limited building for about nine years and News Limited journalists were regular customers. The business closed before the media announcement about the proposed new Lindrum Hotel.

After our several approaches to the developer and his solicitor, and our subsequent approaches to IP Australia had failed my mother, my eldest son (then a 23-year-old law

---

[2] Michael Cave, "Hotels take their cue: billiard legend inspires theme for new chain'", *The Australian Financial Review*, 14 January 1998, 21
  Kylie Hanson, "Lindrum Hotel ball roll", *The Herald Sun*, 14 January 1998, 6
[3] Staged Developments Pty Ltd, Directors David and Elaine Marriner. The Company subsequently changed its name to Australian Super Developments Pty Ltd.
[4] Construction and Building Unions Superannuation is one of Australia's largest public offer Industry Superannuation funds
[5] Irene May Dunn changed her name by Deed Poll to Lindrum in 1966

student) and I started legal proceedings against the developer in the Federal Court of Australia under Section 52 of the Trade Practices Act alleging false and misleading conduct. We argued that the public would believe that the family owned or had endorsed the hotel. We also objected to the registration of the trademark

We could not understand why IP Australia had accepted the application to register the hotel mark, given the organisation's stated view that:

> "If your application to register a trademark is identical to a mark already registered in other classes, or your application is likely to mislead people into believing the mark is associated with another party/mark, then you should rethink your application."

After the proceedings had started, I returned home one afternoon with my two youngest children (then aged 7 and 9) to find the message light flashing on the telephone answering machine. The message, from a person unknown, was this:

> "Miss Lindrum, we have a special for you. Just for the month of August, we can sever your right arm and then your left, painlessly and soundlessly, for only $500."

A few days later, a second message offered to sever my legs for the same price. I know this might sound like a crime novel, but it did happen. I sent the messages to the Federal Police in Melbourne for investigation, to no avail.

Following further threats to my broader family, I reluctantly settled the matter. I have never forgiven myself for doing so, but I acknowledge that, at the time I made the decision to settle, I was living in a state of complete anxiety fearing harm to my beloved family. My feelings of anxiety were further reinforced by threats such as this: "If you lose these proceedings your mother will lose her home and we will bankrupt your son so he never receives his law degree."

Looking back, I probably deserve the white feather.[6] I should have tackled the corporate bullies head on. I tried hard to get leading politicians to hear our protestations; I argued the significance of the Lindrum history and the reality that a family history belongs to a family; I proposed that it was for the family to make decisions on how its history is used; but the leaders of that time were deaf to my protestations. Interestingly, the establishment later acted – by special favour – to protect the Bradman name.

Under the terms of settlement, the hotel trademark was returnable to the family in the event that Staged Developments no longer wished to use the mark.

In 2008, the hotel was put up for sale. I made contact with the selling agent, informing the principal that the hotel trademark was returnable to the Lindrum family. My advice was ignored. I also met with a director of the company that became the new owner of the hotel. The meeting took place two days before the settlement of the company's acquisition. I had made a number of attempts to meet this director before the company exchanged contracts but was informed that the director I needed to see was away in South Africa. At the meeting I learned that the director was aware of the obligation to return the trademark to the Lindrum family. The vendor Cbus had annexed a copy of the settlement deed to the contract for sale, thus evoking the caveat emptor (buyer beware) principle.

Mr Magid asked:

"How much money do you want?" I responded:

"I don't want any money, I want the assignment of the trademark." He ignored my request and the conveyance proceeded to settlement.

---

[6] The badge of the coward

The new owner has continued to trade as the Lindrum Hotel and to promote the story of just one member of the Lindrum family, namely my great-uncle Walter Lindrum. My father Horace, another international billiards and snooker champion, and other prominent champions in the family, have been omitted from the record of this establishment, which exploits the Lindrum name, but has not even consulted with the Lindrum family or traded with us in accord with the terms of the settlement deed. Indeed, because of our stand against this hotel development, I believe that my father's side of the family has been shunned by the Melbourne establishment and by sections of Australia's higher sporting echelons.

For instance, in 1998, the Echo Foundation in Melbourne announced a memorial dinner at the Melbourne Tennis Club to celebrate my great-uncle Walter's centenary. I sent a cheque for $2,200.00 so that our family could attend the dinner. The cheque was returned with a letter saying the dinner had been cancelled. That was untrue. Prime Minister Hawke, prominent radio commentator Alan Jones and Australian champion snooker player Eddie Charlton all attended the dinner.

Subsequently, I have made several attempts to correct misrepresentations of the Lindrum family history. Curators at the National Sports Museum have promised to 'pull up the file', but nothing has happened. A request to *The Australian Dictionary of Biography* to amend the entry on the Lindrums by correcting errors and including Horace Lindrum in his own right were met with "show us your evidence." To which I responded, "show me your homework or research." I have received no response to that request.

In recent times I forwarded a hard copy of my manuscript and dissertation to the National Library of Australia. I expected that the library would commission its researchers to remedy errors in sporting texts published by the library, but I was told that the library does not correct its mistakes. Thus, wrong history remains on the record for public consumption.

On 10 March 2008, Melbourne-based Domain reporter Marc Pallisco reported:

> The former billiard centre – built by the family of world famous billiard champion Walter Lindrum in the 1920s.
>
> [The Lindrum family did not built a billiard room.
> My great-grandfather leased premises in Flinders Lane.]
>
> The former billiard centre will be sold next month – in a deal **expected to pot owner Cbus around $20 million.**
>
> Now branded "Hotel Lindrum," the five-level brick building at 26 Flinders Street, near the corner of Spring Street, was built at the peak of Lindrum's multi-award-winning career.
>
> [The building was built when the Lindrum name was dominant in the market place. The brand was dominant due to the efforts of the family as a whole.]
> Fund manager and developer Cbus inherited the Hotel Lindrum after it split with business partner, private investor David Marriner in 1999. [7]

Cbus did not "inherit" the Hotel Lindrum.

Cbus was the owner of the lands upon which the Hotel Lindrum was constructed. But there is no denying the split with David Marriner.

---

[7] Marc Pallisco, property reporter for the Fairfax property site *Domain* in www.realestatesource.com.au/hotel-lindrum-to-be-sold.html

I believe that the split with David Marriner was most likely a direct consequence of the proceedings instituted by my mother, my eldest son and myself. Those proceedings probably delayed Cbus's plans to develop the hotel.

Curiously, at the time of the sale of the property in 2008 and, despite the alleged split, Staged Developments was still the registered owner of the Lindrum hotel trademark. An application to IP Australia lodged by Cbus via its solicitors, Freehills, claiming common-law rights to the trademark on the basis that Cbus had used the mark for 10 years was withdrawn after I wrote to Cbus requesting the return of the trademark in accordance with the settlement deed between Lindrum and Staged Developments.

Cbus replied: "This matter was settled some time ago."'

The matter was never settled. A contract is only binding if parties to the transaction are fully and properly informed. That is the law as I know it.

Cbus used Staged Developments as a smokescreen. We had no knowledge of their part in the plot until some time later.

In an affidavit to the Federal Court, Staged Developments, via its solicitors, Freehills, declared itself the owner of the land on which the hotel was to be developed.

Media releases, including a release featuring Victorian Premier Jeff Kennett turning the first sod, also referred to Staged Developments as the owner and developer of the lands. That was not true.

After receiving my letter, Cbus withdrew its application to IP Australia and changed solicitors. Staged Developments Pty Limited changed its name to Australian Super Developments Pty Limited which became a member of Cbus for the first time.

One of the tragic consequences of the failure of these entities to act within sound ethical, moral and legal frameworks is that there was no spare money for our mother to take a holiday every year while she was still able to do so. Nor were there sufficient funds to enable her to remain in her own home when she became too frail to do so without full-time nursing assistance. Yet she had done so much for her adopted nation, singing its praises across the globe at her husband's side for 24 years and meticulously preserving Lindrum history. The $10,000.00 per annum license fee we requested for use of the Lindrum name, on terms that would protect the name and history for the family and for the nation was a small request in the big scheme of things.

Another tragic consequence is the deliberate burial of the Lindrum family history, which is a unique part of Australia's national story.

The Uncrowned King is a daughter's attempt to walk from behind her father's shadow to champion a fascinating and intriguing story.

It is also an attempt to turn the tide, swing the pendulum or, as a leading professor has put it, "slow the decay of our society." [8] The reasons for societal collapse are many, but the primary causes are corrupt, unethical and immoral practices, intellectual ineptitude, rapacious greed, disregard for the environment, disrespect for the past and disregard for the feelings and rights of other people (breaches of the dignity of personhood principle). To disrespect the past is to disregard the self as the self is rooted in history. To disrespect the rights of other people is to commit a crime against humanity; others, for example, are entitled to hear and know and comprehend the truth. To keep the truth from others is to strip them of their right to the truth. When that happens, the consequences can affect one person, a series of people, a nation, and, in some circumstances, can extend to the entire global population.

---

[8] Leadership Professor Lin Grier in discussion with Janne Lindrum Austinmer (a northern suburb of Wollongong in New South Wales), 2014

Change now stands as a bailiff on our doorstep. This moment in history might represent our only chance (my generation's last chance) to make a difference. We could leave a meaningful and purposeful legacy to our beneficiaries by the simple act of thinking about how our actions impact on others and admitting our mistakes and making amends. Only then can we be truly human.

Sydney Showground, April 1974

They call him maestro, magician, the man with the golden cue. At 62 he is still the consummate entertainer. A lifetime of practice has given him exquisite control of the audience, has set him apart from the rest. Four years ago, on this same spot, I watched him record his thousandth century with a break of 133. The headline read: "At 58, Horace Lindrum remains king of the table." If you are like me, potting one ball is difficult. We do not have a hope of getting anywhere near a century. I come regularly to watch, to support, to admire.

Memories return of a tiny five-foot-four giant of the green cloth with a mercurial smile who has been bringing happiness to people across the globe for a little over 50 years.

"May I carry your cue case, Dad?"

Off we go, walking side-by-side across the car park, talking about this and that.

Today I am forced to crane my neck to see over 500 heads. Usually I manage to negotiate a position at the front, but not this morning. Fortunately, there are stands and I push my face into a tiny hole between the bony shoulders of those in front of me. At 10.00 am sharp, dad goes to the table. He has two of the most beautiful hands I have ever seen: smaller than Rachmaninov's, bigger than Elton John's.

He tells the audience:

"At sometime or other, especially in your childhood, one or two of you have probably enjoyed an egg for breakfast."

He holds up an egg. "This is the un-cracked variety! Let's see if we can spin it so it runs along the side cushion to pot the red in the top right hand corner."

He points to the red ball, top table, right.

"Then let's see if we can make it travel along the top cushion to pot the red on the left."

We all laugh. I have seen Horace in action many times and these words always get the same reaction. You see, to the ordinary man, the feat he is attempting with his double-jointed hands looks impossible. One British snooker player, Alex Higgins, if my memory serves me correctly, refused to believe the stories of Horace's trick-shot wizardry. When he finally got to see the master in action, he proclaimed him as others had proclaimed him, "The greatest exhibition player of all time". Certainly, in my lifetime there has never been another Horace Lindrum, although there were other Lindrums, all of them great. But none could match the one we dubbed "The Showman".

The egg runs along the side cushion, pots the red in the top right-hand corner, then runs along the top cushion and, with a bit of a wobble, pots the red sitting at the left. The applause is deafening and Lindrum gives his trademark wink to the ladies in the front row.

"Ladies and Gentlemen, forgive me for stopping the proceedings. Allow me to introduce you to an old friend. The great sporting journalist from the *The Sydney Morning Herald* – Mr Les Wheeler. They call him the man with the golden pen. He has with him his beautiful wife, Barbara, and their new addition, son John."

More applause. All smiles, Horace radiates more light than a James Barnet Lighthouse [9].

"This is a little shot for you, young John."

Horace picks up six colours for the steeplechase and spins the balls, one after the other, in quick succession, around the table and into the top pocket. He makes it look easy. It is far from easy. It took years of practice. The steeplechase trick shot is one of my favourites;

---

[9] James Johnstone Barnet (1827–1904), Colonial Architect for New South Wales from 1862–1890. During the course of his service he was responsible for the construction of 169 post and telegraph offices, 30 court houses, 155 police stations, 110 lock-ups and 20 lighthouses. His major works include the Sydney GPO in George Street, Callan Park Lunatic Asylum, the Australian Museum, the Lands Department and the Anderson Stuart Building at the University of Sydney.

and, calling on all my strength and my once pristine ballet skills, I force myself onto *pointe* to watch my father's mastery of the shot.

Two balls thud onto the table, the others roll all over the floor. It is the only time I have ever seen my father lose control and I am certainly not prepared for what follows. Gripping the cushion, he falls forward, removes his glasses which have clouded with great beads of perspiration, places them on the cloth and strokes his forehead with the fingers of his right hand. Then, his motionless body collapses across the table and slumps onto the floor. That's when I hear my mother cry out:

"Please God, someone call an ambulance."

Three months later

Joy stood in the doorway. Fragile and hollow-eyed, she was clutching a tiny box wrapped in brown paper and tied with string. I heard her whisper: "There's nothing left."

Then, one by one, she climbed the stairs. "Twenty-five years gone in a blink."

Later she confided: "When I reached the landing and looked out across the billiard table, it was as if there was a neon sign flashing 'NO LONGER IN SERVICE'." She laid the package gently onto the cloth, walked to the cabinet, poured herself a scotch, placed a record on the turntable and, curling up on the lounge, let Dean Martin sing her to sleep.

> Goodnight, sweetheart, see you in the morning
> Goodnight, sweetheart, see you in the dawning
> Goodnight, sweetheart...Goodnight.[10]

---

[10] A song composed by British song-writing team, Ray Noble, Jimmy Campbell and Reg Connelly (1931). Over time it has been performed by many great artists including Bing Crosby and Dean Martin

Prussia, 1848

A young student of philosophy closed his books for the day, climbed into his coat, wound his thick woollen scarf around his neck, snuffed the candle, walked out into the cold night air and briskly across cobblestone streets, through a labyrinth of narrow corridors towards the town square.

Outside the palace gates, a large crowd gathered. Men, women and children were standing shoulder-to-shoulder about a makeshift dais.

"LIBERTY, EQUALITY, FRATERNITY!"

"People across Europe are taking their lives into their own hands. Germany can no longer look on patiently whilst it is being trod underfoot. You have a right to well-being, education, freedom without distinction of birth and class. We need to be like America. We need to elect our president and be able to depose him if he is bad. When we take this step, taxes will fall away."

Lawyer Friedrich Von Hecker knew how to gather an audience in. He captured them with his wonderfully expressive eyes and men, women and children hung on his every word, vocalising their support when called upon to do so.

Beneath the rumblings of endorsement, the sound of tall winged-leather army boots: The King's men, bayonets fixed. A soldier grabbed a woman at the back of the crowd, tearing her dress. She gave him lip. He slapped her hard.

At this, our student stepped from the shadows and leapt like a tiger. He grabbed the fellow by the shoulder, turned him around and threw a punch that landed squarely on the soldier's jaw.

Friedrich's arrest did not go down too well in the Von Lindrum household. His father, a military general, negotiated the release, but the altercation with his son was anything but pretty.

"Sir, have you forgotten who you are? You will cease your philandering and join the military now or, my God, you will take yourself to the colonies."

A few months later, my great-great-grandfather embarked at Hamburg, aged 20, for a new life in a land of opportunity, far from the turmoil of Germany.

A mighty wave of revolution hit, days after his departure.

Chapter 1
In the footsteps of the Other

The Lindrums were a family of champions, mainly in billiards and snooker, but also in primary industry and entertainment in such fields as winemaking, Dixieland jazz, percussion and the big-wheeled bicycle.

My great-great-grandfather Friedrich Wilhelm Von Lindrum was born in Stralsund[11], Prussia, in 1828. He came to Australia in 1849 as a passenger on the 360-ton sailing vessel *Prinzessin Luise (Princess Louise)*, a ship chartered by the South Australian Colonisation Society. On the passenger list, he was incorrectly described as "Mr Lindnum".

The *Princess Louise,* carried 162 passengers. The list comprised men, women and children and included a mixture of revolutionaries, intellectuals, artists and engineers. The ship was said to be one of the most important vessels to have arrived in Australia. Those aboard left an indelible mark on the history and culture of the Australian nation.

Passengers included botanist Marianne Von Kreusler, journalist Otto Schomburgk, who founded the German newspaper Sud-Australische Zeitung; botanist, author and second director of the Adelaide Botanic Gardens, Richard Schomburgk; artist Alex Schramm; brass founder and winemaker Friedrich Adolph Buhring; music master Gustav Louis Esselbach; pastor Carl Ludwig Mucke who set up the school education system in South Australia; and composer Carl Linger who wrote "Song of Australia."[12]

The lyrics of the *Song of Australia* were written by CJ Carleton. The music was written to be performed *maestoso:* in a stately, dignified and majestic manner. The lyrics run as follows:

> There is a land where summer skies
>
> Are gleaming with a thousand dyes
>
> Blending in witching harmonies,
>
> in harmonies, and grassy knoll and forest height,
>
> Are flushing in the rosy light,
>
> And all above is azure bright,
>
> Aus–tra–li–a, Aus–tra–li–a, Aus–tra- li–a.

The nine-month journey via Rio de Janeiro was largely uneventful, save for the birth of a son to the Lingers.

One can only guess about why my great-great-grandfather left his homeland. Causes could have included poverty; hunger; the onset of the machine age; fear of the wild, undisciplined mobs and growing fascination with the French Revolution, which eventually led angry farmers to don Phrygian [13] hats, swap scythes for weapons and flood into cities chanting

---

[11] Situated in north-eastern Germany in the region of western Pomerania in the State of Mecklenburg–Vorpommern, Stralsund, a seaside city founded in 1234 and was one of the most prosperous members of the medieval Hanseatic League. The city is known for its magnificent red-brick Gothic architecture, of which the most extraordinary landmark is the City Hall

[12] First sung on 12 December, 1859, "Song of Australia" was published by W H Paling & Co. in 1879

[13] A soft, brimless, conical cap associated in antiquity with the inhabitants of Phrygia, a region south of central Anatolia. The cap features in Homer's *Ulysses* and is associated with the mythical twins, Castor and Pollux, patron gods of horses and the Roman social order of mounted knights called *equites,* who appear in a number of Greek and Roman myths. Dubbed France's bonnet rouge, the Phrygian cap was worn by revolutionaries when storming the Bastille

the French cry: "Liberty, Equality, Fraternity". Alternatively, he might simply have been a young man with a fearless and adventurous spirit.

In 1848, three-year conscription into the Royal Prussian Army was compulsory for young men, yet the Prussian government was happy for them to escape their obligation. Perhaps the monarchy, foreseeing the great wave of revolution that was about to hit Europe, sought to preserve the lives of wealthy or gifted citizens. The rulers might have believed that the men and women aboard this ship were capable of establishing a Prussian colony in the Great South Land.

The "Von" in my great-great-grandfather's surname led to the successive naming of children within the Lindrum family:

> Friedrich Wilhelm Von Lindrum I
> Frederick William Lindrum II
> Frederick William Lindrum III, and
> Frederick William Lindrum IV

It is highly probable that the Lindrum family had military, even royal connections, and were supporters of Kaiser Wilhelm as well as the British monarchy [14].

This supposition is based on attributes and achievements of Friedrich Von Lindrum: his superlative skill at the billiard table, which saw him hailed as a great master; his position within the Masonic Temple[15] from which he led the Freemasons into the South Australian Parliament during the visit of Prince Alfred, Duke of Edinburgh (later Duke of Saxe-Coburg-Gotha in 1866); the award to him of Australia's first international gold medal for South Australian Shiraz;[16] and the fact that the Prussian Minister of Customs was godparent at his christening, suggesting a strong relationship with the government elite.

Queen Victoria ordered that a billiard table be installed at Windsor Castle in 1845; another table made by Orme & Sons of 16 Soho Square, London, The Parsonage, Manchester and 69 West Nile Street, Glasgow, recorded that it had been manufactured "By Special Appointment to His Majesty King Edward VII"

Shortly after his arrival in Australia, Friedrich Von Lindrum was granted a crown lease over lands at the corner of Thomas and Edsall Streets in Norwood where he established a vineyard estate.

In 1861 he was granted citizenship. His Naturalisation Certificate lists his occupation as wine merchant. The following year he married Clara Wolff, the nineteen-year-old daughter of a cabinetmaker.

There were three children of the marriage: Frederick William II, Clara and Lavinia, who died of whooping cough before she was one year old. Clara grew up and married John Cawardine and there were two daughters of the marriage, Alethea Ruby and Gwendoline Beavan.

---

[14] Queen Victoria ordered that a billiard table be installed at Windsor Castle in 1845; another table made by Orme & Sons of 16 Soho Square, London, The Parsonage, Manchester and 69 West Nile Street, Glasgow, recorded that it had been manufactured "By Special Appointment to His Majesty King Edward VII"

[15] The first Masonic Temple was built in Marseille, France, in 1765. A decade later (1775), the cornerstone was laid for the Freemasons' Hall in London. The Grand Lodge of England was established on the site of the Goose and Gridiron Tavern. The symbol or trademark of the Freemasons is the square and compass with the letter "G" in the centre. Whilst Freemasons follow no specific religion, but members are required to believe in a Supreme Being as the "Grand Geometrician of the Universe" and Freemasonry is a way of life rooted in morality

[16] This award was presented to Friedrich in 1873 at the inaugural celebrations of the London Wine Society held at the Victoria and Albert Hall by the President of the Society, Prince Albert Edward, later King Edward VII. The following year Friedrich was invited to be a Brandy Judge at the Paris Exhibition (1874)

The daughters died, aged 20 and 17, without progeny. Clara Cawardine and her daughters are buried in my great-great-grandfather's grave in the West Terrace cemetery in Adelaide: originally Common Ground Road, path 36, allotment 22 east, now road 5, pathway 4, 2E, number 2225.

Fame for a Lindrum forebear at the billiard table can be traced to the first professional billiards championship event staged in Australia. Held at the York Hotel in Adelaide in 1865, Friedrich's win against the great British champion John Roberts Senior generated great excitement and triggered a trade boom in the export of award winning billiard tables. The tables, crafted from the finest Australian timbers were covered with five yards of material finely spun from merino wool. Big match-play followed. Then, on 31 January 1885, John Roberts and Field Marshal Horatio Herbert Lord Kitchener; Kitchener, a graduate of the Royal Military Academy in Woolwich (founded 1741), who won fame in military campaigns in Egypt, Khartoum and the Sudan, together, established a governing body to oversee the rules of the sports of billiards and snooker, the British Billiards Association and Control Council.

Friedrich's win against Roberts signalled the start of the Lindrum legend: five world champions in the same discipline in only four generations.

My father was the last of this great line.

Friedrich, hailed as a national hero for his billiards and winemaking success, died on Anniversary day, 26 January 1880.[17]

In respectful silence, 700 hundred men and women mourned his passing and remembered his accomplishments for Australia and Adelaide as they marched behind the casket to the railway station, where they formed a guard of honour to say their last farewells. On arrival in Adelaide an elected body of pallbearers lifted the casket into a horse-drawn, glass-fronted hearse. With the body laid respectfully upon the slate slab, as artist Vincent Van Gogh's body had been placed lovingly upon a billiard table, the cortege made its way to Friedrich's resting place; hearse and carriages lumbered over unmade roads to the toll of church bells and the beat of a solitary drum.

Waiting at the graveside was a boy, not yet 15, my great-grandfather Frederick II. He had learned enough billiards from his father to leave men and women gasping as he waltzed around a billiard table. Six years later, his love affair with one of the maids in his mother's household caused a family rift which would never be healed. Harriet Atkins was not pregnant but she came with a two-year old daughter, Florence Lilian born 1 December 1884.

Clara Wolff had been raised a staunch Lutheran. She had been brought up to believe that a woman conceiving a child out of wedlock was morally wrong and socially unacceptable. So she withheld her consent to the union, an act that led to a row with her son so furious it sent her servants flying for cover. "Your life will amount to nothing", she told him.

He responded by storming out of the house and slamming the door behind him.

The wedding took place 13 days after Frederick's 21st birthday (1886), his mother's consent being no longer required by law. A few days after the marriage, great-grandfather, his wife and daughter left South Australia and spent the following 10 years criss-crossing the nation in a horse and cart with a billiard cue strapped to the back. Tragedy! The best billiardist in the world roaming the Australian countryside scavenging for a crust. But the news was not all bad. Lady Luck dealt a few good cards. His win against Harry Gray was an ace.

---

[17] Now known and celebrated as Australia Day, commemorating British settlement of the land

The following enthusiastic report of the event was found buried in an early scrapbook:

May 6, 1887.

The Athenaeum Hall, Melbourne

Australia has a new champion. Lindrum defeats Harry Gray

Last night at the Athenaeum Hall our Pioneer of the Long Red was no match for his opponent. Frederick William Lindrum II dealt him a knock-out. Boy, oh boy, what a spectacle! There are all sorts of adjectives I would pluck to describe the incredible display but none seem as appropriate as "extraordinary".

Our thanks must go to King of the Ring, Smokin' Joe Thompson, for promoting what was surely the most stunning piece of theatre we have seen at the Athenaeum for a very long time. If I could find fault with anything it would have to be Joe's cabbage tree hat.

Joe, what on earth possessed you to put that silly thing on your head? It looked ridiculous mate. Poor Billy Winter! [the referee]. Billy had a tough time keeping a straight face. He told me after the show:

"If Joe wears that ruddy hat next time I'll get my cricket bat and whack the bloody thing for a six".

Whatever happened, great-grandfather was determined to make something of himself in order to prove his mother wrong.

The win against Gray, the first of many milestones, provided the seed capital to open billiard rooms in Western Australia. Great-grandfather saved the profits from these enterprises for a return to the east coast, where he established The Classic on George Street, Sydney, and acquired a lease on a store on the corner of Glenmore Road, Paddington. The profits from these ventures provided the deposit for Lindrum's of Flinders Lane.

Lindrum's started as a commercial enterprise and ended up as a shrine to a family whose name became synonymous with the games of the green cloth.

The success of the business was largely attributable to great-grandfather's ability to train others in the art of billiards.

Firstly there was my great-uncle Frederick Lindrum III. Australians dubbed him "The Great White Hope". In the family we knew him as "The Perfectionist".

Next came my great-uncle Walter. He was known as "The Man of Figures" because of his mathematical scoring ability.

And then there was my father Horace "The Showman". Dark-haired, barely 5 feet and 4 inches tall and notably handsome, Horace was a favourite with the crowd wherever he went. My father could be seen as the most important and influential of these men.

As the chairman of the Indian Billiards Association, MM Begg said:

"Horace probably did more than any other player to raise the sports of billiards and snooker to new heights of popularity as much by the magic of his genius as by the charm of his personality.

A great champion, his modesty was invincible. With the charm of his manners he combined his greatness as a player and made himself one of the most authentic champions. It has often been said there are no 'born' billiards and snooker players. Only those who worked hard got where they are. To some extent this was true of Horace Lindrum but, if ever a man was born with genius for snooker, he was that man."[18]

Over a career spanning an incredible 50 years, Horace was at the forefront of his profession as a world professional snooker player. He was the subject of intense media coverage in an era when technologies were nowhere near as sophisticated as they are today: he frequently featured on the front pages of newspapers across the globe and was almost continuously in the spotlight.

Overseeing this remarkable progeny was "The Ringmaster extraordinaire."[19] In the photo below, the Ringmaster is third from the left, eyes fixed, arms held tightly behind his back.

Horace, Walter, Frederick II , Frederick III

The Perfectionist is smiling on the far right.

The Man of Figures is second from the left.

Shoulders forward, there is a certain arrogance in the stance.

The Showman is far left, quite clearly the kid.

Shared characteristics are apparent: fine, high foreheads and large ears.

They were the personification of billiards perfection, geniuses.

Three personalities central to my story are missing from this photograph. My grandmother Clara Violet Lindrum "the Entertainer'"; my mother – Joy – "the Black Poker"[20]; and my great-grandmother "Harriet-the-hard-as-nails". Harriet, with one eye on the till and the other on the stocks and shares section of the newspaper, knew how to turn a dollar. Pressmen regularly sought interviews with the matriarch. The lust for "the story" was strong. But Harriet did not care for the limelight and refused to talk politics. In fact, talk of politics was forbidden in the Lindrum household. There was a belief that political talk caused arguments. Opinion was okay, but not political opinion. Opinion had to be okay because every member of the Lindrum family had an opinion.

Between them, this fascinating family created a unique piece of history, sending newspapers flying off news-stands for over a century.

---

[18] These words belong to MM Begg, Chairman of the Indian Billiards Association and were published in the 1952 Souvenir Program commemorating Horace Lindrum's official visit in his capacity as world professional snooker champion

[19] My great-grandfather, Frederick William Lindrum II

[20] My mother was dubbed "The Black Poker" by Britain's Lord David Quibell because of her incredible PR and marketing skills and her undying enthusiasm for the games of the green cloth. Joy stoked the competitive fires in the cue sports in both the men's and the women's game which resulted in the revival of the women's game and big box office sales

The Uncrowned King

Melbourne 1921

Down narrow Flinders Lane, in among the vibrant Jewish rag, tag and bobtail operations,[21] was the House of Lazar Slutzkin, the first Jewish clothing manufacturer in Melbourne.

The House of Lazar Slutzkin was the lifeblood of the lane, its heart and its soul. Lazar, a kind and generous man welcomed newcomers, shared his knowledge and skill and encouraged everyone he met to love their neighbours, to work from the heart. Budding entrepreneurs built their enterprises on Lazar's business model and, as a consequence, boom or bust, business in the lane flourished.

I stop to imagine the old days when the lane was the meat and wine of the Australian fashion industry. I see the tailor Mendel, a tape measure buried in the thick folds of flesh around his neck. He is greeting the machinists in Yiddish:

"Shah-lolhm. Mah hah-in-yah-neem."[22]

"How are things?"

No material today.

Today is Friday.

There will be the usual morning prayers and, at the end of the day the afternoon prayers, then the machines will be covered and the material stored with the multi-coloured pin-cushions, cotton–reels, cutting scissors, thimbles, buttons, braids and all the other paraphernalia of garment–making. Managers, staff and their families will then ready themselves for Shabbat. It takes time to make the Challah[23] and the chicken turkey soup, set the table, and light the candles. One must not be too tired from the day to concentrate on the most important part of the week.

Henry Haskin (winner of Melbourne Gown of the Year two years running), Charlotte of Fifth Avenue, Cherry Lane, Hartnell, Saba, Lindrum's – all were born in Flinders Lane.[24] I want to tell you about Lindrum's.

It was a billiard room like no other, before or since. The only place that matched Lindrum's of Flinders Lane was its sister, Lindrum's of Pitt Street, Sydney. The Sydney room was built on the same business model as the Flinders Lane original: wholesome and elegant service, starched aprons and caps. no gum, no hard liquor, no smoking, no swearing, no spitting, no pickpockets, no prostitutes, no gambling men. The ideology on which the Lindrum billiard room was founded was a creed of excellence first formulated by Philip Astley "The Father of Modern Day Circus"[25] and later adopted by British–American entrepreneur Fred Harvey. Harvey's lunch rooms, built along the Atchison Topeka and the Sante Fe railway line, were the first restaurant chain in America.

Great-grandfather thought Harvey was a genius. He sold the dream based on the images of the 'little house on the prairie', the white picket fence with a pretty girl at the gate and a delicious dinner bubbling away on the stove. The Harvey girl did not quite mirror Shakespeare's Rosalind (from *As You Like It,* Shakespeare's "it" girl[26]) but, in her little black dress and Elsie collar, she came close.

---

[21] Jewish peoples ran clothing manufacturing industries popularly known as "the rag trade" from Melbourne's Flinders Lane
[22] Hello/good morning. How are things?
[23] Jewish egg bread that is carefully plaited. Other wonderful Jewish foods enjoyed at Shabbat include freshwater fish, meats and horseradish sauce
[24] Today Chanel has a flagship store at the "Paris end" of Flinders lane
[25] Philip Astley (1742–1814) was a British equestrian, circus owner and inventor. The circus industry, as a presenter of an integrated entertainment experience that includes, music, domesticated animals, acrobats and clowns, traces its heritage to Astley's Amphitheatre, a riding school that Astley founded in London following the success of his invention of the circus ring in 1768
[26] A term for "ideal woman"

Today, the Harveys and the Lindrum's, along with Mrs Hordern's Leghorn hat[27] and Keith and John's Gainsborough House [28], are no more than a glorious memory of Bombe Alaska and Blue Nun[29]. Yet, when I walk down Flinders Lane or stroll down Pitt Street, I can still hear the click, click, click of the billiard balls and the roar of the waiting crowd.

Contemplating my family's past in this way, I wonder why I have chosen to write their story? Am I up to the task? Can I do it? Even as we speak I feel my skin burning like crackling on a pig that has been roasted for too many hours in an overheated oven. Many a time I have thought of giving up the ghost, of having a party and heaping the whole bloody lot on a bonfire but the perfume of my family history clings to my flesh and I am haunted by a vision of great souls riding around and around on a carousel. Music. Bright lights. Painted horses. Heady days.

> Wherever I look the ghosts are there.
> Wherever I go, the ghosts go with me.

Not so long ago a certain politician told me to commit my family story to memory. I don't know what to think about him.

I lie!

Family stories are important because it is through the experience of family that we learn about ourselves.

Before I sail much further into the Lindrums' world, of incredible highs and devastating lows, let me pay homage to the unsung heroes, those who stand largely in the shadows: the journalists, publishers, editors, cartoonists, cameramen, interviewers, filmmakers, scholars, friends and fans – who captured the evolution of my family story for 109 years. Without their contribution, this book, this opportunity to "bind the past with the future"[30], would not have been possible.

I touch my father's cue case. I run my fingers across the plaque on the front. I open the case. I lift the cue nestling inside. I hold the cue high above my head as one holds up an Olympic torch. A gesture to the men and women who parted with hard-earned cash to buy a newspaper and those dripping in talent who wrote articles with great headlines like:

> **"Lindrum brothers seesaw during week's play"**
> **"Mussolini of billiards holds pistol to their heads"**
> **"Here comes the next Lindrum...Horace's star in the ascendancy"**

Headlines like these turned the Lindrum billiard rooms into iconic landmarks and catapulted the Lindrum name into households, initially across Australia and later across the globe.

My family story started the day my great-great-grandfather strode up the gangplank of the *Princess Louise;* it gathered momentum the day his son opened the door to Lindrum's in Flinders Lane.

---

[27] Italian wheat-straw woven into hats. Mrs Hordern, a regular attendee at race meetings was renowned for her fashionable dress, especially her stylish Leghorn hats

[28] Fine dining restaurant, Cambridge in the Waikato, 20 kilometres from Hamilton, New Zealand, run by my dear friend Keith McDonnell and his long-time partner, John, Hospitality was paramount. Today it provides bed-and-breakfast accommodation

[29] German wine brand launched by H Sichel Sohne (Mainz) in 1923 with the 1921 vintage

[30] Australian sculptor Linda Klarfeld (1976–), whose bronze and granite works focus on the human figure. (Hunter Valley Gardens – a grandmother plays with her grandchildren – emphasising the reality that every link in the chain of the human family is important to the whole)

In 1921 Melbourne was not the sophisticated metropolis it is today. Largely populated by ordinary Joes who could not afford to buy themselves a vanilla slice, the little municipality was a somewhat divided space. On the south side of the Yarra, known back then as "Smellbourne", were pubs, brothels, boot factories and betting shops. On the north side, a sprinkling of dramatic, federation-style mansions, clubs, including the Melbourne Cricket Club, Victorian Racing Club and Tattersalls Club, and theatres such as the Velodrome and the Athenaeum. The latter was the Australian equivalent of Laura Henderson's Old Windmill Theatre in London, famous for its *nude tableaux vivants* [31] that landed many a performer and audience participant in the lock-up.

Maximilian Ludwig Kreitmayer's waxworks museum was also in the theatre district. The waxworks came to be known as a Gallery of Reference for displaying sexual organs decayed by venereal disease and the head of bushranger Joe Byrne, which was well caked in blood.

Sandwiched between these establishments were bookshops, shooting galleries, Parliament House, Old Melbourne Gaol where they hanged Ned Kelly, the Russell Street police station, barristers' chambers, the Supreme Court (where His Honour Mr Justice Redmond Barry conspired with a Victorian Premier to deprive poor Ned Kelly of a fair trial), St Paul's Cathedral, the Princes Bridge and Flinders Street Station.

Big-name celebrities graced the Opera House stage, including Hungarian–American illusionist and magician Ehrich Weiss "Ehrie" known as Houdini, and comedian and juggler William Claude Dukenfield known as WC Fields. But times were tough. The Depression was brutal. Gone were the days when you could walk in off the street and get the bank manager's nod for a "Variety" store [32] in Collingwood, so the idea of opening a billiard room was a hot topic at the pub.

Critics at the Duke of Wellington fell into two camps:

one thought my great-grandfather was as mad as a cut snake; the other believed he was a bloody Einstein. The debate attracted wide media attention but the story of the room was not the first Lindrum story. The Lindrums were already a household name. Newspaper moguls James Joynton-Smith and Robert Clyde Packer had been championing the Lindrum brand for some time and had a vested interest in ensuring the name remained at the forefront of sport.

As joint proprietors of *The Sporting Referee*, the leading sporting newspaper in Australia, Joynton-Smith and Packer's interests extended beyond the paper. Packer had a passion for polo and Joynton-Smith loved jumping onto tables in restaurants and pubs and delivering impromptu performances of "Down at the Old Bull and Bush"[33] to the accompaniment of the concertina he carried with him everywhere he went. He could also go quite a few rounds in the boxing ring and, at his wife's behest, had worked hard to make race tracks more "lady friendly".

The Packer–Joynton-Smith partnership sponsored the Wallabies and the Kangaroos and, when the pair heard of a nine-year-old prodigy at the billiard table, they set out to see whether what they had heard was true. After seeing my great-uncle Frederick play, they decided to keep a close eye on the boy's progress and, when he won the Australian title[34] from the more seasoned billiardist Charles Memmott, they pulled him into their fold.

When you see my great-uncle's photos, it is easy to understand why we called him the Perfectionist. He always took aim nine inches in from the ball, always well down. The straight cue between the two eyes created a harmonious union between cue and cueist. The

---

[31] Nude living pictures that created quite a sensation
[32] Sir George James Coles, CBE (1885–1977), founder of the Coles supermarket empire. The first store was established in Smith Street, Collingwood, Victoria, opening on 9 April, 1914, and promoting in the window: "Nothing over a shilling". Before the the opening of the Coles store Australians purchased their produce from street barrows. The Coles store revolutionised the way people shopped
[33] English music hall song composed by Harry von Tilzer around 1905. Lyrics by Andrew B Sterling, the song was popularised by Florrie Forde
[34] Frederick William Lindrum III won the Australian professional billiards title in 1908, when he defeated the renowned Charlie Memmott. Frederick III retained the Australian professional billiards title for 27 years

bridge arm seems unyielding and there is a certain amount of weight on the bridge occasioned by throwing the body forward. Pressure on the bridge hand ensures its steadiness. This weight is borne by the thumb and tips of the fingers. The stance denotes perfect balance: knees bent; left foot in a perfectly straight line six inches in front of the right; right foot turned slightly to the right; the distance between the feet precisely 12 inches.

Frederick won the Australian title for the first time in 1904, the same year my great-grandfather became a bookmaker for the Western Australian branch of Tattersalls, an exclusive club network established to provide a social outlet for "gentlemen only", and where the elite could gamble on the races. The art of bookmaking[355] – like the arts of speech, dress, statesmanship, service, journalism, film-making, good sportsmanship, billiard playing and polite manners, as well as the dramatic arts and the culinary arts – all have been or are being progressively diminished.

Experts argue that subversion was triggered by the bank crash of 1893; it was during Australia's darkest decade that a "set of men" infested the places of public resort. These men saw an opportunity to make vast sums of money by making the practice of business and, especially, gambling, more accessible to workers in the engine-room of the nation who were struggling, much as they are today, to put bread on the table. These workers were men and women who wanted nothing more than an opportunity to improve their lot.

Meat tray lotteries, chocolate wheels, one-in-a-hundred spinning-wheel raffles: taking these chances drew great numbers into a deep sea in which many gamblers could not stay afloat. They were seduced into an addiction that is even more widespread and damaging in our times.

The lyrics to the old song "Burlington Bertie from Bow" serves as a reminder of what happens to those who become addicted to industrialised gambling practices.

> I'm Burlington Bertie I rise at ten-thirty
> and saunter along like a toff
> I walk down the Strand with my gloves on my hand
> Then I walk down again with them off
> I'm all airs and graces, correct easy paces
> Without food so long, I've forgot where my face is
> I'm Bert, Bert, I haven't a shirt
> But my people are well off you know.
> Nearly everyone knows me from Smith to Lord Rosebr'y
> I'm Burlington Bertie from Bow. [36]

By 1913, the seeds of a mature sporting culture had been planted and gambling was beginning to play a powerful role in Australian society. It was during this period that my great-uncle Frederick's star was in the ascendant and the Australian public, not only got behind him, they pinned all their hopes on his ability to win the world crown.

"The Great White Hope is off to London to take on the Brits."

---

[35] Bookmaking was perceived to be a mathematical way of making a living through calculation of the odds
[36] A music hall song composed by Harry B Norris in 1900 and sung by Vesta Tilley. The song was parodied in the now-much-better-known version in 1915 which is credited to William Hargreaves and performed by his wife, Ella Shields, while dressed in male attire as the sort of character known as a "broken-down swell"

A young Frederick at the table in London

Dame Fortune did not deal him an ace.

"What went wrong, Mr. Lindrum?" a journalist asked after his defeat. "I'm sorry. That's all I'm going to say. I'm sorry I let Australia down."

According to family legend, the Perfectionist collapsed in Trafalgar Square.

On hearing the news, the Ringmaster ran into the street and hailed a Hackney carriage to take him to Charing Cross Hospital in Fulham Palace Road.

"I'm looking for my son," he told the woman sitting at the reception desk. "Ah, here he is. Ward number 10."

Seconds later: "Frederick, get up. I didn't come ten thousand miles for nothing. Did you hear me? I said, get up!" The Ringmaster stormed across the room.

The Perfectionist looked up from his pillow. He knew instinctively that his father was coming towards him.

"Did you hear me, son? I didn't come ten thousand miles for nothing." The Perfectionist rolled over.

"Get up, Frederick. You're coming with me." The Ringmaster ripped back the cover.

For the first time in his life he did not think he could do his father's bidding. "Excuse me, sir, what on earth do you think you're doing?"

The thick Welsh accent belonged to a young nurse tending a patient on the far side of the room.

The Ringmaster told her to mind her own business. "He is my business. Your son has pneumonia."

"I don't care what he's got, he's coming with me."

The nurse scampered off to get help but the Perfectionist was already in a cab on the way to his Waterloo.

The British billiards champion, Willie Smith of Darlington, was waiting patiently in the reception rooms. He was not waiting for the Perfectionist to walk through the door. That was the last thing he expected to happen. He was sitting upright in a high-winged blue leather chair waiting for formal notification of the cancellation of the match.

Although the media attack about this incident was savage, it was nothing compared to the siege from within the household. Great-grandfather wanted the world cup on the wall at Lindrum's and he was prepared to do just about anything to that end, including weight (handicap) his eldest son as men weight racehorses. He eventually succeeded in breaking the boy's heart and, with his heart, his spirit.

The Perfectionist worked hard to meet his father's expectations by recording some phenomenal world-record breaks; then, out-of-the-blue and without consultation, he took a public stand against the slaughter of elephants for billiard balls, and the Ringmaster and the media resumed their attack.

"If it's okay for President Roosevelt, it ought to be okay for the Australian champion" one newspaper commented.

Cartoonist Tom Webster jumped to Frederick's defence with a cartoon depicting half-a-dozen elephants dancing to the song "For he's a jolly good fellow".

Various dramas unfolded in the Lindrum household during the next decade and a half (1913–1928). More drama in 15 years than most families experience in a lifetime. It all began on 4 October 1913, the day the Royal Australian naval fleet steamed through Sydney Heads:

> Since Captain Cook's arrival, no more memorable event has happened than the advent of the Australian fleet. The former event announced the birth of Australia. The latter event announces its coming of age.
>
> Minister for Defence
> Senator Edward Millen

To entertain the officers and men, Frederick and Walter went head-to-head for the Australian professional billiards title. Frederick emerged the victor. A year later, in 1914, as Australians pledged their loyalty to the Mother Country, the Lindrum brothers contested the title for a second time, performing for the troops on the eve of their ships sailing for the Dardanelles. Again, Frederick emerged the victor.

Recurring theme
The Sporting Referee May 30

My great-uncle Walter Lindrum wanted to be the Australian champion. He threw a real tantrum when he lost the second time and then flatly refused to have another crack.

He told the press the Australian title was not important to him.

The reality was, he liked to be in control of the game; he did not like losing in front of the Navy men and he did not want to risk losing for a third time

A few months after the declaration that the war was over, the Ringmaster sold The Classic billiard room on George Street in Sydney and the family moved to Melbourne.

Joynton-Smith and Packer were not happy about the Ringmaster's move to Melbourne and they had every right to be upset. They had made a significant investment in Lindrum's billiard room and in building the Lindrum brand and they had a sneaking suspicion the Ringmaster was planning to move in on their turf.

A war of words ensued. Nobody knew when it would end nor did they know who would emerge the victor. The Ringmaster got the publicity he wanted for his youngest son and Joynton-Smith and Packer got a terrific return on their investment. So it might be argued that both sides were winners.

The Lindrum story was not the story of a single champion, it was an epic, a saga, a legend with more angles than those to be found in E White's famous *Treatise on the Game of Billiards*. A reporter called Jack Oake covered many of those angles. In his memoir he said interviews with my great-grandfather had included some of the most engaging discussions of his career despite the fact that great-grandfather made him feel like he was standing in a dock with Jesus on the one side and Sir Redmond Barry, "the hanging judge", on the other. His first impression: "Fred was a cranky, old bastard. On the day I first met him I found him sitting in a chair directing the action. He was very good at directing the action and his sons and his staff did exactly what they were told to do."

Oake was particularly interested to know how great-grandfather had managed to scrape up the money to set up a billiard room. Opening a new business in the midst of a recession was a brave move. Billiard tables, scoreboards, equipment, racks, framed copies of rules and so on: it was an expensive exercise. The simple answer to that question was great-grandfather's swaggering self-confidence. (He had saved the deposit and had, somehow or other, secured a loan from the bank at a time when the bank had declared a freeze on lending.)

Oake was also interested in great-grandfather's personal life. "There was a barney in the Lindrum household over his marriage to Harriet," great-grandfather told him. His mother disinherited him. That caused him a great deal of pain and he never spoke to nor saw his mother again.

Sometime later, he fell in with the touts (gambling men). Card playing followed, and betting on the gee gees, prize fighting and wood chopping, the whole box and dice. He had made a tidy sum out of the gold prospectors in the west. "Those boys would gamble on just about anything...a fly climbing up a wall...a mosquito poised to draw blood."

Oake wanted to ask about the little girl. Instead, he made a mental note to do his homework and, later, reflected on the certificate from the Registry of Births, Deaths & Marriages. The birth was registered a month after the delivery by a Susie Atkins. Was she Harriet's sister? Lindrum was listed as the father but he was not a "painter", as the certificate stated. A burning desire came over him. "I need to don my archaeologist hat and do a bit of excavation" he said to himself. He found some interesting facts and fascinating coincidences.

For example, my great-grandfather was born the night his father defeated John Roberts Senior at the York Hotel in Adelaide, and my great-uncle Walter was born the night my great-grandfather won an important match at the Shamrock Hotel in Kalgoorlie. Hearing of Walter's birth, the actor and opera singer Wallace Brownlow suggested the babe be given the initials W A after the State of Western Australia. (Brownlow was my great-grandfather's landlord.)

"You remember Wallace Brownlow?" my great-grandfather had asked Oake, rummaging in a drawer and finally producing a photograph of Brownlow playing the role of the Sultan[37] in the Australian production of Paul Lacome's "Ma mie Rosette", a musical so popular it sold out when it opened at the Globe Theatre in London in 1892.

The hand-painted photograph was like a single frame from a Melies[38] film. Caught in the moment, great-grandfather pulled out a second photo. "Do you remember George Sorlie?"

---

[37] Reference to first performance of "Ma Mie Rosette" presented by Williamson & Musgrove's Royal Comic Opera Company "The Firm", at the Miner's Institute in Kalgoorlie as reported in *The Kalgoorlie Miner*, 21 June 1898. Brownlow's leading lady was Nellie Stewart
[38] Marie-Georges-Jean Melies (1861–1938), French illusionist, filmmaker and prolific innovator in the use of special effects, Melies was famous for leading many technical and narrative developments in the early days of film

he asked, not waiting for the reply. "Sorlie made tough men cry. Why, when he played Simon Legree in *Uncle Tom's Cabin*[39] you could hear a pin drop."

Sorlie got his big break in show business when Billy Brown, a brilliant ad lib comedian, wanted a song-and-dance partner for a new act. The pair brought the house down at the Tivoli with the song "I Want to Be a Song and Dance Man". The press dubbed Sorlie Australia's answer to Al Jolson. His wife argued that he was better than Jolson, which did not make her too popular with Americans.

Oake enjoyed the theatre but he wanted to know more about the Lindrums so he put the interview back on track by asking great-grandfather why, given his success in Western Australia, he had moved back to the east coast and, more particularly, why Melbourne?

Great-grandfather told him: "Harriet and I fell in love with Melbourne. Our daughter Clara was born here. When the bank crash came in 1893 we couldn't afford to stay but vowed when we made our fortune we'd come back and spend it in dear, old Melbourne Town." Then, to Oake's surprise, he broke into song.

> Goodbye Melbourne Town, Melbourne town, goodbye.
> I am leaving you today, for a city far away.
> Although today I'm stony broke, without a single brown,
> when I earn my fortune, I'll come back and spend it in
> dear, old Melbourne Town.[40]

Oake then asked the question journalists were still asking five decades later. "How did you to learn to play billiards?" Great-grandfather told Oake he had grown up in an atmosphere of billiards; his baby memories were stacked with talk of billiards wizards and three-ball miracles. The world of billiards, of pure science and mathematics, so fascinated him that he could not remember a day when he was not exercising his cue.

"My father sought perfection on the green baize in the same way Paganini searched for perfection on a violin. His teaching methodology did not allow for minds to wander or feet to slip from the stance chalked to the floor to which I was glued for hours on end. Instructed to execute the same shot over and over and over, a slight smack across the back of my legs with a cane served as a reminder to maintain focus. Sticking to the one-ball shot was exhausting. When my back ached, which it frequently did after eight hours of practice, my father told me: 'Begin again, son.'

Training also included "fresh air revives". Eyes needed rest after playing billiards. Walks on the beach or in the park followed by a strong cup of tea, a light meal and an early night.

Great-grandfather adopted the same method to teach his sons and provide early instruction to his grandson, continuously reminding them that billiards was a clean, healthy, manly sport, played by Royalty, and that they were obliged to represent the sport to the very best of their ability.

This included starching their shirts and polishing their shoes till they could see their faces in the shine. Respectability was paramount.

"The practice regime sounds like child abuse!" Oake proffered knowing full well he would be slapped in the face.

"Don't be ridiculous," great-grandfather barked.

"You have to put your shoulder to the wheel if you want to make something of yourself. There is no escaping the hard yards, not if you want to become a craftsman. Tea?"

Later, Oake discussed this interview with an old friend over a pint of Victoria Bitter. "There was a bit of a fracas in the household when Lindrum came to teach his eldest to play. He told me, there was no way on God's earth he was going to teach a left-hander.

---

[39] An anti-slavery novel published by Harriet Beecher Stowe in 1852
[40] Great-uncle Walter used to sing this song to me on the billiard room step at Albert Park. To this day I still remember the tune

Left-handers cavort with the devil." A commonly held belief in those days. Ironically, my great-grandfather was later forced to tutor my great-uncle Walter to play billiards with the left hand as Walter severed the top of the index finger of his right hand in a terrible accident in the washhouse. His sister said: "The accident just happened." Walter said: "Clara goaded me to stick my hand into the jaws of the mangle." We will never know the truth but I can tell you the sibling rivalry was something fierce.

Great-grandfather would not be quizzed on the rivalry. Thankfully, Walter was right-eyed and the right-eyed player should play with the left hand because it balances the body. Of course, inherited genius was a factor, but the ability to make a break of 1000 was not written on any of their birth certificates. Training the eye, repetition, coaching in the essentials, the arts of patience and confidence, the science of critical evaluation – these were the factors that turned the Lindrums into champions.[41]

The hard yards, long hours of practice, and adoption of the Harvey and the Slutzkin business principles turned Lindrum's in Flinders Lane into an overnight success. Over three generations, not a day passed without a story, so you can only imagine how some of us felt when the demolition boys moved in. Ah, well, you cannot halt progress! Fortunately, the Ringmaster, the Perfectionist and the Man of Figures were not alive to see them stripping the walls and chucking billiard balls into boxes. It cut the Showman to the core. I still carry the pain and pull myself through it by dredging memories from the depths of a place deep within me that I would not know was there except that I do. Chilean poet Pablo Neruda (1904-1973) referred to it as "the space between the shadow and the soul."

Turning the page of an album, I sit for a time admiring a black and white photograph of the two brothers. The Man of Figures wears a cheeky grin. The Perfectionist is poised for the shot. In the shadows is a young man in his early teens. He is supposed to be ironing billiard tables. Instead, he is watching his uncles at play. The look on his face says: "I want to be doing what you are doing."

Walter on the left, Frederick poised for the shot

How he came to be in the moment is a story in itself. For the present all I am going to say is that his mother, my grandmother (Clara Violet), had landed herself in a sticky situation, really a mess. The Ringmaster felt that it was in the boy's interests for him to spend time in Melbourne whilst she sorted herself out.

When Horace first arrived in Melbourne in September 1924, the boy who became my father resided with his grandparents and uncles and his cousin Irene May Dunn, at number

---

[41] The Lindrums reached the Inner Temple by developing the essentials – the patience of Job, the eye of the surgeon and the judgment of Solomon

4 Church Street, South Melbourne. Midway through 1928 the family purchased a house in Kerferd Road. It was described by the agents as:

> Within easy walking distance of the tram to the city, this substantial four-bedroom home is situate on a large corner block, a cooee from Port Melbourne and St Kilda, and a short distance to the best milk bar in the country. [That milk bar made sensational lime-green spiders!]

In the 1920s, Albert Park was not a chic suburb but was awash with bordellos. Great-grandfather figured that the council would flush the whores out sooner or later, which they did. The big attraction was the shed at the rear of the house which was big enough to accommodate a full-size practice table.

For Horace, living in Melbourne had its pluses and its minuses. He missed his Mum terribly but loved life in the billiard room, especially when the Ringmaster was not around and he could practise his snooker. When the Ringmaster caught him in the act he would lock the snooker balls in the cupboard and lecture Horace on the billiards tradition.

The Perfectionist went to London for his second crack at the world crown shortly after the family moved to Albert Park. While he was away, Horace made his debut in the professional league.

Now that is a story and a half!

Chapter 2
Horace's star in the ascendant

In 1927 Al Jolson's film "The Jazz Singer"[42] steamrolled the world into a new chapter in the history of moviemaking. By the 1930s "talkies" had become a global phenomenon: so, too, had Sir George Alfred Julius's invention, the totalisator. The invention was designed for fair voting, but State Premiers in Australia refused to adopt it, so Julius converted the machine for gambling. The first totalisator was installed at the Ellerslie racecourse in Auckland. By 1970, gambling had become Australia's biggest export.

Inside the Lindrum household, life went on as usual. Practice sessions followed, one after another, which might sound like drudgery but life as a Lindrum was anything but mundane. It was a circus, a great vaudeville performance with all the razzle-dazzle of sideshow alley. It is no exaggeration to say that there was more razzamatazz in the Lindrum household than you would ever find on stage at the Princess Theatre.

For me, it was like sitting in the front row watching Elaine Paige[43] making her debut on Broadway.

I could smell the grease paint.

I can still smell the grease paint.

> Horace's diary of 7 May, 1928, notes:
>
> Aviator Bert Hinkler has just completed his record-breaking solo flight from England to Australia. Fifteen days and one hundred and twenty-eight flying hours.
> Boy, oh boy!
> What an achievement.
>
> Me? Well, I've just made my debut at the billiard table.
> My uncle Walter gave me a thrashing.
> I was so nervous, the sweat was pouring out of me.
> Why did I agree to be his punching bag?
> That was a big mistake.
> Goodness knows what Mum is going to say about it.
> The press had a field day.
> They kept asking me how I felt.
> How do they think I felt!

---

[42] The maverick Warner Brothers had backed a winner, but it was Thomas Edison who believed movies could talk
[43] Born Elaine Jill Bickerstaff (1948–), English singer and actress Elaine Paige made her West End debut in the musical "Hair" at the age of 16 (1964). In 1978 she performed as Eva Peron in the musical "Evita", winning the Laurence Olivier award for her performance. Paige made her debut on Broadway to critical acclaim as Norma Desmond in the musical "Sunset Boulevarde" (1996)

Uncle Walter clearly had something on his mind the day he suggested to Horace that they go for a walk together. Horace could see trouble written across Walter's face as he had the look that men get when something is gnawing away at their insides. Horace asked him: "What's up, uncle?" Walter put his arm around Horace and said:

"Come on, let's go down to the St Kilda Pier."

Albert Park to St Kilda Pier is a long walk of about five kilometres. It took them an hour, maybe a little longer. Horace did not mind the walk to Luna Park because there was always the chance of a ride on the Big Dipper. On this occasion he did not count his chances very high as his uncle Walter did not look to be in the mood for the roller-coaster. He bought Horace an ice-cream and he was half-way through it when Walter asked: "Tell me, how would you like to make your debut in the professional league?"

Walter had an innovative strategy aimed at catching and frying two big fish. The first fish was British billiards champion Willie Smith of Darlington. Some say the game plan was born out of revenge. Walter had not liked Willie beating his brother in the world championship. Horace, however, believed that Walter just wanted to be somebody, and to do that, he had to beat Willie Smith of Darlington because Willie Smith of Darlington was the greatest scoring force on the planet. Walter had every confidence that he could beat Smith.

The second big fish was a known associate of his grand-dad's. His name was John Wren. Walter wanted Mr Wren to sponsor his passage to the Mother Country. Horace had heard the name Wren and racked his brain to remember exactly what he had heard about him. Then it came to him. Mr Wren was the ex-factory worker who had made a fortune betting his life savings on the horse Carbine in the 1890 Melbourne Cup. He used the windfall to establish an illegal betting operation in a coffee shop in Collingwood. Horace did not know how many times the police raided that place but reading about the raids was like reading a comic book: police hiding in hay carts, masked men jumping fences and disappearing through trap doors.

Wren rose to prominence and became one of the two kings of illegal SP (starting price) bookmaking in Australia. The other king was racehorse owner and head of the Tattersall's club in Melbourne, Solomon Green. Rumour had it that to get anywhere with Wren or Green you had to be "liked". This is where uncle Walter's confidence came into play. Uncle Walter was not afraid of anybody. He was the possessor of his father's indomitable confidence. This was the figure of Walter: short, stocky, black-haired, big-eared, square-jawed and pudgy-faced, he was an almost freckle-less version of the archetypal bully. You only had to take one look at him to know he would never be backwards in coming forwards. Grandma Violet (Clara) told me her brother was a handful to bring up. He was the sort of kid you would send to do the shopping and he would come home with a whole heap of things that were not on the list.

She also told me about the squabbles between Walter and her and said that, when Walter was not fighting with her in the washhouse, he was bragging like a trooper in the middle of Page Street. The bragging led to fisticuffs and to her Mother's downing tools and racing out to break up the great war her son had started. "Christ! Dearie, your son's a match for Ned Kelly," the next-door neighbour used to say.

Great-grandma turned the hose on uncle Walter more than once. Not that the hose would have done anything to wash away his belief in himself. If the family had slapped him in a straitjacket, he would have still performed like Harry Jansen, aka Dante, King of all Magicians.

Uncle Walter was a brilliant billiards player. He thrashed the locals. As an adult, he even had the Russell Street police wrapped around his little finger. Anyone else would have been booked for leaving their model-T Ford in bumper-to-bumper traffic and catching the tram home, but not Walter. Police washed and polished the car and drove it back to Kerferd Road. He was given no warnings because warnings would have been a complete waste of time. If they had given Walter a warning, he would have shot back: "There is no way I am going to sit in traffic jams when I could be practising billiards. You blokes need to fix the roads.'"

Horace confessed he was concerned about Walter doing business with Mr Wren and he wanted to know and understand where Walter saw him fitting into the picture. Walter confided that he had been cabling Willie Smith for months pleading with Smith to play him. Willie told him to get lost. Smith did not play just anybody. You had to prove yourself before he would throw down the glove (which is what great sportsmen did in those days). Even great-grandfather's line to the British press: "Walter is the greatest thing since sliced bread" failed to draw a reaction from Smith. It did, however, spark British curiosity. The full-faced, heavy-eyed Claude Falkiner and the pretty Harry W.Stevenson (known as the Beau Brummel of billiards because of his striking good looks) were sent to play Walter and report the results.

Walter played well against Falkiner and, in the first of two matches against Stevenson, outscored him two to one, but his play was inconsistent. In the second match, Stevenson got his own back. Scoring at phenomenal speed, he completely demoralised his opponent. After Walter's loss to Stevenson, the Fleet Street press wrote: "The Colonial ego is bigger than Everest. Today Everest is looking more like Mount Blanc." Headlines like this one did not worry great-grandfather nor did they worry Walter. On the contrary, it was "Cry God for Harry, England and St. George!"[44]

The tragedy of the publicity campaign was that it gathered momentum and, over time, served to displace the Perfectionist and dilute the real story of the Lindrum family. Maybe this is just the way of the world but I do not know that for certain. I cannot know because the distillation of stories is not something that happens over night; it takes time to build a fictitious mythology. Frederick, for example, was still hallowed by the public and the media as "the greatest billiardist Australia had ever produced" when he met my father in the final of the Australian professional billiards championship in 1933. It is only in very recent times that history has been rewritten: contemporary critics have served readers with the spirit of the Perfectionist and the Showman in a form far removed from the authentic versions of these champions.

Years later my great-uncle Walter told Horace he had been studying Smith's play by standing on a crate and peering through a vent into the billiard room where Smith was practising and he had found a way to outscore him by concentrating on nursery cannons (delicate, gossamer-like shots, keeping the balls close to the cushion and in the "nursery"). "I knew if I could get him to the table, I would beat him and then I would be home and hosed." By this he meant that he would get the sponsorship needed to get to Britain.

"Think what a world title would mean to your grand-dad, Horace." Horace had absolutely no idea what "home and hosed" meant, but he did know what a world title meant to his grand-dad, who, was forever telling him that his dearest wish was for a Lindrum to win one. He had even carved out a special place for the trophy and described in great detail how it would look on the wall. The fact that the trophy was perpetual (it could not be brought home to Australia) did not seem to bother him one iota.

"I need a sparring partner, young Horace. Someone good enough to play me and good enough to let me win. This is your big opportunity."

"Why don't you play uncle Frederick?" Horace asked.

"If I play Frederick, he won't play ball with me and there is no guarantee I will win and, if I lose in front of Smith, Smith won't have a bar of me nor will Mr Wren. You are my only hope of putting my hat in the ring and getting to London." This was probably true as there were no other billiardists in Australia at that time who could match skills with the Lindrum aristocracy.

---

[44] Last line of the famous speech beginning with the words: "Once more unto the breach, dear friends, once more", from Act III of Shakespeare's play Henry V, thought to have been first performed at the Curtain theatre in 1599, the same year the Lord Chamberlain's Men opened the new Globe theatre. The play was performed by the King's Men at the new Globe on 7 January, 1605. It is believed actor Robert Burbage played the role of Henry V on that occasion

My great-uncle Walter explained to Horace that if they worked together to convince Smith that Walter was a threat to his supremacy, Smith would throw down the glove and, when that happened, Mr Wren would not be able to resist the thrill of the contest. Gambling was deeply ingrained in Wren's psyche and there was no limit to the amount of money he would pay out if Walter could prove himself capable of beating the British at their game. Horace harboured his concerns. He wanted to make his debut in the professional league, but at what cost? Walter could see his nephew was having reservations and he knew his sister would be furious when she found out he had used Horace as an instrument for his own ends.

Walter offered Horace a carrot. "Let's play snooker as well as billiards." That set the ball rolling on Horace's professional career but not before Horace expressed his concerns to his grandfather, who told him that it was a good plan and raised the issue of his surname. "Your uncle Walter and I have been talking. We think you should change your name. Bloody good publicity if another Lindrum enters the ring and you, my boy, are more than good enough to carry the Lindrum flag." And, from that time forward, Horace became known as Horace Lindrum.'

Reporting on Horace's debut, *The Sydney Morning Herald* reported:

> Coaxing the balls with deceptive ease and a firm but delicate touch, this was a display of superlative skill. Horace and Walter Lindrum made the balls do everything but beg!

Horace and Walter were forces to be reckoned with, geniuses who, as time passed, came to be identified, first as brothers (they were uncle and nephew; master and apprentice) and, later, as the same man.

Smith read the review but he did not throw down the glove as Walter had expected him to do (probably because Horace had put on such a fine performance against Walter), so Walter was forced to plead with Mr Wren for assistance. Wren told Walter he liked his form, issued a media release dubbing him "The Phar Lap[45] of Billiards" and suggested to Walter that they set up an appointment to see Smith together. Clearly, Wren saw the potential to make a killing. Inside he was like a wild dog; on the outside, cool as a cucumber.

"I am sure we can persuade him to play you. Where did you say he was staying?"

"The Lord Nelson."

"You know, Walter, I meant what I said, there is no limit to the amount I am prepared to outlay if I think you can beat the British at their game. If you have any doubts as to my capacity you should speak to Plugger [46] (the famous cyclist, Hubert Opperman). Plugger and I go back a long way."

Wren and Lindrum arrived at the hotel for their meeting with Smith. Smith listened intently to their proposals and spent some time staring at the sizeable cheque Wren had placed on the table in front of him. Finally, he picked it up, held it to the light as if he were checking the validity of the signature, walked to the bar and whispered something to the bartender who nodded. The eager pair were too far away to see what Smith was doing but it soon became apparent. Holding a lighted match between his thumb and first finger, Smith slowly connected the match to the corner of the cheque and, throwing the burning paper into the fireplace, bowed and bid the pair, "Good evening, gentlemen".

---

[45] Phar Lap (1926–1932) was a famous thoroughbred racehorse during the Depression years that captured the imagination of the Australian nation. Foaled in New Zealand, Phar Lap "the Wonder Horse" was trained and raced by Harry Telford. Winning 36 of 41 starts, Phar Lap was struck down by a mysterious illness a fortnight after winning America's richest horse race, the "Agua Caliente" handicap, in 1932. The death was attributed to foul play

[46] Sir Hubert Ferdinand Opperman OBE (1904–1996), known affectionately by Australian and French crowds as "Oppy". Opperman was an Australian cyclist and Liberal politician whose endurance cycling feats earned him international fame in the 1920s and 30s

Wren was not used to people saying "No" to him.

"Leave this to me," he ordered.

The glove was delivered to Kerferd Road two days later. The amount Wren paid Smith remains commercially in confidence, as does his deal with Walter. The only thing we can know for certain is, the handshake was cosmetic. It was the type of handshake that only ever sees money going one way.

When Clara saw the headline "Horace Lindrum makes his debut" she was as happy as a lark. When she learned the price her son had paid to enter the professional league she read the riot act.

Clara believed a youngster appearing for the first time in public, even though he was the better performer of the two competitors, would inevitably succumb to the superior tactics and greater confidence of the more experienced player.

This fact was well-known to both her brother and her father, whom she believed had taken unfair advantage of her son. Horace refused to talk about the row but told me his mother insisted he memorise these Commandments of Sport:

> Thou shalt not quit. Thou shalt not alibi.
>
> Thou shalt not gloat over winning.
>
> Thou shalt not sulk over losing.
>
> Thou shalt not take unfair advantage.
>
> Thou shall not ask odds thou art unwilling to give.
>
> Thou shalt always be willing to give thine opponent the benefit of the doubt.
>
> Thou shalt not underestimate an opponent or over-estimate thyself.
>
> Remember that the game is the thing. He or she who thinks otherwise is no true sportsman or sportswoman. Honour the game, for those who play the game straight and hard win even when they lose.

Much later, great-grandfather informed Clara that he had cut her out of his last will and testament. "You don't need my money, you've got a son to look after you." That did not bother Clara. The only thing that had ever concerned her was getting the right messages through to her son.

"You will never, never, never have anything to do with gambling men. Do you understand me, Horace?" She then set about devising a scheme to put her son on an entirely different pathway. The Great White Hope played an important role in the execution of his sister's plan.

While Clara was planning her son's career, Walter was falling in love with Rosie Coates.

Ah sweet mystery of life at last I've found you Ah!
At last I know the secret of it all...
And my heart has heard the answer to its calling
For it is love that rules for evermore.[47]

---

[47] Song composed by Victor Herbert with lyrics by Rida JohnsonYoung from the Broadway two- act operetta "Naughty Marietta" (New York, October, 1910) which was Victor Herbert's greatest success. The song was sung by Jeanette MacDonald and Nelson Eddy in the motion picture adaptation in 1935. Tenor Richard Tauber recorded the song in his album "Will You Remember?"

Jan Lindrum

1928–1929

Rosie was sitting in the front row when Horace made his debut. She was also sitting in the front row at the Sydney Town Hall for the opening night of the week's match-play between Walter and Willie Smith. All was going well until midway through the week. What happened after that is anyone's guess. Rosie was admitted to the Omrah private hospital in Darlinghurst[48] around 10 am on Thursday morning. Rumour has it she was hit by a bus. The hush-hush circumstances surrounding her admission to hospital suggests something else altogether. Members of the press noticed the empty seat and were dying to ask: "Where's Rosie?" but the opportunity did not arise.

At 2 pm sharp the referee made the introductions. Walter and Willie came together and shook hands. The atmosphere was one of absolute decorum. Well-known critic C D Dimsdale[49] described the scene:

> "Except for the occasional applause, voices were subdued, cigarettes and pipes lit almost furtively for [fear of] disturbing a player on his stroke. The only noise was the click of the balls, the crash of one driven hard into a pocket and the referee calling score."

Willie Smith moved to the table. A practical man, he wasted no time with preliminaries. He chalked the tip of his cue. Not a sound except for the soft scrape, scrape, scrape. Cue levelled like a rifle, he held the butt lightly, eased his chest along the tubular body and took aim. A soft tap, tap, tap. Smith gained position. Then, tightening the grip on the butt, the cue tip struck the ball low and hard with the force of a boxer's half-arm jab.

One, two.

Ker-plunk.

Walter sat quietly on the sidelines. The Prince of Players oblivious to the first-class billiards being played out in front of him. He was thinking of Rosie and the son or daughter he would never come to know.

A ball skidded across the cloth. A drop-cannon; the first object ball, cue ball and second object ball joined together at the top of the table. From a positional perspective the drop-cannon can be deceptive. Although easy to score from, it can leave a player with a liability. The ball stopped a fraction of an inch short. A fatal blunder! Smith shrugged his shoulders; he had been playing billiards for a long time and knew that balls can sometimes run unkindly.

Walter pulled himself together and walked to the table. Practice, the right-royal road to success, was to serve him well. Delivering his cue straight and smooth he began to score at an amazing speed with inexorable precision and uncanny manipulation of the balls.

Stunned, Smith sat on the edge of his seat. The maestro had miraculously found his form and the brilliant technical performance now being played out before a packed house overflowing into the street was one of such perennial importance it had nowhere else to go but into the history books as one of the greatest sporting feats of all time.

Loud applause drowned the referee's voice as the Man of Figures allowed a wry smile to creep across his face. Rosie's silver tea service was nearly in the bag.

Straightening his back, Walter paused to wet his vocal chords. It was a long drink, his eyes fixed on the three balls lying close together at the top of the table.

---

[48] Darlinghurst is on the outskirts of the Sydney CBD near the fashionable and trendy suburb of Paddington

[49] Born Rodolphe Louis Megroz (1891-1968), British writer, critic and poet – C D Dimsdale – (who also wrote under the pseudonym Roy Cumberland), trained as a journalist, worked as a freelance writer and, during World War II, was engaged by the BBC

Smith winced, looked down at his shoes. Two thousand. Two thousand and two.

The bagman's[50] saturnine malaise turned to red-blooded euphoria. "Ladies and gentlemen, Mr Lindrum's break of 2002 is a personal best."

Mr Lindrum's previous best was 1461. The break of 2002 is the third-largest on record. The other two records belong to Mr Lindrum Senior with a break of 3000 and Mr Lindrum's brother Frederick Lindrum with an unfinished break of 2196 against that great master of the long red, George Gray. We will now proceed to an interval of twenty minutes."

Pressmen took to telephones, cameramen grabbed their cameras but the subject had flown the coop. Twenty minutes later the referee declared a forfeit.

On the way to the Omrah Private Hospital in Darlinghurst Road Rosie's words were ringing in Walter's head.

"Don't worry, Darl, I'll be okay. I want you to concentrate on winning me that silver tea service."

"Why did I go along with it," he asked himself. He was still playing the reel when he pushed the door into Rosie's room. Startled by the sudden entrance, the doctor finished taking Rosie's pulse then, putting a hand on Walter's shoulder, directed him back into the corridor.

Once out of earshot of his patient he gave Walter the news. Two hours later, pallid and weak, Rosie lifted her body to place an 'X' on the marriage certificate. Minutes later she was dead.

Walter lost something of himself that day.

The part of him that stayed behind never stopped loving Rosie.

A few days later Walter took Rosie's body back to Melbourne on the Wodonga Express. I have often imagined the scene. Central station, pigeons fluttering on the steel and glass roof overhead. The famous clock under which everyone arranged to meet. The hustle and bustle of the porters and the teary farewells.

"Everything is in order, Mr Lindrum. Here are the papers.

Arrangements have been made for my colleague to meet the train at Flinders Street station. Please accept our heartfelt condolences."

Walter thanked them, placed the papers in the inside pocket of his coat, hugged Willie Smith and Hughie Boyle and boarded the train. Once in his compartment, he opened the window and leaned out. Willie was breathing into his palms and rubbing them together to keep himself warm.

"Willie, you're cold. Best get going, my friends. A big thank you to you both for looking after me. Rosie's death may delay my departure to Britain but you know I'll keep faith with the contract. I'll get there sooner or later. In relation to 'The Sun competition', I intend to write to Sir Hugh Denison and suggest that the trophy be presented to you."

Smith would not hear of it.

"Don't be daft. I can't claim the match on a forfeit not with the kind of lead you had. You won the silver tea service, fair and square. You can serve me a cuppa and a scone or two next time we're in town together. That's what Rosie would expect you to do. See you in England."

Willie and Hughie waited for the train to disappear then, retraced their footsteps and rejoined sports buff Eric Callaway. "Let's go, catch up with Duggan and get ourselves a stiff drink," Willie suggested. A regular daddy-long-legs, Duggan was propped against the bar at the Fortune of War.

"Sorry I couldn't get to the train, boys. I've been covering the Twickenham Rugby."

---

[50] A bookmaker's employee or associate, responsible for settling debts

"Looks like you're covering something else." Boyle's eyes floated in the direction of the barmaid.

"How was Walter?" Duggan asked, ignoring Boyle's cheeky grin.

"Very good, all things considered. Walter's a man of his word. He'll play in England this year."

The barmaid hovered. A bee around a honeypot. "What'll it be, boys?"

"Pint of VB for me, thanks,' Boyle responded.

'Make that two, Deary. What about you Eric? Willie?" Willie thought for a moment.

"Jack Daniels on the rocks." Callaway settled for an OP rum.

"I hear you don't practice before a match, Mr. Smith?"

"Never have, my boy. At the end of the playing season, I put my cue away until the start of the next one. I prefer to play myself into form with match-play. I get more than enough practice throughout the season, what with two, two hour sessions a day, six days a week, week in, week out. In the break I re-read the classics."

"Do you find match-play a great physical strain?"

"The strain is not so much physical strain as strain on the nervous system. You need physical stamina and you need nerves of steel to compile big breaks." Duggan lit a cigarette.

"You don't seem to suffer any nerves."

"No, I'm fortunate. My big breaks have been made under pressure." "Do you think Walter suffers from nervous tension?"

"I don't think Walter has a nerve in his body." "What about his brother, Frederick?"

"Frederick is a rare gem. You won't find too many players in history who have dragged themselves from a hospital bed to play in a world title. Frederick won our match in Melbourne recently. He is the most stylish all-round player I have ever seen. Some players are artists. Some players are men of science. In bygone days the artist was number one and there are those who still prefer art to science."

When Smith's head finally hit the pillow his mind continued to churn. His adversary had become a friend. He had also become, wittingly or unwittingly, an accomplice.

Walter switched off the small reading light near his head, shivered and pulled the railway blanket up to his chin. He was having difficulty with his body temperature. Gazing into the darkness, he listened to the rhythmic,

KER-PLAK, KER-PLAK, KER-PLAK...

"If only I could turn back the clock'" he thought to himself. He pulled the papers from under his pillow.

Rose Ellen Lindrum – Cause of death "Peripheral Toxaemic Pyelonephritis"[51]...

"What are you doing, Rosie?"

Rosie was folding the blue dress he liked so much and packing it gently into a suitcase.

"Darl." She threw her arms around his neck. "You take that glum look off that lovely face of yours. Don't worry about a thing. I will be just fine. Nobody has to know."

She smiled sweetly. "Your father is right."

Burying his head in the pillow, Walter, grief-stricken, sobbed his heart out over what might have been.

Two years later Clara and Frederick pushed the button on their plan.

---

[51] The most severe form of urinary tract infection associated with the *Escherichia coli* pathogen that leads to the rapid destruction of the kidneys

The letter

To: Mr Frank Smith, the World beating Champion of Australia

Dear Mr Smith,

    I have been in awe of you for some time and feel that I am now ready to challenge you for your title.

    Yours sincerely,
    Horace Lindrum

The response

My dear Mr Lindrum,

    I accept the challenge with one stipulation.
    The event will be played in Sydney.

    Sincerely yours,
    Frank Smith Junior, Esquire
    Champion of Australia

The event was played out before a capacity crowd at the Elysian Parlours, number 147A King Street. Before the event *The Sporting Referee* reported: "New Lindrum in the field."

After the event, the headline in *The Sydney Morning Herald*[52] read: "'Here comes the Fourth Generation. Another star rises in the Lindrum family."

> Handsome, modest, finicky and punctual, 19-year-old-Horace Lindrum has just become the youngest player to win the Australian professional snooker title, but it is his speed play that stupefied the spectators. Breaks of 97 in 4 minutes and 49 seconds
>
> He is not only the greatest player at his age in the world but the last of the wizards is the perfect billiard picture.

Frank Smith Junior was devastated by the loss. Anticipating a counter-challenge, the Showman kept himself to a rigid routine. He was keen to stay at the top, did not smoke or drink, watched his diet and made sure he got enough sleep, exercise and fresh air. When the challenge came, he was ready to meet it head on. *The Sydney Morning Herald* reported:

---

[52] 23, September, 1932

Lindrum won't be 20 until January 15 but you can count on the fingers of one hand the players who are capable of extending him in a game of snooker. As a billiardist, too, he is uncanny.

In the final match against Smith he cleared all the colours from the table three times, twice in 32 seconds and once in 30 and won the final frame 126 to 2.

Elated at his successes, which had exceeded his wildest dreams, Horace was sad for his opponent; he did not possess the killer instinct. Even so, great-uncle Walter was not taking any chances. After Frank Smith's defeat he refused to play his nephew in competition.

Labor Daily, Thursday 4 August, 1932...

In 1932 Walter embarked on a line voyage to London on the *Cathay*.[53] He thought he was going to play for the world title. Although Rosie was long dead, his grief still travelled with him.

I picture the scene.

"Hello there. Hello there." Smith yelled from the deck. "Ahoy, there. Yoo-hoo!"

---

[53] *SS Cathay* was built by Barclay, Curle & Co., Glasgow for the Peninsular and Oriental Steam Navigation Company, London, and launched in 1924

The boys could not see nor hear him so he flew down the ship's staircase, reaching the top of the gangway in time to greet them as they came aboard. "Walter, Big Horace, Mac – good to see you."

From a distance Walter looked okay. Face-to-face was a different story. Pale and pitifully thin, the Trumper of Billiards [54] was a shadow of his former self. Smith, shaken by his friend's appearance, pulled Big Horace and Mac to one side to express his concern.

"Walter doesn't look too good. I've promoted the exhibition events as 'The Greatest Show on Earth' and we've banked the gate [the price of the tickets]. If we are forced to cancel it will cost us."

"Don't worry, he'll pull through. The sea voyage will do him a world of good." During the daylight hours, fellow passengers gossiped about the man in the steamer-style lounger chair who pulled a blanket over his head when he saw them coming.

"Tut, tut, tut, how rude! What can he be thinking?"

They would have been horrified to know the answer to that question. Walter's thoughts were of Rosie's coffin, of his beloved buried under all that soil with only the Megascolides Australis[55] to keep her company. Rarely did he come to dinner and, when he did, ate like a sparrow, excused himself, returned to the cabin, lay on his bunk and listened to his gramophone play "Walking my Baby Back Home".[56]

Low spirits took his soul to a place where it had never been before and two weeks into the voyage he attempted suicide. Big Horace found him just in time.

"Christ Almighty, Walter."

The doctor listened to his patient's stomach then reached for the Ewald tube. Over the following days, he counselled Walter and confided: "You and I have something in common."

The doctor had lost his wife and daughters in a house fire caused by an undetected gas leak.

"Didn't you feel like giving up?" Walter asked him.

"Of course, I did. I felt just like you do and I asked myself the same questions about life that you are asking yourself. See this photo." He picked up the framed picture sitting on his desk.

"My girls gave me the answer. The purpose of life is to come to know the self. Your Rosie came into your life to help you to achieve that end. You must not rob her of her purpose."

Walter thought long and hard about the doctor's philosophy. By the time the *Cathay* reached Colombo he was enjoying the odd Fox Trot and, on the final leg, the boat train from Southampton to Waterloo, he joined Mac in his exercise regime. On the train Mac was limited to eye-rolling, push-ups, flexing of finger joints and signing of autographs. That is what they were doing when the train slid into the platform.

"Come on, boys," Willie yelled. "We have arrived."

The London welcome was first-rate.

---

[54] Victor Thomas Trumper (1877–1915), considered to be the most stylish and versatile batsman of the Golden Age of Cricket. Great-uncle Walter was compared to two human heroes and a horse: Bradman, Trumper and Phar Lap.
[55] A species of Australian earthworm
[56] Popular song published in 1930 with lyrics by Roy Turk and music by Fred E. Ahlert. The song inspired the 1953 musical of the same name starring Donald O'Connor, Janet Leigh and Buddy Hackett

Third from the left, New Zealand champion Clark McConachy. shaking hands with the chairman of the Association. Walter Lindrum is fourth from the left. Dressed in a light-coloured suit , he is looking straight into the lens. Willie Smith of Darlington, gloves and bowler hat clasped in front of him, stands to the chairman's right.

"Willie, my good man, good to have you home. London hasn't been the same without you," chortled James (Jake) C. Bisset, the chairman of the Association, grabbing his friend warmly in a bear hug.

"Morning, Mrs Jenkins," Bisset had chirped, tipping his bowler hat. "I'm off to the station to welcome my international visitors. No idea how long I will be. I'm sure you can manage." Jenkins, a damn fine bookkeeper, had been Bisset's personal assistant at the Arundel Hotel for longer than either of them could remember. The truth was that she was in love with him.

On a normal business day Bisset skipped down the steps at about 8.30 am and set off on his stroll to Cecil Chambers in the Strand. In summer, there were daffodils. In winter, he wore a black wool coat with Persian lamb lapels to shield him against the sleet. No matter the weather, his was a confident stride to the swing of the conventional black umbrella.

He travelled a regular route: from Knightsbridge to Hyde Park corner, past the Duke of Wellington and up Constitution Hill to the Queen Victoria Memorial, down the Mall to Admiralty Arch, arriving at the offices of the Control Council at about 9.30 am. Bisset would spend the next three hours reading mail, issuing instructions to staffers, playing politics and dictating letters to an assistant whose Pitman's shorthand was the talk of the town. Finishing at about 12.30 pm, he would make his way to Ye Olde Cheshire Cheese to indulge in a fat slice of steak & kidney pud swimming in a thick gravy sauce and listen to the local gossip.

Bisset was a man of few and direct words who spoke directly: he ran a tight and profitable ship which funded his good life. There were annual escapes to Tunisia, the occasional weekend at Maxims and Le Palais de Glas and the special hobbies of billiards, ballroom dancing and ornithology[57], each occupying a separate compartment in his life.

Mac followed Smith from the train. Mac was tall, slim, confident and imbued with a great sense of calm: his long lantern jaw gave him a somewhat melancholy appearance. He maintained this stern countenance throughout his career, delighting audiences with his stupendous play and acknowledging the applause with only the slightest of nods. Rarely did the real Mac show through, the man with twinkling eyes who knew how to make people laugh till their cheeks ached and was known to cartwheel down Oxford Street.

[57] Ornithology is a branch of zoology concerned with the study of birds

British journalists compared Mac to the great hypnotist Svengali as it was so easy to fall under his spell. Australian journalists compared him to the British champion Diggle. Yet Svengali and Diggle were Mac's polar opposites. Svengali went around laughing at the wrong thing at the wrong time which was something Mac would never do. Diggle, despite physical similarities with Mac, was aggressive by nature and horribly awkward at the billiard table; he stood upright and his bridge hand looked like a huntsman spider.[58] Mac's body fell beautifully over his cue and his magnificent long-fingered bridge was as delicate as rose petal jelly.

Minutes after Mac stepped from the train, Walter emerged and stood framed in the carriage entrance. The language of Walter's body said: "I have arrived."

Walter's Fedora[59] was set at a jaunty angle, his left hand clutching the cue case. Frank Barnes, sports writer for the *The Daily Express*, gave his first impressions in an article on the front page.

Clark McConachy (left) Walter Lindrum with cue case (right)

---

[58] Sparassidae are known as huntsman spiders because of their speed and mode of hunting. They are also known as giant crab spiders because of their size and appearance. They are long-legged and grey-brown in colour and often live in sheds and garages. Larger members of the species are known as wood spiders

[59] A felt hat with a wide brim and indented crown. The word "fedora" comes from the title of a play by the same name written by Victorien Sardou in 1882 for the famous actress Sarah Bernhardt. The play was first performed in the United States in 1889 and the heroine in the play wore a fedora, making the hat a symbol for women's rights. After Prince Edward started wearing it in 1924, it became popular among men for its stylishness

Here we were, expecting a loud-mouthed, big, burly bushman and Lindrum was charming and refreshingly down to earth.

Clearly overwhelmed by the welcome, we couldn't get a bloody word out of him for the first hour. After that he chatted away as if he'd known us all his life. If first impressions count for anything, he's top-notch.'

Barnes turned up at the Strand Palace Hotel early the next morning in the hope of an interview. The concierge was helpful, directing him to Covent Garden. Barnes thanked him and walked the block. The Australian would not be hard to spot. Walter, hat perched at the same angle, was leaning on a pillar outside the Theatre Royal. A crowd had gathered, highly amused by the Australian twang; their interest turned to hysterics when the little Australian jumped upon a ledge, curled his body around a lamp-post and started singing: "You made me love you! I didn't want to do it. I didn't want to do it." [60]

Barnes shook his head.

"Gracious, Walter, you're a character! We'll have to get you a busker's license. Now…" glancing at his watch, "I've got a political luncheon today, but it's still quite early, shall we grab a coffee?"

"That sounds like a good idea. I had planned on walking to Frascatis for a Hazelnut macaroon."

"Walter, Frascatis is in Oxford Street."

"I know," Walter responded cheerily. 'The concierge gave me directions." He pulled out his map.

"Walking is the only way to get to know a city. I like to look into people's faces and I've been told not to come home without a bottle of Penhaligon Bluebell and some Lavandula hand cream."

"Mmmm!" Barnes responded. "Breakfast with a weapon [fresh orange juice laced with ginger] at the Wolseley. Afternoon tea at the Ritz. Bag of Blueberry Marshmallows from Fortnum & Mason and a night at the Royal Opera. I get the general idea."

"I came prepared." Walter pulled out his wallet, flicked the notes inside and grinned from ear to ear.

While Frank and Walter were walking across London, Jake Bisset was locked in discussions with his second-in-command, the slightly built and enigmatic A Stanley Thorn. Mild and gentle on the outside, Thorn was hard-boiled at the core.

"Cuppa, JB?" Thorn asked.

"Later, Thorn. I've been thinking about Walter Lindrum. If he's as good as they say he is, he will be a great asset to our next championship. What do we know about his contract with Willie Smith?"

Thorn fell to twisting the corners of his handlebar moustache and studying the picture of Brizzie Lizzie on the wall.

"Well, Mr Thorn?" Bisset sounded impatient.

"I don't think we know anything other than a contract has been signed between Lindrum of Australia, McConachy of New Zealand and our Willie Smith." "Have you considered the implications, Mr Thorn?"

"I am not sure that I follow, sir," he replied, tapping his pipe for a refill of Hermit's Ten Russians.

---

[60] *News of the World* greatest song of the year, 1913. Composed by James V. Monaco with lyrics by Joseph McCarthy, the song was published in 1913 and recorded by Al Jolson on 4 June 1913. Jolson later performed the song on the soundtrack to the motion picture *The Jolson Story* (1946) starring Larry Parks

Bisset passed a hand over his forehead, fingering the small cyst near his right temple which got bigger when he experienced a blinding shot of the obvious.

"Smith is under contract to table manufacturers Burroughs & Watts and I'll make you a bet the contract dictates he can only play on a Burroughs & Watts table. The contract Lindrum and McConachy have signed may place the same restriction on them. That means the world's greatest players might be prevented from vying for the world crown." Bisset stared into the soft blue cloud of smoke pouring from Thorn's pipe. The smell was intoxicating.

"Close the door, Mr Thorn. Close the door.."

The Times reported:

> The arrangements for the competition for the professional championship will be considered at a meeting of the Billiards Association & Control Council tomorrow and everyone will be hoping that there will be a settlement to the present predicament. It will be regrettable if a championship cannot be arranged in which **all** and not some of the leading players can participate.
>
> The remarkable form shown by both Walter Lindrum of Australia and Clark McConachy of New Zealand has proved that if either of these players challenges for the title – which at present is held by Joe Davis – there will be a very big chance of the championship being won by a competitor from overseas.
>
> McConachy has beaten Davis in the two games they have played, while Lindrum has shown that – on the balance of results in matches between them – he is a more powerful scoring force.
>
> While the complications that have arisen may have been avoidable, there is no reason to suppose that the difficulties cannot be overcome and, in the interests of the game both here and in Australia and New Zealand, it is to be hoped a compromise will be found.

Burroughs & Watts, whose role in bringing my great-uncle and Clark McConachy to Britain is unclear, refused permission for them to play on a table other than one manufactured by their company. Despite earnest pleas from every conceivable bona fide source, the directors of Burroughs & Watts held their ground. Barnes was so upset about what he referred to as 'Hanky-panky', that he wrote the following article in *The Daily Express*:

> There should be no question of the authority of the Control Council, and no attempt on the part of any other group or individual to dictate the conditions of the world championship.
>
> The competition should be wholly dissociated from the use or advertising of billiard tables or implements of any particular manufacturer. It should be so arranged as to afford to all players the opportunity to take part, and then it should be possible to hold a competition for the championship which would be worthy of the name, otherwise we might as well hand Joe the title without asking him to pick up a cue.

Walter was prevented from participation in the world championship. Before disappointment could hijack him, he set out with his gramophone on an exhibition tour, reaching Toronto, Canada, in March 1932. "The gramophone prevents me from getting headaches," he told a journalist at *The Toronto Star*. What the reporter did not know was that the gramophone and a recording of "Walking my Baby Back Home" were clamped to

Walter's soul as an anchor to a sea bed. With Rosie forever in his sights, Walter walked the road to glory.

Headlines such as, "Another Big Break for Lindrum and Lindrum's brilliant form" were common. Strangely, his success did nothing for his bank account. An unusual suspect was the primary beneficiary; gambling giant John Wren, who had made sure, from the outset, that the financial arrangements were weighted in his favour.

Wren loved the gamble. It was the one thing in the world that made him feel alive, that made blood flow faster through his veins and his pulse beat more quickly. It gave him the thrill that nothing else could provide. But why my great-uncle Walter passed the right to use the name "Walter Lindrum" on the products of British cue-maker Perdons for "eternity" and why he returned to the sporting capital of Australia owing money remains a mystery.

Perhaps he took his chances and Lady Luck failed to deliver the ace. Lady Luck runs in streaks and one can have an exceptionally bad run of luck. On the other hand, doing business with Mr Wren may have been a stupid, fatal blunder on Walter's part.

Walter's tours were filmed by Movietone news. As one reporter noted:

Not since the days of the great John Roberts has there been so much interest in the game of billiards. Australia's Walter Lindrum has today taken the world of billiards by storm by defeating long-term champion, Joe Davis, for the world professional billiards title. It remains to be seen whether Davis can win it back. Meanwhile, Lindrum has told the press:

'If Davis wants the crown back, he'll have to come to Australia to get it.'

Walter holding the Gold Cup. Group photograph taken shortly after his World Championship win. Frederick II (left)

Australian reaction to this news was entirely predictable. "Walter Lindrum is the greatest nugget to come out of the west." The British response was outrage. As for family sentiment towards Walter's registry office marriage to Alicia (Auntie Pat) on 9 April 1933, well, that was infused with a similar tone. We all liked Auntie Pat. Well, some of us liked her. Great-grandfather did not care for Rosie or Pat. In the codicil to his will he accused both women of causing trouble. What sort of trouble they caused is not made clear but, although news of Walter's marriage to Pat was not viewed with pleasure, news of the Control Council's ban on the nursery cannon[61] was received with indignation and triggered

---

[61] Delicate shots, keeping three balls together, as if in a "nursery", and moving them along the cushion

a furious response from Albert Park and an even more furious one from the desk of John Wren.

New Zealanders, on the other hand, were popping champagne corks. Their champion had been lobbying the governing body for a change in the rules, spending hours at the billiard table to prove his point, finally demonstrating to the council that nursery-cannon play breached the fifth commandment of sport; "Thou shalt not take unfair advantage." But what might appear to have been an obsession with upholding the commandments of sport was also Clark McConachy's concern for falling box office receipts. The monotony of nursery-cannon play was sending the audience to sleep. Shortly after McConachy proved his point, the chairman of the governing body announced the ban and the introduction of the "Baulk-line" rule, which required competitors to display all-round billiards artistry to entertain the audience. There were at that time only a handful of players left in the world who possessed the skill to play all-round billiards, and those who could rose to the top of the snooker tree. Horace Lindrum was one of them.

Then, there was a terrible accident. The Commissioner at the Russell Street Police Station took it on his shoulders to make the journey to Flinders Lane.

"Good afternoon, Fred. I need to see your eldest."

"Is there a problem, Commissioner?"

Frederick appeared.

"Best sit down, me boy…

2 August 1932.
The Sydney Telegraph

Famous Billiardist's wife killed in terrific smash

Mrs F Lindrum, wife of Mr F Lindrum, a leading billiard player, and sister-in-law to Walter Lindrum, champion billiard player of the world, was fatally injured today when a motor car in which she was a passenger was sandwiched between two electric tramcars in Sturt Street, South Melbourne. The driver, William Addison, 43, of Moonee Ponds, lost a finger. Another passenger – Ruth Dale – escaped without injury and – although the car was so much crushed that it broke into pieces when the trams were backed away – the couple's eight-year-old son – Frederick Lindrum IV – survived.

His war records tell the story of a young man who never recovered from post-traumatic stress disorder, battled alcoholism and exhibited anger at the world.[62]

---

[62] Army number VX61110. Frederick's war record reveals that he was battling alcoholism and, on 13 July 1945, he was charged with the offence of "conduct to the prejudice of good order and Military Discipline" and fined three pounds. On 6 March 1946 he was "Marched in for disposal" and transferred out for discharge. His home address is shown as the family home in Albert Park and his profession is shown as billiardist.

Chapter 3
Clara's story

Clara (Violet) Lindrum

"I won't get through the day without a Newman's chocolate bar," Clara thought to herself as she lay listening to the rattle of the milkman's cart. The milko loved to make a noise as did the rabbitoh, a pasty-coloured fellow with a grumpy nature who courted a constant scowl on a face comprised almost entirely of the enormous mouth.

"Rabbitoh!...Rabbitoh!"

On the third cry his knees creaked into action, his joints rusted like the chain on an old bicycle.

Rat-a-tat. Rat-a-tat.

Think Ravel's *Bolero*.[63]

Paddington was teeming with characters like the rabbitoh. Remember the peddler in the story of Aladdin? The one who went about the city calling: "old lamps for new". In Paddington the peddler was the rag-and-bone man who pulled a big-wheeled cart of the Ali Baba variety. If you needed to barter with him you kept your distance for he wore oilskins and stank to high heaven.

Then there was the fishmonger, a happy chappie whose lips resembled those of a Mooloolaba King.

---

[63] A one-movement orchestral piece composed by Maurice Ravel (1875–1937). Originally composed as a ballet commissioned by Russian actress and dancer Ida Rubinstein, the work premiered in 1928

"Get yer fishies….Get yer fishes."

"Any old iron."

"Rabbitoh!"

Washed and dressed, Clara grabbed hold of the bedpost and heaved herself upright. She had passed a bad night. It was so difficult to get comfortable these days. Her back ached. Her poor feet were swollen and, no sooner had she emptied her bladder, than it was full again. Par for the course when soon to give birth. Pulling the curtains, she looked out the window. The birds were chirping and the milko was running from house to house, whistling like a cockatiel. The tune was not easily recognisable. It sounded like "Hitchy Koo" but it may have been "Good night Nurse".

"Better get downstairs," she said to herself checking the money in her pocket. You didn't leave your milk money under the doormat. No way! Blasted hooligans. The milko thought the police could do more. "If you ask me they're taking a backhander. Turning a blind eye. They turns a blind eye to a lot of things. Council's the same. I sees those rats in Wynyard park. Big as possums. Hot today, isn't it love? Humid. Don't look as if you've got too long to go!" "Any day now," Clara responded.

"That'll be two and sixpence."

Clara fumbled with the coins.

So much for Caroline Chisholm's much-trumpeted meat three times a day.[64]

Clara put the milk can in the icebox, filled the kettle and lit the gas. Usually sweet and smooth this morning's brew was bitter on the tongue. A few sips and she left the rest. Five days later the cup was still sitting on the ledge with that nasty mould that cold tea gets when it has been left for days.

"You need to walk, lassie," the doctor had told her. During the winter months, from June to September, she walked from Paddington to Susannah Place in the Rocks and back. In the spring, from September through November, she managed the distance by taking a break at the tree arch in Hyde Park. There she would sit for a time watching small children chasing giant bubbles as they floated towards the Archibald fountain and, on occasion, she would debate with the man on the soap box.

If there was any spare money, she would make a second stop at the Tea Cosy for a cuppa and a freshly baked scone with Barambah cream and fig jam.

Today, it was stinking hot. The walk would be a short one, to the corner shop and back. She donned her wide-brimmed, rose-coloured straw hat and pulled the shopping-list from the front of the ice-box. Ginger, lard, Lyle's golden syrup, Lakersteen's marmalade, Society tea, Lively Polly – but the contractions started before the money changed hands. Twenty minutes later a kindly midwife in a Peter Rabbit apron was wheeling her off to the delivery ward. She spoke in a heavy Scottish brogue.

"Yer must-ner be worrying about a thing, ma dear, the wee one will be with us before ye know it. Remember, breathe, breathe."

---

[64] That promise was used to populate the nation

15 January 1912

Horace was born into the Lindrum family as Horace Norman William Morrell on 15 January 1912 at the Royal Hospital for Women in Glenmore Road, Paddington. He was named after the Roman poet and philosopher Horace, who believed that memory was a marvel, that happiness came from within the self and that great gifts for humanity lay in places where we least expected them or came to us in disguise. Horace the philosopher also believed that mankind should aspire to fairness, justice and forgiveness and that there was something to be said for the private man.

Governor Arthur Phillip described the city where Horace Morrell grew up as a "kind of heath, poor, sandy and full of swamps."

In the third volume of his *Antipodes* or *Residence and Ramblings in the Australian Colony* (London, 1852), British-born soldier and historian Lieutenant-Colonel Godfrey Charles Mundy wrote that "on one side, towards Port Jackson, the prospect is full of cheerful beauty: on the other, the direction of Botany Bay, it is desolation itself."[65]

This perception of Paddington changed after a committee headed by colonial Governor Richard Bourke made the decision to move the Redcoats from their ramshackle premises in George Street, Sydney to brand new premises built on land between Oxford Street and Moore Park Roads.[66]

Completed in 1846, the Victoria Barracks, a magnificent conglomeration of Hawkesbury sandstone buildings in the Georgian style, housed government business, the engine of the local economy. By 1912, however, the once-gentrified village of Paddington had managed to turn itself back into a slum with a Jekyll-and-Hyde personality: respectable on the outside, underbelly at its core. Street after street was inhabited by families – mum, dad and five or six ragged-arsed kids – living on the smell of an oily rag and teetering on the brink of bankruptcy; side alleys were infested by thieves, murderers, rapists, con artists and drug dealers.

At the historical root of the urban expansion of Paddington, of what is today a chic, elegant, distinctive, sophisticated, aesthetically pleasing, cosmopolitan suburb was an eclectic mix of transported convicts, corrupt politicians, unethical businessmen, immoral servants of the Crown, hard-nosed criminals, female gossips, talented tradesmen and struggling families.

Those families, ordinary men and women of the city, were the carefree, hard-working, hard-drinking backbone of the State of New South Wales. Many were of Cockney, Irish, Welsh or Scottish extraction; they brought to Australia their twinkling eyes, their craftsmanship, songs, culture, energy, enthusiasm and philosophy of a shared space. It was the combination of these qualities that fostered the spread of the intricate, neat, tidy, well-constructed terraces that stretched along narrow lanes.

According to social historian Max Kelly, who captured the rich day-to-day life of the early Paddingtonians, the area prospered at the height of Sydney's first real-estate boom in the late 1830s. Land and house prices soared, but it was the drinking holes that fared best of all: they included the Sussex Arms, the Britannia, the Rose and Crown, the Londonderry, the Rifle Butts, the Colonel Bloomfield's Arms, the United Service and Cross Guns, the mere shanties and grog shops.[67]

---

[65] Max Kelly, *Paddock Full of Houses*, Paddington: Doak Press, 1978, 51
[66] Built largely by convicts under the command of Lieutenant-Colonel George Barney of the Royal Engineers and, later, his successor Lieutenant-Colonel James Gordon and constructed of Hawkesbury sandstone on a section of a 1000-acre reserve set aside by the visionary Governor Lachlan Macquarie, the Victoria Barracks is a stellar example of Georgian architecture and of great significance to the military and colonial heritage of the state of New South Wales. The Officers' Quarters were completed in 1842. The Barracks, built to accommodate 650 British Army soldiers, was completed in 1846
[67] Kelly in *Paddock Full of Houses*, 140

The Oddfellows and the Union were among the most popular pubs, but the Greenwood Tree[68], the Coachman's Arms[69] and the Paddington were particular favourites of the contemporary establishment. At the Paddington Inn, the 25-year-old proprietor, an attractive widow by the name of Jane Beard, was the main attraction. At weekends, crowds came by the bus-load to meet her which suggests that Beard was a big personality and that going to the pub for a few pints was as important as turning up to Mass on Sunday.

In the pub men, were known to vent their spleen. The target of their angst was the heartless establishment.

"After I feed and clothe the wife and kids and pay the mortgage I am bhail bhris;[70] I've less money than a frog's feather."[71] The complaint was spoken in such a way as to make the barman wilt like a violet. Cynical jesting and bawdy laughter followed as tears over the miserable wage packet were drowned in raffle tickets and liquid amber.

Father Birch, being well-acquainted with the sins of his parishioners, especially their employer-bashing, drinking, gambling, wife-beating and fondness for a good yarn, called them to account. If he ran into them in the street he would give them a tongue-lashing that made them feel as if they had been smacked across the head with a shillelagh[72]. If they managed to escape the priest's hot breath in the streets he would hurl fire and brimstone at them from the pulpit. "You lousy rotten ungrateful wretches, you are well on yer way to roasting in hell," he would scream.

The little children suffered abuse on all fronts. In the home they copped it from their drunken fathers. In the pew the priest berated them. In the classroom they were thrashed by the nuns and brothers who were always at the ready to belt the hell out of anyone who did not know their 5 x tables.[73]

"You flaming dunce," was the regular catch-cry.

Children were grabbed by the earlobes, marched to the corner, walloped with a rattan cane, forced to wear a cone-shaped cap. In the afternoons, victims of the abuse gathered together under one of the giant figs where they would play knuckle-bones, listen to the clip-clop of passing horses hooves, the rattle of gunfire from the barracks and sometimes the tinkle of rain on shingled roof-tops. On occasion they pulled branches from the trees, imagined the branches as rifles and marched like soldiers, caking their bare feet in mud.

Aside from government business and what was transacted in public houses, the chief industries of the time included ribbon-weaving, boot-making, tailoring, dressmaking, hat-making and baking; the manufacture of soda water, confectionery, soap, coaches, furniture and saddles; and tanning, butchery and brewing. Of these, brewing was probably the most successful industry as an insatiable thirst had gripped the colony. By 1890, for example, "Marshall's Brewery was producing 600 hogsheads, as well as a very large quantity of ale and porter per week."[74] and, throughout the day and into the night, the roadways were alive with the sound of "bullock trains hauling their loads of gin."[75]

The ubiquitous corner stores (which could be found on just about every corner) were another hive of activity and they were a critical element in the flowering of an emerging community spirit. For the women of Paddington, gossiping was more important than stocking the larder and there was plenty to gossip about. The conversations might have gone something like this:

---

[68] This hotel was further along Old South Head Road
[69] This hotel was further along Old South Head Road
[70] Irish term for "broke, penniless
[71] Kelly in *Paddock Full of Houses*, 192.: "On fifty bob a week, with a wife and five kids, a man was scratching himself to keep his head above water," 194
[72] Believed to have originated in the village and barony of Shillelagh, County Wicklow, and traditionally made from blackthorn (sloe) wood or oak, the shillelagh (shi-lay-lee) has a long and rich history. Originally it was used for settling disputes in a gentlemanly manner, the knotty club, which was often filled with lead, has also been smeared with butter or lard and placed up chimneys to cure and used for self-defence and the martial arts. Horace Morrell (Lindrum) maintained his childhood connections with the Irish people. A treasured piece of Lindrum memorabilia is a shillelagh presented to Horace on one of his many visits to Ireland
[73] Kelly in *Paddock Full of Houses*, 192.
[74] Ibid, 140
[75] Ibid, 166

"Did you hear about the doctor on the corner of Oxford and Queen? Terrible business. Judge found him guilty of cutting off a boy's whistle."

"I did hear that story, my dear, I didn't believe it when it was told to me the first time around. What about the father of three hung last week for slitting his daughter's throat. Fancy a father doing a dreadful thing like that. Pressure must have got to him. His poor, poor wife!"

"Do you know she comes from Manchester?"

And so it went.

The gossips, male and female, came from all walks of life. They were produce merchants, water-carriers, wheelwrights, plasterers, quarrymen, fencers, coach-builders, blacksmiths, turnkeys and dairymen.

Local identities included:

>midwife Mary Mitchell [76]
>
>pork butcher Nora Hall
>
>stove-maker Bill Hughes
>
>music store owner Robert Crooks
>
>manager of the Kooloo Tea Company George Jacobson
>
>organ-builder Charles Richardson
>
>dyer of ostrich feathers for ladies of fashion Frederick Williams
>
>picture framer James Gleeson
>
>operator of the Paddington Marble Works Mr Tremlett
>
>milliner Mrs Power
>
>carpenter Mr Power
>
>operator of the oyster saloon George Marshall
>
>proprietor of one of Sydney's five "massage establishments" Mrs Drabble
>
>the clothes-prop seller, who staggered along under a load of trimmed saplings on his shoulder, shouting "Sixpence a pair!", and
>
>the bottle-ohs, one-armed Dan and Raggedy Bill, who pulled a small dray, their poor red-raw chests pressing on the crossbar of the shafts, sweating and stinking to high heaven.

Not to be forgotten:

Old Jimmy Powell the lamplighter, the Broken Biscuit man, Abby Symond who ran the hock shop where the faithful on Mondays would be waiting their turn to go through the side door into two little compartments (something like a confessional) where they would beg and plead for an extra bob on a suit or watch, Nosey Bob the hangman, the Cockeyed tailor, Fishbones and a lot whose nicknames are long forgotten.

God rest their souls, poor benighted buggers.[77]

---

[76] Kelly in *Paddock Full of Houses*, 194
[77] Ibid

This great mix of labour and skill contributed to the rapid development of Paddington and ensured that the area's needs were met. Medical, dental, legal, everything from music lessons and music hall performances of "Poor Little Nell" to steel-rimmed glasses, furs, spuds and stewing chops. Fresh rabbits from the rabbitoh at nine pence a pair. Milk from "a fly-by-night milkman [in tinsel coat] at tuppence a quart. (The hungry and needy waiting on the kerbside in the lane to buy the skim)."[78] Honey from the honey man who either gave the spoon a hearty lick himself or offered it to a child willing to do it for him in much the same way as our mothers gave us the spoon from the cake mix.

If you needed to travel, you caught the bus. Driven by a clay-smoking female, the omnibus was the principal form of transportation into and out of the village until the steam tram came along. That did not happen until 1881 and, when it did, the following post from *The Sydney Morning Herald Centennial Supplement*, 17 January 1888 suggests that there was still quite a bit of competition between the bus and the train:

> It was amusing, sometimes, when the tram, owing to greasy rails would get stuck on the Hill. The bus would struggle past, loaded with lads coming home from work, the boys jeering at the halted tram as the engine-driver made frantic efforts to get the wheels to grip. No love was lost between the trams and busmen, the bus driver always trying to beat the "puffing billy" on the run home.[79]

Economic downturn triggered Paddington's decline.[80] From the day the moneymen packed their trunks of cash and mortgages and abandoned the suburb to invest elsewhere abject misery took hold.

Stripped of assets and income, the destitute went to jail. Those who managed to cling on took up residence in boarding houses, joined soup kitchen queues and were counted among the poorest in Sydney's Depression-era society.

Horace's early years, growing up in a slum where beggars bartered their clothes to the proprietor of the gin shop and stiffs queued at the Pig & Whistle for a porcelain bowl of tripe and onions, were very strange and, looking back, he felt he missed a great many of the joys of childhood. His home was surrounded by the crazy whirl of the theatre; the sole means of putting bread on the table; rehearsals and performances one after another meant little time for traditional family life.

Morrell's Dixieland Jazz Band, the first such band to be heard in Australia was topping the bills. Below is a photograph of my grandmother (Clara Violet) with one of her performers (holding the balloon); my grandmother has the pearls hanging down from each side of her hat. The photograph was published with the following caption:

"Come on all your bright young things, come and have a PEPPY TIME! You too can dance like Eugene Stratton."[81]

---

[78] Kelly in *Paddock Full of Houses*, 172

[79] Ibid, 172

[80] The downturn appears to have coincided with the opening of Paddington Town Hall in 1891

[81] Born in Buffalo, New York, American dancer and singer Eugene Augustus Ruflmann (1861– 1918) (stage name, Eugene Stratton), travelled to Britain in 1880 as part of a minstrel troupe. His career was largely spent in British music halls. Perhaps his most famous song was "Lily of Laguna"

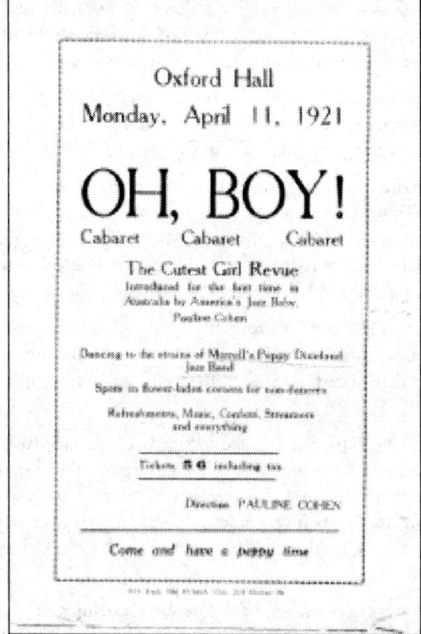

Original promotional flyer

Clara was a fine pianist and she was fabulously extravagant, changing her gowns six or seven times during every performance.

It was often said that Horace's father was quite a card. Billed as "the singing drummer", he could play several instruments and enjoyed a stellar reputation for his performances of popular favourites: "Jazz Baby,"[82] "Look for the Silver Lining"[83] and "I Wish I Could Shimmy Like my Sister Kate."[84] He inherited his passion for theatre from his mother. Her name was Mable Staunton ; she was a jack of all trades. Most artists were in those days.

---

[82] Composed by Blanche Merill and M K Jerome (1919). In 1926 the rights were acquired by Wheaties cereal for use as an advertising jingle. The song was revived in original form and context for the motion picture *Thoroughly Modern Millie* (1967)

[83] Composed by Clarence Williams and Armand Piron (1919), believed to be derived from a bawdy tune by Louis Armstrong about murdered brothel madam Kate Townsend

[84] Music by Jerome Kern, lyrics by B C DeSylva (1919), written for the unsuccessful musical *Zip, Goes a Million*. Popularised in 1920 and popularised by Marilyn Miller in the musical *Sally*

Mable was singer actress, and Penny Farthing cyclist. She would appear as Mable on stage and Dot on the big wheel.

Big Horace was a fine swimmer and a member of the surf life-saving movement. His approach to life was light-hearted and gay but he could be a hard taskmaster, as Horace found out when his father caught him riding on the running boards of a Sydney tram. He could not sit down for a week after the walloping his father delivered with a leather strap.

As the jazz band became in greater demand, Horace was left more and more to his own devices. He spent hours reading about ships and distant lands and consuming geography as a hungry wolf devours its prey. In fact, he became so preoccupied with his ambition to travel that it came as something of a shock when he first learned that travelling to distant lands was not quite as easy as jumping on a magic carpet.

He was also shocked to learn that things were not going well between his parents. After that awareness kicked in, he found himself crawling deeper and deeper into his shell, away from what became a highly disagreeable and discordant atmosphere. The whole business was a mystery to him for a long while; only as he grew older did he learn the truth of the story that hit the headlines in 1926. It was a story so fantastic that he left it as a skeleton to be pulled from the cupboard by another when the time was right.

At school, Horace was not a star pupil. He played truant more than once or twice to go fishing and read. However, as a young man he obtained an education as good as any of us can ever hope to obtain. First-class honours on the stage of life.

One of the most pleasant memories he had of his young days centred on the time his uncles Frederick and Walter came to Sydney and, without any warning or explanation, he found himself journeying back to Melbourne with them. Snuggled against his uncle Walter's coat, his eyes heavy with sleep, he surveyed his uncle Frederick sitting opposite him. He was puffing on his pipe and Horace was moved by the kindness in his eyes.

Horace's experiences in Melbourne were happy and sad. He missed his Mum dreadfully and news of his Auntie Florence's death came only a short time after his arrival. His grandmother took the news hard, of losing her only daughter, and wore black for years afterwards.

Auntie Florence died giving birth to her second child, a little girl, Irene May Dunn. Harriet travelled to South Australia to bring the little girl home. The infant's brother, William (Billy) Dunn, was left with his father, Percy Henry Dunn. Percy was not welcome in the Lindrum household. He was a staunch trade unionist and Horace's grandparents believed their daughter had married beneath her station. Billy joined the Lindrum household much later.

Horace's grandmother was a woman of many fine qualities. However, her forthright approach to life was sometimes as cold as steel and Horace often felt that his presence was on sufferance. He was not the only one who felt that way. The children were well fed and well dressed but there were no cuddles from grandmother, only polite greetings.

Cousin Irene became known as Dolly and Dolly was more of a daughter than a granddaughter. She took her mother's place in grandmother's heart. To say grandmother spoilt Dolly would be an understatement. Everything a child could possibly want was bestowed upon her, but for her brother it was an entirely different story.

William remained Billy Dunn and he was treated as an errand boy. During World War II he served in the army and had the terrible misfortune to be imprisoned in Changi. Even this episode failed to bring him closer to his grandmother. He was always an outsider in the Lindrum house.

Horace started studying the art of billiards while he was in Melbourne. He was coached a little at first by his grandfather, usually when there was a gap in play on one of the 20 tables in the billiard room, and he remembered meeting some of the old stars, including John Roberts Junior. His uncles worshipped the ground John Roberts walked on. Walter told him: "I was knee-high to grasshopper when I first saw Roberts play and what I saw was an education and an inspiration. Roberts was a genius, an incredible technician and a brilliant showman, and I would proudly have sat at his feet."

Horace's grandfather had no intention of turning his grandson into a professional, let alone a great wizard like Roberts, so Horace was left to his own devices. He was about 12 or 13 when he began, on his own initiative, to practise seriously. In the beginning he modelled his play on that of his uncle Frederick and later improved it after seeing Willie Smith perform in Australia. Willie had a pair of perfect eyes and his cue action was beyond criticism. He was not the showman that Roberts was, but he played a highly varied game and was a fascinating player to watch.

When Horace's mother eventually returned to bring him home, he was already proving himself a capable addition to the line of Lindrum champions and, on the 12 September 1933, she suggested that he change his name by deed poll. Horace thought that was a good idea as everybody knew him as Horace Lindrum anyway and he referred to himself as Horace Lindrum. He was proud of his connection with the great Lindrums but, without a shred of conceit, felt he would have scored the same successes if his name had been Brown or Smith and it would certainly have saved him from the many pin-pricks directed towards him over the years.

"You're not really a Lindrum, are you!"

"How come your name is Lindrum when Lindrum was your mother's maiden name?"

"It must be a great advantage to be called 'Lindrum'?" "Were you adopted into the Lindrum family?"

He used to ask himself: "Where does all this come from?" He never did find out.

The day Clara opened the letter from the Department of Health advising the results of a blood test taken at the time of Horace's birth she was so shocked she drowned her sorrows in Society tea and Kolay Glucose Biscuits.

Glucose biscuits using pure malt and milk

The full implications of the test would not be understood by Horace until many years later, as explained further on in this story. Two days after receiving that awful news Clara caught Morrell having it off with the hussy in Number 10. That was the straw that broke the camel's back. She went home, packed his bags and threw them into the street. Big Horace continued to float in and out of her life until Horace was nine years old; then he disappeared until 1957.

A man of sound mind might have felt some sort of remorse for being caught in the act, but not Morrell. He just picked up his bits and pieces and moved on to the next set of vacant loins. He did not give a fig for Clara and the boy he had sired. It may have given Clara hope knowing that her own mother had survived the stigma of sole parenthood but Clara and her mother lived in societies that viewed sole parents as one might view the tea leaves in the bottom of a cup. It had not been easy for Clara growing up in a house of boy champions in an era when women felt the need to die for the feminist cause.[85]

All Clara had been expected to do was wash and clean, and throw her body under the body of a respectable man.

For someone with Clara's fierce ambition to succeed on her own account that was an intolerable expectation. Was she not the one that Paderewski had identified as "The genius of the family"?

Survival meant hard work. She wrote music, taught dancing, played piano, knitted socks for the Comforts Fund, took in mending and alterations, tended her baby and, for relaxation, read the adventures of Birtles & Ferguson [86]and the works of Australia's first literary treasure, Charlotte Atkinson[87]. It did not help that her father had stopped talking to her. To rub salt into the wound, he put Big Horace on the Lindrum payroll. But things are

---

[85] On 4 June 1913, Emily Wilding Davison threw herself under the King's horse at the Epsom Derby. She died four days later
[86] Described in an article in *The Barrier Daily Truth*, Tuesday 15 April 2014 as "One of the greatest adventure stories in motoring history. Two men in a "Brush" and a dog called "Rex",is the story of a famous adventure undertaken by long-distance cycling champion Francis Birtles and driving enthusiast Sid Ferguson who travelled from Freemantle to Sydney in March and April of 1912 in a one-cylinder 10-horsepower "Brush"runabout manufactured in Detroit in 1910. Birtles and Ferguson, sponsored by Canada Cycle and Motor Company and Dunlop Tyre Company, were the first to undertake the arduous trip across the wild Australian bush
[87] Charlotte Atkinson nee Barton was the author of Australia's earliest known children's book. *A Mother's Offering to Her Children* by a Lady, Long Resident in New South Wales, Sydney, Gazette, 1841. The text reflects on the high value and importance of family dialogue

not always as they seem. This will become clearer as my story unfolds, but that is how Morrell got to stand with my great-grandfather, my two great-uncles and my dad in a press photograph. I took a pair of scissors and cut him out of the frame.

On 14 April 1912, three months after my father's birth, the ship *Titanic* hit an iceberg. On the eve of that event, Captain Edward Smith followed an order from his superior, J Bruce Ismay (an executive of the White Star Line), to set the ship's engine to full steam ahead. Ismay wanted to beat the record for crossing the Atlantic and his directive was driven by pure greed. When Smith acted on Ismay's Order, he acted against his own better judgment. He had seen the iceberg warning and knew the danger. The world changed forever the day the crystal, silverware and bone china slid off the tables in the first-class dining-room. In the after-shock of that terrible calamity, Australian society morphed from bushman to digger and the hymn, "Nearer My God, to Thee"[88] became an anthem.

For two years after the calamity, days and months came and went as if they had never existed. Then came the terrible news that Archduke Ferdinand had been assassinated in Sarajevo.

---

[88] Hymn composed by English poet and Unitarian hymn writer Sarah Flower Adams (1805– 1848) at her home in Loughton, Essex in 1841. It was first set to music by her sister, the composer Eliza Flower, for William Johnson Fox's collection *Hymns and Anthems*

1 August 1914

John Wren did not go to war. He enlisted but the enlistment was a ploy to get 14-year-old boys who had never been to the barber to offer up their lives for the nation.

>*The Bulletin*[89]
>
>25 November 1914
>
>> Please don't. This is no laughing matter. John Wren went on a 16-mile route march the other day and now has varicose veins or something and won't be able to go to Gallipoli. He's just a miserable lucre-loving trafficker in the temple.
>>
>> FULL BLOODY STOP!

Wren's rhetoric lent weight to the Prime Minister's pleas for a referendum on conscription and, as Lieutenant-Colonel Peter McGuinness says:

> "They marched them down to Woolloomooloo in single file, impossible to march otherwise on account of the crowd, took about two hours to get there, embarked on ferry steamers which conveyed them to their ships, were fixed up with their quarters and then went on deck to see swarms of small boats with friends encircling the ship, saying goodbye. Steamed out at 4 pm amidst great noise from the surrounding ships and ferries."[90]

Sailing towards what Bea Miles[91] called a "grand strategical blunder", the consequences of which spread far wider than the Dardanelles: a monumental gaffe that is now touted as the birth of the nation.

Whatever the reality, Germans who had pledged their allegiance to Australia were spat at, dismissed from their jobs, removed from their university posts, imprisoned and forced to change their names. Hence, "Von Lindrum" became just plain "Lindrum" and the history of the Lindrum family was buried in a tin the size of a rectangular money box.

In May 1915 the Zeppelins bombed Britain and another bitter wind swept the world. Six months later men scrambled onto wrong beaches. I guess there's not much point replaying the reel but I can't help wondering how much blood has been shed on this earth of ours. I mean, how many dams would we have filled? And how much greater might we have been if we had put our energy into something other than warmongering and our money into something other than the manufacture of weaponry? All that friendship we might have enjoyed. All that culture we might have shared. All that tradition we might have taken and turned into something truly wonderful.

---

[89] Australia's longest running magazine. The Bulletin was founded by J F Archibald and John Haynes. The first issue was published in 1880 and the final issue in January 2008. In its early years the magazine comprised political commentary, sensationalised news stories and Australian literature; it featured the works of many writers and poets, including Dorothea Mackellar, Banjo Paterson, Henry Lawson, Mary Gilmore and C J Dennis. The magazine played a significant role in the encouragement and circulation of nationalist and republican sentiments: Australia for Australians and Australia for the white man. The magazine remained an influential and controversial publication through the 20th century and into the first decade of the 21st

[90] Lieutenant-Colonel Peter McGuinness MBE, RFD, ED (Retired), *Boldly and Faithfully, The Journal: The Official History of the Australian Imperial Force March 1915–October 1918*, (1/19 RNSWR Association Incorporating 2/19 Australian Infantry Battalion, AIF Association, 2011),

[91] An "iconic eccentric", Beatrice Miles (1902–73) was known for her outrageous and disruptive conduct in public places, outspoken criticism of political and social authority, altercations with taxi drivers and famous performances of the Bard in exchange for money and goods

Shell-shock, alcoholism, sleepless nights, nightmares, depression, loss of limbs, loss of sexual drive, the trauma never goes away it stays with a man or woman, forever, and bleeds into the family chain and into the chain of humanity.

Of course, these echoes of war's thunder rang through the Lindrum family too, as with all other Australian families who were affected, during and after the war.

Horace was three years old at the commencement of World War I. In 1917 he was five when Brigadier-General Reginald Dyer gave the order to raise rifles and point them at the exit gates in Amritsar. Seconds later, Gurkhas and Sikhs under Dyer's command, some standing, some kneeling on one knee, raised their .303 Enfields and opened fire on their own people: innocent non-violent protesters and Baishakhi pilgrims who had come together to celebrate the annual Baishakhi (harvest) celebrations, a religious and cultural festival for the Punjabis. The festival space of some six or seven acres was walled on all sides save for five exit gates. The order was based on the false belief that there was going to be a major insurrection against British rule.

In all, 1650 rounds of ammunition were fired.

How much of our warmongering has been based on false beliefs?

Three months later Lenin ordered the slaughter of the Russian Czar, his wife, children, servants and family dog. After that, woolly caps and fingerless mittens prepared for Armageddon, preaching Chapter Three of the Second Epistle of St Paul, Verses 1-8.

> This know also in the last days, perilous times shall come.
> For men shall be lovers of their own selves, covetous boasters,
> proud blasphemers, disobedient to parents, unthankful, unholy.
> Without natural affection, truce-breakers, false accusers,
> despisers of those who are good. Traitors, heady high-minded
> lovers of pleasures...lustful...never able to come to the knowledge
> of truth.

Poverty, war, family upheaval, anxiety about the potential collapse of a world he was only just coming to know: these infused Horace's youth with dread but, in contrast, also with an inner belief in himself.

The sounds of London overtake Duncannon Street and the aroma of chestnut and hot custard draw people to the crypt. My fingers are starting to hurt and I try desperately to focus on making my way to the Italian restaurant on Shaftesbury where Linguini Putanesca is a regular special. But how does a writer, how does anybody, liquidate thoughts of dug-outs and megaphones and long sermons and never-ending choruses of "Onward Christian Soldiers, Marching as to War, with the cross of Jesus going on before". Or, in today's lingo, expenditure of billions of dollars "to become more powerful on land and in the skies, and more commanding both on the seas and beneath them."[92] Sure, manufacture of weapons creates jobs but how many people do those weapons kill? Should we not be investing in education, science, culture, health, peacemaking and caring for the elderly? Should we not be planting forests? Should we not be remedying the horrific art and sport imbalance? Should we not be returning to craftsmanship before human effort is supplanted?

If, sometime down the track, we come to know an enemy, the "big fight," kill people we know and people we love and people who look just like us, we will build hatred in an already brutal world. Then again, 220,000 people were killed when President Harry S Truman put his finger on the button that triggered the atomic bomb,[93] so nuclear bombs, if used, would be likely to obliterate the greater part of the world as we know it.

Funny how we are always too busy folding the washing to see the Gospel Truth. Guess that is why we ultimately end up dressed in our top hats and tailcoats, banging our fists on a table inside a ruddy cold tram or, in contemporary terms, sitting, cold-eyed, in a wing-backed lounge chair inside a palace bedecked with chandeliers "shirt fronting" the leader looking back at us.

> The reality remains.
> Johnny enlisted.
> Johnny never came home.

I stand for a time reflecting on the words of Admiral Gene La Rocque[94]:

> "I hate it when they say, 'He gave his life for his country.' Nobody gives their life for anything. We steal the lives of these kids. We take it away from them. They don't die for the honour and glory of their country. We kill them."

With La Rocque's thoughts still spinning in my head I am drawn to a man standing on a fruit crate near Nelson's Column:

> "Rule of law gone. Justice, gone. Remember that ruler who brought disaster upon the French? These men are a law unto themselves. The people are their vassals. Ask yourself, what did they achieve? Nothing! Bloody

---

[92] Front page of *The Sydney Morning Herald*, Friday, 26 February, 2016, "Malcolm Turnbull has unveiled his blueprint for the military, with plans to pump $195 billion over the next decade into new hardware. At the centre is a submarine program that could cost $150 billion by the middle of the century." Analysis pages 8 and 9. David Wroe, National Security Correspondent., 'Navy building response to region's rapid change.'. Tony Wright, 'Flagging PM fails the patriot test'

[93] On 6 August 1945, American B-29 "Enola Gay" bombed Hiroshima. Three days later, the Americans bombed Nagasaki

[94] An advocate for peace, Admiral Gene La Roque (1918–), is a retired rear admiral of the United States Navy who founded the Center for Defense Information in 1971

massacre. Murdered and terrorised their own people. Clung to power as the fiery monkey clings to a tree. Wake up, I say unto you. Accept that the devil devours his own children. Stop making the excuse...we didn't understand until it was too late. This is history, people and history is not always written on trophies. I say this because you can't always believe what is written, even if it is written in stone. We're heading for storms. You might think it is over but I am telling you we are heading for storms and we are not prepared for them."

The bobbies arrive and, ever so gently, put a hand on his shoulder.

"Come along, sir, we don't want to alarm the people."

He keeps up the fight as they cart him away:

"Ask yourself, what would you do if your neighbour's house was on fire and your neighbour inside it? Would you stand there and let the house burn down or would you try to wake him up?"

> All things bright and beautiful
> All creatures great and small
> All things wise and wonderful
> The Lord God made them all.

"Mummy, will you please tie my laces?" Clara bent down to help her son.

"I love you, Mummy.' "Do you now."

"Yes, Mummy, I love you because you dress me and feed me and take care of me."

"Thank goodness you are not yet a man," Clara thought, her mind travelling to the picture on the front page of *The Sydney Morning Herald*.

"Now, off you go." She kissed Horace on the cheek, turned him around and directed him through the school gate. He gave her a smile and a wave and she watched and waited until he disappeared from view.

Horace was a pupil at the Sacred Heart primary school in Darlinghurst. He was not a Catholic. It was unusual in those days for a non-Catholic to be permitted entry to a Catholic school but Clara had developed strong ties with the Irish Catholics in the area and the local priest and the nuns turned a blind eye. In his manhood, Horace did not align himself with one religious sect, he believed in a Supreme Being and adopted Mahatma Gandhi's philosophy, "I am Christian, I am a Muslim, I am a Jew, I am a Buddhist......" This is borne out by the photographic evidence of Horace with so many people of the world.

Pauline Cohan and her Bottom Wigglers arrived in Sydney in 1921 for a series of concerts at the Oxford Hall. A "New Age Woman" – bobbed hair, painted lips, pencilled brows – Cohan took the city by storm. She had everybody doing the Bunny Hop, Charleston, Cake Walk and Turkey Trot. "We're looking for a pianist. He or she has got to be good," Cohan told the Australian Opera. "Clara Lindrum can play anything you throw at her. Why don't you give her a go?"

A member of Nellie Melba's Sock-knitting for the Comforts Fund Patriotic Circle, Clara had made quite a name for herself playing request programmes in the town halls for international opera stars[95], Galli Curci and Toti Dal Monte, who were engaged in Melba's touring company. Cohan accepted the recommendation and asked her secretary to write the following letter:

> Dear Miss Lindrum,
>
> Pauline Cohan has asked me to write to you.
> We are looking for a pianist for our new show. You come highly recommended…

Clara could not believe her good fortune. "Thank you, Miss Cohan," she whispered, kissing the note then racing to the jam jar where she kept her savings: 24 shillings and 11 pence, enough for an imported corset, dress, hat and overcoat. She had already fallen in love with a hat. In fact, she had spent the last few weekends glued to the front window of the local milliner's shop. Now she sat imagining the work of art on her head. A snazzy cream number, it had a wide band of navy blue silk drawn into a huge bow at the left-hand side, secured by a bunch of bright pink cherries.

"Delicious! I will make a name for myself in that hat," she giggled.

Then she remembered the appointment she had made for young Horace to have his hair cut.

Horace, then nine, was about to experience a metamorphosis from Gainsborough's *Blue Boy*[96] to short back and sides. On the same afternoon he was caught by the ear lobes for stealing ice-cream. The proprietor of Peter's reported him shimmying up the drainpipe of the West Street terrace, a plastic bucket in one hand and a spoon in the other, climbing through the window and scooping Neapolitan from the makeshift die.[97]

Clara had her hands full.

Raising her son, working her fingers to the bone during the day and playing the piano seven nights a week did not leave her much time for anything else.

Victor Lindley arrived on the scene mid-way through 1923.

---

[95] Among others, Clara played for Amelita Galli Curci who was under contract to the Victor Talking Machine Company, and Toti Dal Monte who was engaged to the famous tenor, Enzo de Muro Lomanto. Dal Monte eventually married Lomanto in St Mary's Cathedral with the Cardinal presiding

[96] Oil on canvas painted by artist Thomas Gainsborough (c. 1770), the *Blue Boy* is said to be a portrait of Jonathan Buttall (1752–1825), the son of a wealthy hardware merchant. The painting is held at the Huntington Library in San Marino, California

[97] Peters' ice-cream company was established by American expatriate Frederick (Fred) Augustus Bolles in Paddington in 1907 under the trading name "Peters' American Delicacy Company"

Sydney, 13 September 1924

Horace was 12 when Clara married Victor at the Church of Christ in Petersham. The sole pictorial record is a photograph taken inside the church. Clara looks as if she has been plucked from the chorus of Leslie Stuart's *Florodora*.[98] Bathed in silk tulle, the cream-coloured flapper-esque lace dress with its dropped waist and tea-length hemline suited her to a tee. Lindley wore pin-stripes. A barley-twist watch-chain dripped from the pocket of his waistcoat. At 193 centimetres, he commanded attention.

The Reverend Reginald Provan Arnott stood on an elevated platform to the right of the couple.

Nobody gave a reason that the pair should not be joined.

After the wedding the bridal party retreated to the Oxford Hall for refreshments.

At about 10.30 pm, Clara, Lindley and best man Douglas Birrell took their leave.

"What a bloody awful night," Birrell said as they dashed to the car.

The ants were swarming and you could feel the southerly bluster on its way. "Another ten minutes and I reckon' she'll be pelting down," Birrell continued, jumping in the back. Lindley nodded, settled Clara into the front seat and cranked the engine. They did not get far. A few streets at best before Birrell leaned forward.

"What did I tell you. Here she blows."

Again, Lindley nodded. He did not like driving in the rain and the rain was now bucketing down.

"Wow! That wind is really something."

Lindley had to work hard to keep the car from veering to the wrong side of the road.

"I can't see a bloody thing," he told Clara as he wrenched the car into second gear.

"Take it slow, love."

"The lighting is so poor down this end of town. I'm going to pull over and adjust the lamps."

"You'll get drenched."

"Christ almighty," he shrieked as he pushed open the door, the wind whipping at his face.

Thunder rolled overhead; he lost his grip and the door slammed shut.

"That was a beauty," he said to himself, watching Clara's reaction through the windscreen.

He managed to adjust the light on the left without too much difficulty but the wires on the right headlight had come loose and he could not get them connected.

"Damn it," he said to himself, "We've only got one light."

"Look at you. You're soaked to the skin," Clara observed as Lindley climbed back into the front seat. He looked and smelled like a wet labrador.

Birrell offered to have a go. "Best wait a bit mate."

A terrific clap of thunder caused Clara to throw her hands onto her ears and sink further down in her seat.

"It's only thunder, Duckey," Lindley comforted. "I'm not too keen on thunder," she mumbled. Giant pieces of ice were hitting the bonnet.

---

[98] Based on the book by Jimmy Davis, using the pseudonym Owen Hall, *Florodora* was an Edwardian musical comedy; one of the first successful Broadway musicals of the 20th century; music by Leslie Stuart additional songs by Paul Rubens and lyrics by Edward Boyd-Jones. It was first performed when the iron curtain was raised at the Lyric on Shaftesbury Avenue, London, in 1899. The song "Tell Me Pretty Maiden" was a big hit

"That hail is the size of golf balls. I hope you don't get too much damage to the paintwork, Lindley. We haven't had a storm like this one for as long as I can remember." At Birrell's words, a fork of lightning sizzled and ripped through the cloud cover to the ground.

"Spectacular. I wish we had a camera."

Neither Lindley nor Clara shared Birrell's enthusiasm. "As soon as it eases, I'm going out again."

Lindley was shivering so badly now his jaw was trembling.

"I'll have another go at connecting the light and then I'll crank her up again.'" The journey down Macquarie Street was painfully slow. The rain had stopped but sections of the road were blocked due to flooding, and a thick mist was rolling in. To make matters worse, the windscreen wipers were not working properly so Lindley was forced to steer with his right hand and use his left to push the rubbers backwards and forwards. Next, the front wheel got stuck in a large pothole.

"Hell!" Lindley slammed the car into reverse and pushed his foot hard onto the accelerator. The whirring noise told him it would take more than acceleration to get the car out.

"I best take a look."

"You're going to catch your death," Clara harped.

"I'm soaked already, it's not going to make any difference."

"Well, at least put this blanket around you." She pulled a picnic rug from the back seat. Seconds later, Lindley, draped in the blanket, his torso caked in mud, came to the window.

"Sorry, mate, I'm going to need your help. You take the wheel and I'll push." Birrell clambered into the front.

"When I yell 'foot down', slam her into reverse and give her all you've got." A few seconds later:

"Okay, Doug, foot down."

The engine laboured and the wheel dug deeper into the mud.

"Bloody hell," Lindley exclaimed, slamming the flat of his hand on the bonnet for a second time.

"We need something to jack her up and we'll have to go gently so we don't damage the suspension."

It took them nearly an hour to get the car out. By that time, Lindley could feel a virus coming on. His immune system was not strong at the best of times.

The weather finally eased as they came into the Parramatta Road.

Then sudden disaster. At a few minutes past midnight, Victor Lindley ran over and killed Robert Walker and seriously injured two other men near the intersection of Johnson Street.

Birrell was to tell the court:

> "I estimate we were travelling at about twenty miles per hour. I saw three men a few yards ahead of us, trying to cross the road. One of them looked as if he had been drinking for he was swaying all over the place. The car swerved and there was a jolt.
>
> I must have been knocked unconscious because all I can remember after that is waking up in the hospital with a broken cheekbone and a dislocated jaw."

According to Lindley, he swerved to avoid a collision with another vehicle. He told the magistrate he slammed his foot on the brake and the car mounted the footpath, twisting the front wheel on the left-hand side, damaging the suspension and coming to a stop short of somebody's front wall.

> "I got out and, to my horror, found three men lying unconscious on and near the tram lines. I looked for the other vehicle but it had disappeared. At the time, I had no idea whether I had hit the other vehicle or whether the other vehicle had hit my vehicle nor did I know which vehicle had hit the men. I was in such a state of shock and simply did not know what to do. I remembered something about not moving an injured person and this thought was running through my mind. I cried out for help but nobody came so I ran to the nearest house and started yelling and banging on the front door. A light came on and a fellow opened up. He was holding a stack of blankets and told me he was coming to help.
>
> I returned to the car. Clara was hysterical, so I shook her and told her she needed to calm down. Next I checked on Douglas. He was unconscious and clearly in need of medical help so I decided to drive to the Royal Prince Alfred Hospital. On arrival at the hospital, I ran straight into the emergency department and cried out for help. Douglas was subsequently admitted and two ambulances dispatched to the scene. The rest is history."

The prosecutor at the committal hearing was a warrior who knew how to read a jury.

"Mr Lindley, had you been drinking?"

The prosecutor's eyes were hard, cold as the ice at the summit of Everest.

"No, Sir."

"Mmmmmm. A dry wedding!"

A cynical tone. "Surely you can't expect this honourable court to believe you did not consume some liquid refreshment at your own wedding?"

"Starkey ginger beer, sir."

"Starkey ginger beer! Are you sure it wasn't Jamaica Green?"

Then a rattle-snake change in direction.

"What do you say about the blood on the bonnet of your car?"

Lindley responded quickly.

"I did not know about the blood on the bonnet of my car until Sergeant Mackay told me there was blood on the bonnet of my car."

"You didn't hear the thud, thud, thud when you hit the victims?"

"I don't believe my vehicle hit the victims."

"Do you have a hearing problem, Mr. Lindley?"

"No, sir, I do not."

"Were your senses impaired by the hair of the goat?" "No, sir, they were not."

"Mmmm!"

A long pause and more shuffling of paper. "The other vehicle?"

"Yes, sir."

"Tell me about the other vehicle."

Lindley explained that it had all happened so quickly and he could not remember the colour nor the model of the other vehicle, so the prosecutor put it to him that he was lying. There had been no other vehicle. He had been driving in a manner dangerous and, although dear jury, one should never speculate, the likely case scenario was that Mr Lindley was intoxicated.

Lindley's solicitor strenuously objected to that allegation. The objection was sustained.

Ethel Thorneycroft of 85 O'Connor Street, Haberfield informed the court that she had been returning home from the theatre when she saw a car pass at high speed. A few minutes later there was an awful thud, thud, thud. On being asked to assess the speed of the vehicle, she said it must have been travelling at least 35 miles an hour because it skidded, burning rubber on the roadway and there was a terrible screech of brakes before it mounted the footpath.

Unexpectedly, she turned to Lindley and screamed:

"You're a murderer. You were going too fast. You killed that poor man." At this outburst, the magistrate slammed his gavel onto the bench.

"Madam, you will keep your opinions to yourself. The jury will disregard the last statement." Turning to the court reporter, he ordered: "Strike that statement from the record." The reporter nodded, pushed her glasses up her nose and scrubbed out the words with her graphite.

Later, council worker Thomas Leonard Day of Leichhardt told his version of the events. He said he had been sweeping the roadway when the accident occurred. He heard a terrible thud, saw a body fly up into the air and then fall like a stone. The vehicle skidded 50 yards before it finally came to stop. He had written the registration number down on a cigarette packet. 14205. He produced the piece of paper and held it up for all to see. A murmur swept the courtroom and Day waited for it to pass before continuing with his evidence. Minutes earlier he had seen three men attempting to cross Parramatta Road. They were shaky on their legs and swaying all over the place. He thought they must have been drunk.

The prosecutor quickly intervened.

"But you can't possibly know whether or not the pedestrians had been drinking, can you, Mr. Day?"

"Well…"

"Can you, Mr Day?"

Reluctantly, Day conceded he could not say for certain.

"Did you see any other vehicles on the road?" the prosecutor continued. "No, sir, I did not." Another murmur swept the court.

Day had heard the driver's cries for help and, within a short time, neighbours from around the district were tending the injured men and redirecting traffic from the scene. The driver had disappeared.

"Did I hear you correctly, Mr Day? The driver left the scene of the accident?" "Yes, sir."

Yet another murmur.

Francis Joseph Smith, rubber worker of Matraville, was not fit to appear at the committal proceedings. He was still unconscious in the hospital. Later, at the trial he denied the drunkenness. He told the judge:

"My lord, we was perfectly sober."

Alfred Ephraim Mitchell, his iron-moulder friend who had been out to the world in the bed next to him during the preliminaries, backed up the story. Constable Littlefair gave his summary of events

> "It is alleged, your Worship, that at approximately 12.30 am on the morning of 14 September 1924 said defendant drove his vehicle along Parramatta Road in a manner dangerous and did occasion grievous bodily harm, running down three men, killing one and seriously injuring the other two and that he did leave the scene of the accident. We estimate that the vehicle was travelling at more than thirty miles an hour. Twenty over the speed limit."

Lindley was committed for trial on a charge that he did:

> "On Sunday 14 September 1924, feloniously and maliciously murder one Robert Walker and cause grievous bodily harm to Alfred Mitchell and Frank Smith."

The media had a field day.

"Petersham motor tragedy"
"Sensational police story"
"Mitchell and Smith remain in critical condition"
"Bridegroom on murder charge"

Mr Jennings then heard an application for bail, which was set at 500 hundred pounds. Lindley was thankful to have been granted bail and was relieved to hear that Mitchell and Smith had regained consciousness. He was far from happy, however, about the publicity poor Clara was receiving. Headlines like:

"Jazz Baby – charged with bigamy" and "On cue for conviction!"

were splattered across the front page of *The Sydney Morning Herald*.

They say there is a reason for everything in life. The Lindley case led to Horace's moving to Victoria.

Clara was in a sticky situation. She was concerned for Lindley but she was also concerned for the wellbeing of her son and did what she had to do in the circumstances. Her bigamy case came before the magistrate's court a few weeks after Lindley's committal hearing.

There she stood, solemnly answering the judge's questions, attempting to maintain her Lindrum dignity.

"State your name." "Clara Violet Lindrum."

"I don't suppose you could be related to…?" Mr Jennings SM asked. "Yes, your Worship."

"Oh, my, my. Can you play billiards, my dear?" "No, your Worship. I play the piano and snooker."

The prosecutor gave a little "ahem", to remind the magistrate that he was in the court room not the billiard room.

It was alleged that:

> "On Saturday 13 September 1924, said defendant, Clara Violet Morrell nee Lindrum, married Victor Lindley, at the Church of Christ in Petersham. Her husband, Horace Staunton Morrell, to whom she was married in 1911, being alive."

Under cross-examination, Horace Morrell informed the court that he had only lived with his wife for a short time. There was a child of the union but he did not support him. The jazz band was the common thread, Clara being a pianist and he being a timpanist, who were hard to find. The defendant reserved her defence and was committed for trial. Her lawyers, Messrs Abigail & Millar, warned her not to speak to the press. Before Clara's case came to trial she learned that Lindley had been acquitted of the murder charge and other charges following the road accident.

The trial took a terrible toll on Horace.

On 20 October 1926 he wrote:

> Dear Mum,
>
> Just a few lines hoping you are well and not worrying. I suppose you know that you get nothing from worrying. I am writing to tell you that I am in the fittest condition and I am wearing a smile even though Mr Millar has been in to see me since he came back from seeing you and tells me you are looking very tired and feeling worried, the latter which I keep telling you not to do. Do you know when your case will be on Mum? Please write soon and, don't forget – WIN OR LOSE – come home with a SMILE. Well, I have to wear my grey suit now because my black one is worn out and, just the other day, I made breaks of 108, 123 and 125. This is all the news at present.
>
> From your loving son,
>
> The Marbles Champion of New South Wales
>
> PS: Grandpa backed Manfred to win the Caulfield Cup.

At about the same time, Horace wrote to his father.

The letter is dated 23 February 1926.

The handwriting suggests a strong level of hurt and anger.

The ink is heavy.

> Dear Mr Morrell,
>
> Just a few lines to let you know that I do not wish to recognize you as my father on account of the way you have treated Mum. If you was any decent father you would have written a letter to show respect, as I used to have for you.
>
> My opinion about you is that you are a coward when you want to fight a lady in the street. But still you know it comes to those who wait.
>
> From the one who is never going to be a drunkard.
>
> Horace

PS: I forgot to tell you something, I am never going to be a lady-chaser either.

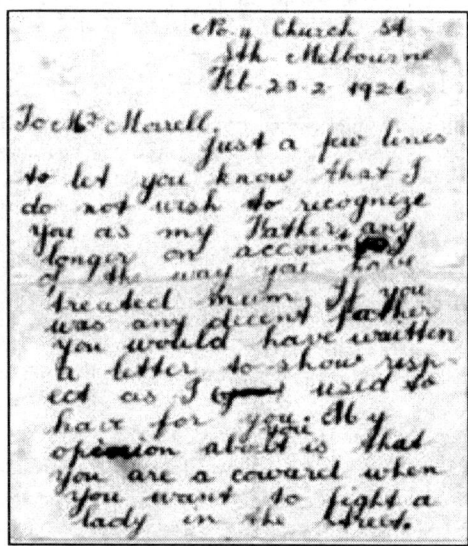

Original letter written by Horace in his own hand 23 February 1926

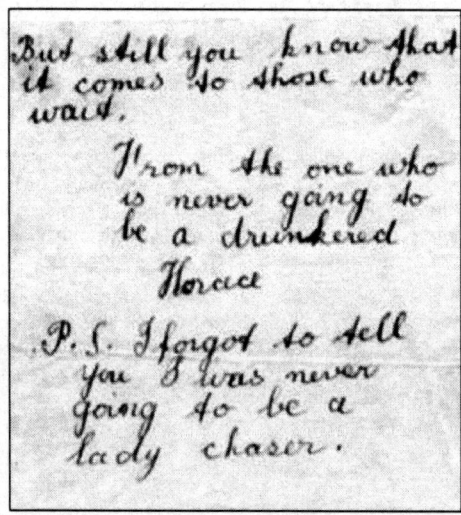

Eighteen months passed before Clara's case came to trial. Every month there was a new headline.

"Married at 14. Dancing Mistress Charged – BIGAMY ALLEGED."

"Fateful Honeymoon. Recent Bride Charged with Bigamy."

Clara was 29 at the time of the trial. Mr Justice Davidson presided. Mr Mead appeared for the prosecution. Mr ER Abigail for the defence. Called over by ballot, the jurymen answered to their names.

Leaning on the bar table, Mead turned the pages of his brief as a mother turns the pages of a fairytale. A Cicero of the first order, he had served his profession with distinction for many years and had recently taken silk.

> "Gentlemen of the jury, the defendant is indicted for having committed the offence of bigamy, that, whilst still married she knowingly married another man, one Victor Lindley, on the 13 September 1924. This is the kind of heinous act that serves to corrupt the moral fibre of decent society and must not go unpunished."

Clara had written in her affidavit:

> I, Clara Violet Morrell nee Lindrum, being duly sworn make oath and say, as follows:
> 1. I am the defendant in these proceedings.
> 2. I was married to Horace Staunton Morrell on the October 09, 1911 at St. Bartholomew's Church, Pyrmont near Sydney in the state of New South Wales, according to the rites of the Church of England.
> 3. There is issue of the marriage, one child to wit, Horace Morrell, aged thirteen years.
> 4. At the time of and prior to my marriage to Mr. Morrell, my mother had a shop at Glenmore Road in Paddington and the Respondent was constantly coming in to the shop and asking me to go out with him but my mother refused to permit him to take me out.

One evening he came into the premises through the back entrance and I was downstairs in the basement cooking the tea. Morrell was there for a few minutes when he put his hand over my mouth and threw me down on the floor. I tried to scream but he prevented me and Respondent had intercourse with me. [Clara was 14 at that time]

The rest is history.

> t the time of and prior to my marriage my mother had a
> shop in Glenmore Road Paddington, and the Respondent was
> constantly coming in to the shop and asking me to go out
> with him but my mother refused to permit him to take me out.
> One evening he came into the premises through the back
> entrance and I was downstairs in the basement cooking the
> tea. Morrell was there for a few minutes when he put his
> hand over my mouth and threw me down on the floor. I tried
> to scream but he prevented me and Respondent had intercourse
> with me.

The above is an extract from Clara's original affidavit

During the course of the trial, evidence of Morrells' womanising was tendered. Private detectives had caught him in bed a number of times, usually with another man's wife. His conduct gave Clara grounds to petition for divorce but her petition delayed the hearing of the bigamy proceedings because, in those days, it was extremely difficult for a woman to secure a divorce from her husband. Legal advice provided to Clara at the time was that, even though she had grounds for a divorce, her chances of securing a divorce from Morrell were slender unless Morrell cross-petitioned her on the ground of adultery owing to her recent marriage to Lindley. If Morrell did that, the court would expedite the hearing. Morrell took his time, allowing Clara to languish in jail. He eventually filed a cross-petition whereupon the bigamy and divorce proceedings were set down for hearing.

"Members of the Jury on the matter of bigamy have you reached your verdict?" "We have, your Honour."

"How say you?"

"We find the defendant…"

Clara took a deep breath.

…"not guilty."

On evidence, the jury determined that Clara's marriage to Morrell had been a sham. Morrell had gone to her father with a proposition. He would make an honest woman out of Lindrum's daughter in exchange for Lindrum putting him on the Lindrum payroll. Lindrum could go to the police and report the rape but the publicity would not serve the family well and what man would want to marry his daughter after that. In the early 20th century, in the aftermath of the Victorian era, Clara would have been seen as "used goods."

The judge turned on Morrell and told him his conduct was unacceptable in a moral society. He then dissolved both marriages and awarded sole custody of Horace to his mother.

The headlines:

> "Jury brings down verdict in Jazz Baby case. Mother gets custody…"

> Mrs Morrell says: "She won't remarry Lindley."

> "Fake Marriage. What Wife Thought. DIVORCE AT LAST."

> "QUEER PATHS TO DIVORCE."

Of the petition brought forward in the Supreme Court of New South Wales, Matrimonial Causes Jurisdiction No. 118 of 1926, the judge said: "The whole affair was stranger than fiction."

The judge's comment came and went but stories about the trial continued for months.

Clara reverted to her maiden name and waited patiently for the hullaballoo to subside before heading to Melbourne to collect the Marbles Champion of New South Wales. While she was waiting she read and re-read her son's letters.

> Dear Mum,
>
> Just a few lines hoping you are well and not worrying. I suppose you know you get nothing from worrying. I am to tell you I am in the fittest condition through wearing a smile. Win or lose, come home with a smile, Mum. I have been treated very well since you have been away. Grandpa bought me new shirts and socks. I have to wear my grey suit now as my black one is worn out……….
>
> Your LOVING son xxxxxxxxxxxxxxxxx

What Horace had not told her was that his uncle Walter had taken the reins on his career. Horace's moving to Melbourne had provided Walter with an opportunity – at least that is what Walter thought at the time – it also provided Horace with an opportunity that would otherwise not have existed.

"11-year-old Horace Morrell is the goods alright. He will be a world-beater in my opinion. No question about it"[99]

Like the hero in Celtic myths Horace followed his uncles into a world he had never visited before. At first glance he had no idea what he was doing in that realm. He eventually succumbed to the magic of the green baize; the adventurer in the boy turned into the man who wanted to share his talent wit the world.

---

[99] *The Sporting Globe* by Masse, Saturday evening 28 April 1923

Chapter 4
The Real McCoy

Horace had grown up. He was still enjoying the Wurlitzer[100] and The Man of a Thousand Faces[101] but he was no longer a boy.

Clara, stony broke after paying her legal bills had no idea how she was going to help her son to achieve his dreams. She did not have have sixpence to get him to Penrith let alone enough for a boat ticket to London but this "exceptionally single-minded and wilful character" possessed an entrepreneurial spirit; the initiative that flowed from that spirit laid the foundations for Horace's future.

Clara did not conjure a fancy business plan. Her plan was ridiculously simple. She was her father's daughter and she did what her father did. She opened a billiard room. In the absence of paternal support, opening another Lindrum's was going to be an annoyance at best, but it was not the decision to open a billiard room that rocked the family foundation stones. It was Clara's decision to take back the reins on her son's career. The last thing her father and Walter had expected was for Clara to waltz in and steal their thunder, but that is exactly what she did. Her father and Walter had set up the long reds. Clara came along and pocketed them.

Five years later the family tiff had turned into a glacial rift.

---

[100]The Rudolph Wurlitzer Co. was established in Cincinnati, Ohio and North Tonawanda, New York in 1853 by German immigrant Rudolph Wurlitzer. In the beginning Wurlitzer imported stringed, woodwind and brass instruments into the United States. The company began manufacturing pianos in 1880. Products included the Band Organ, Orchestrion, Nickelodeon, Pipe organ and Theatre Organ, all of which were popular during the days of the silent movie. Manufacture in the United States ceased in 2009. Wurlitzer pianos are still manufactured in Germany

[101]Famous vaudevillian silent screen star, Lon Chaney (1883–1900). Born Alonzo (Leonidas Frank) Chaney to deaf-mute parents, it is thought his efforts to communicate with his parents is the chief reason he became so expert at his acting craft. Chaney was dubbed "The Man of a Thousand Faces" for his uncanny ability to transform himself into many types of characters through make-up, mime and pantomime. Lon Chaney's life inspired a motion picture *The Man of a Thousand Faces* (1957), directed by Joseph Pevney and starring actor James Cagney in the lead role

"There will be no more new billiard champions for at least 10 years," Walter told a journalist at *The Evening Herald*.

Clara retaliated. "My brother, Walter, doesn't know what he is talking about." Sibling rivalry had, once again, surfaced.

A 12-month rent-free lease on the Mechanics Hall in Goulburn was offered with a pledge to smarten the place up. Scrubbing brushes, a few pots of zinc oxide, half a dozen Aladdin and Tilley lamps, two Hercules fire-proof partitions courtesy of Fred K Jones & Co. Add tables and equipment, Bob's your uncle!

> **LINDRUM'S opens for business tonight...**
> **Be there! All welcome.**

The room was a great success and the first week's takings, all 15 pounds of it, was enough to launch Horace's first big tour of Australia and New Guinea. Fifty years later he had travelled the world.

"What did your Dad do for a living?" "He was a cueist," I say.

"A what?"

"A remarkable man with a remarkable talent. He travelled 18 times around the globe on a piece of wood."

The earnings from Lindrum's in Goulburn provided the seed capital for the establishment of Lindrum's in Pitt Street, Sydney.

With eight tables and an exhibition table, the room was next to the Liberty theatre. The number-one table overlooked Pitt Street. My grandmother kept this table for herself and for my father. The Showman practised on this table in the evenings in full view of the patrons. How do I know that? Les Wheeler told me and Les would know. He knew my father long before my mother and I sailed into view.

At the very beginning of his career, Les worked for *The Sportsman*,[102] an in-depth form guide and Australia's most authoritative racing journal. After that he was racing writer for *The Sydney Morning Herald*, then sub-editor and sporting editor. He was also a major contributor to the English publication, *Snooker Scene*.

Les used to visit Lindrum's in Pitt Street. His father would take him there on a Saturday evening but only after he had shined his shoes, scrubbed himself from top to toe, poured himself into his Sunday clothes and combed his hair.

Les told me: "Only the well-groomed got through the door at Lindrum's." Les was a 15-year-old schoolboy when he ventured into Lindrum's. If first impressions count for anything, his vivid memory of a well organised and immaculately maintained billiard room managed by a "firebrand" (my grandmother) has to count for something. Les confided, "Why, if anyone even said 'I'll bet you two bob' Miss Lindrum would fly down like a rocket and not only stop it, she'd throw you out. What is more, you didn't argue with the boss. She'd rouse on you if you so much as thought about backchat. It was as if she could read your mind. I can still hear her giving one fellow a good dressing-down."

---

[102] *The Sportsman* was "The Bible for students of racing. Committed to the provision of clear and comprehensive form analysis and the latest inside information." First established in 1900, Banjo Paterson was editor of the publication from 1921–1930. The establishment and the evolution of *The Sportsman* can be traced to the Australian nation's love affair with racing and the racing industry.

"Did you drop that match, Mr Brown? Would you do that in your own home?' Of course, you wouldn't, so don't do it here. If I catch you doing it again, you won't get back in. Do we understand each other?" Brown nodded his head and mumbled 'Sorry, Miss'."

Les's observations are shared by the German author, Rudolph Brasch. In his book *How Did Sports Begin? The origins of Man at Play*, published by Longman Australia in 1972, Brasch refers to Lindrum's in Pitt Street as "the best billiard room in the world", to the Lindrum family as "the aristocracy of billiards", to the exemplary manner in which my grandmother ran the billiard room as being evidence of "their expressive love of the game" and to Horace as "The greatest exhibition player the world has ever seen."[103]

I wanted Les to tell me about the Showman. "What was he like?" I asked. Of course, I had my own opinion of my father but I wanted to hear what Les had to say about the young Horace I never knew. "Well, Jan, it was such a pleasure to know him. You didn't have to be afraid because he was a champion. He loved to joke. Loved to laugh. My word, he was a popular fellow. He knew all the customers and would walk down the room and go out of his way to say hello. He was easy to know. There was nothing distant about him. Do you know the handwriting story, Jan?"

"I know my father wrote in copperplate with a great flourish."

"Yes, he did. That came from his schooling in Victoria. I developed my handwriting skill in north Queensland and wrote in a more severe, plain style. Your father used to say to me: 'That's not a T. That's an S'

"Tell you what," I said to him, "let's select a passage out of Shelley's *Frankenstein*[104] and you write it out and I'll write it out and we'll see what people think about the writing'. I lost that competition!"

Les went on to tell me that my grandmother gave him his first job. He collected the money from patrons and set up the tables. He also acted as a marker on the Kelly Pool table, ensuring that players kept to the rules.

One evening my father called him over and told him a patron had arrived for a game but he did not have a partner so he should take his cue and give the fellow a game. The patron turned out to be one of his school teachers. Les beat him. Two days later, the school sent another teacher along and, over time, Les gained quite a reputation in his class for beating his teachers.

There was so much I wanted to ask Les Wheeler. Did he know Bradman did not have to turn his head to look at the bowler? Of course he did. He told me, Bradman had the "strong eye". So did my great-grandfather.

"The Ringmaster was the man I wanted to meet but I didn't make my first visit to Melbourne until 1949 and your great-grandfather had already passed away. He was the genius, Jan. One of the great coaches in the history of our nation, the greatest if you take into account the number of champions he produced from the same family and in the same discipline. He woke up to the reality that the opposite-eyed player had the real advantage. If you are right-eyed, you need to play with your left arm. If you are left-eyed, you need to play with your right arm. As for Horace, well Horace had the Magic Eye." He laughed, a delightfully wicked laugh.

"I've told you something of your father, did you know billiard tables are like people? Oh, yes, Jan, billiard tables have their own character and personality."

---

[103] Rudolph Brasch, *How Did Sports Begin: A Look into the Origins of Man at Play* (Australia: Longman Australia, 1971), 44

[104] British author Mary Shelley's *Frankenstein* or *The Modern Prometheus* was first published anonymously in London in 1818. The second edition was published under Mary Shelley's name in France in 1823. It might be argued that the fictional story of Victor Frankenstein – a young scientist who creates a monster – is a reflection of Mary Shelley's somewhat tumultuous life and makes a fascinating study. Mary's father was the philosopher William Godwin (1756–1836). Her mother was the author, philosopher, feminist Mary Wollstonecraft (1797–1851). Mary eloped with romantic poet and philosopher Percy Bysshe Shelley (1816–1822) whom she married in 1816 after the suicide of Shelley's first wife, Harriet, in the same year. . Mary Shelley's story has inspired a number a motion picture treatments and remains a fascinating case study. Perhaps the most famous motion picture is "Frankenstein" (1931) directed by James Whale adapted from the play by Peggy Webling, loosely based on Mary's novel, starring Colin Clive, Mae Clarke, John Boles and Boris Karloff

After my several conversations with Les Wheeler, I reached a greater understanding of what it must have been like to be a Lindrum growing up in an Australia I never knew, in a profession I only ever knew from the sidelines.

I found myself reflecting with great sadness on the request made by the President of the Victorian Association who (representing unknown people) wanted my sister and I to agree to the sale of the family billiard table located at Albert Park to the National Sports Museum at the Melbourne Cricket Ground and to consent to the legs of table being severed so that it could be mounted on the wall.

To a Lindrum, cutting the legs off a billiard table would be akin to cutting the ears off an elephant. (The table is half-owned by my mother and Irene May Ellis née Dunn by the bequest of Beryl Elaine Lindrum known as June Lindrum née Carr, Walter Lindrum's third wife).

Clara Lindrum demonstrating her skill at the billiard table . Horace gave his mother lessons before he left on his first international tour

Lindrum's, Pitt Street, Sydney

Before I take you back to Horace, I have to pull another billiard room story from the family tucker-bag. During World War II, the Duke of Edinburgh, then Prince Philip of Greece and Denmark, made a visit to Lindrum's in Pitt Street in the company of his emissary. The Prince's emissary approached my grandmother and informed her that the Prince would like to play a game. My grandmother responded:

"Sir, can you see all those tables? They are currently occupied by my regular customers. If His Royal Highness would like to take a seat over there I will let you know when a table becomes available."

The room went silent. The players froze in the moment. Clara smiled, curtsied and returned to her office.

The emissary walked back to the Prince and whispered something that nobody could hear whereupon the Prince turned, walked to the lounge, politely took a seat and waited patiently for a table to become available.

When a table eventually became available Clara danced across the room and, in a loud voice, announced:

"Righto Admiral, it is your turn now." The press had a field day.

When my grandmother relayed this story to me she confided that the Prince was one of the handsomest men she had ever met, and she told me there was something about a man in a uniform.

Jan Lindrum

22 March 1928

Jack Oake published an article about Australia's new boy wonder in *The Sporting Globe*. The article was a significant milestone in Horace's career. Oake proclaimed:

> Horace Lindrum is the greatest player of his age in the world, his love for the game practically compels him to be its slave.

After reading that article, Horace began to give serious thought to his own type of play, from an "entertainment" rather than a "competitive" perspective.

Oake had seen the Showman in Horace before Horace had seen the Showman in himself. He started carrying images of certain strokes in his mind so that he could develop them from an artistic perspective. He asked himself over and over: "What does the audience want from me?" The answer to this question did not come quickly because the fierce competitive spirit inside the Lindrum household forced Horace to spend much of his time proving himself as a billiards player; the game that he loved had yet to gain popularity. When the answer did come, it was as if Edison had switched on the light. The Everyman wanted to be entertained.

Horace had worked hard on developing his artistic skills on his last tour. By the end he was tired. He felt he had earned a rest. A stint at home. Mum's cooking. One or two early nights away from the shaded overhead light on the green cloth of a billiard table and the click, click of the balls, crawling into bed well after midnight. It did not seem like a lot to ask but it obviously was not going to happen. Something had come up. Clara had made plans.

Clara, diminutive, with violet eyes and flaming red hair, had more tricks up her sleeve than the devil himself. Nobody, not even her own son, could read what was going on in her extraordinary and always original mind. In many respects she was as eccentric as the man who had dubbed her a genius – the pianist and composer Ignacy Jan Paderewski. He had turned up at the Lindrum household in Albert Park for a game of billiards, in the company of a wife draped in furs. Paderewski also brought 25 caged parrots. He spent the evening competing with Clara on piano.

Horace reappeared.

"Righto, Mum, before you tell me, how about we sit down and have a cuppa with a couple of those scones?"

Moments of uncomfortable silence followed.

"I've entered you in the Australian professional billiards championship." There was a pause before Clara delivered the punch line.

"You play your uncle Frederick tomorrow night…"

The World's Best Boy Billiards Player had toured the country with his uncle Frederick performing exhibitions for hundreds of people but he had never contemplated competing against his uncle for his uncle's crown. Overwhelmed, Horace propped his right elbow on the table, rested his head in his hand and reflected on the forthcoming foray with his uncle Frederick. The night of his debut still haunted him and it is probably fair to say he carried the scars for a lifetime.

A beating. It was a brutal beating. The 16-year-old Marbles champion of New South Wales pitted against the 30-year-old seeded professional Walter Lindrum. Indefinable anxiety versus nerves of steel. Why had he agreed to be his uncle Walter's punching bag? He had asked himself that question I don't know how many times. He never found an answer and lived with the regret, largely because his countrymen, who saw Horace and Walter as equals rather than master and apprentice, remembered what they wanted to remember.

"Where on earth have you gone?" Clara asked, placing a hand on her son's shoulder.

"You haven't been listening to a word I've said."

Clara explained that she had raised the money for Horace's entry into the world professional billiards championship. She had played her fingers to the bone on the piano to put the fees together. Mysteriously the entry had gone missing. She could not prove it, but believed that the gambling boys had scratched her son and her brother just as they had scratched Phar Lap in the Caulfield Cup.

Horace looked horrified. His uncle Frederick was the Australian champion so it was only appropriate for him to represent the nation and he could not understand why anyone would want to scratch the Australian champion and the Boy Wonder from the competition. The event would be far more exciting with them in it than out of it. Clara saw the puzzlement on her son's face. "The betting boys couldn't have you and Frederick in the same race with Walter. One of you would put a spanner in their works and men like that don't like spanners. Walter has played right into their hands. If he's not careful…"

Clara stopped short.

"One must focus on winning strategies. Remember that Horace. I got on the phone and organised your debut in the United Kingdom. I told the British Association that this was their big chance to book the dual title-holder before anyone else. Win tomorrow, my darling, and you will be on the *Strathaird*[105] on Wednesday night."

The words whirred around and around in his head.

"To go on this trip, I need to beat one of the greatest billiard champions this nation has ever seen."

Clara read his thoughts.

"That's true, my darling, but the time has come for an old lion to pass the baton to his cub. I believe you can beat my brother and I also believe my brother will be proud to pass the torch to a fellow artiste."

That was all true, but Clara probably had not considered the impact the loss of the title would have on a brother who had just lost the love of his life.

She pulled the boat ticket out of her pocket and danced around the room, waving the ticket high above her head.

"Here's your rite of passage."

Horace watched his mother then looked across at his cue case. This was, without question, his big break, but could he do it? Could he beat his uncle Frederick?

Did he want to try?

Twenty-four hours later he walked down Pitt Street, looking intermittently at the billboards plastered on shop fronts.

LINDRUM versus LINDRUM

"See the Perfectionist and the Boy Wonder go head-to-head for the Australian Title – tonight – be there."

---

[105] *RMS Strathaird* later *TSS Strathaird*, a vessel of the Peninsular & Oriental Steam Navigation Company, launched 18 July 1931

Horace stands watching his uncle – Frederick III

An onlooker saw a young man about to run. At least, that is what he thought he saw but the young man kept walking, kept putting one foot in front of the other reminding himself of what he needed to do to win. He knew winning was "Fifty per cent – skill. Twenty-five per cent – control your nerves. Twenty-five per cent – Dame Fortune."

The room was packed to the rafters and Horace could hear the noise a block away. Hundreds of people crammed into a small space. Behind the scenes, Clara was busying herself laying out the clothes. Dinner suit, waistcoat, starched white shirt, bow tie, cummerbund, braces, socks, suspenders, shoes – highly polished with Nugget – the whole kit and caboodle purchased a week ago at a clearance sale at Gowings.

Glancing at the clock, she pulled the hairbrushes and the Brylcreem hair gel from the top drawer. An hour later she watched as her brother walked to the table. Tall and slender, he looked every bit the champion. Nobody, except Clara, dreamed that he would lose the title that night; a title he had held for 27 years.

Frederick's attitude at the table, and his delivery, were near perfection; he began scoring at an extraordinary rate. Meantime, his nephew sat silent as a mouse. If the hand of fate had twisted ever so little, Horace would not have taken passage on the *Strathaird* for this was battle between a Knight of the Inner Temple who could execute amazing technical shots and a journeyman who was yet to be dubbed a Knight.

A day later, Clara, in turquoise coat and picture hat, stood on the dock living the second-most-important moment of her life. She would not see written into history the chapter that she had sacrificed her whole life to see.

> Should old acquaintance be forgot and never brought to mind?
> Should old acquaintance be forgot and days of ol' lang syne
> For auld lang syne, my dear, for auld lang syne,
> We'll take a cup o' kindness yet for the sake of auld lang syne.

"For auld lang syne", she whispered. "Don't blink. The worst thing you can do is blink."

Standing at the ship's rail Horace reflected on his remarkable past. He had not had much time to think about a childhood bent over a billiard table. Living in the present was about all he had ever been able to manage. Then, embarking for the UK, he found time to think back over the past few years. So much seemed to have happened. The professional marbles title of New South Wales. Quite a feat for a boy of 14. First snooker century at 16. An unheard-of achievement. Australian professional snooker title at 19. Australian professional billiards title at 21. Wunderkind! But it was his mother's chance meeting with a man by the name of Bill South that had really changed his life. "Chance" is a relative term. Clara never did things by chance. She was a planner not a gambler.

Horace recalled the first time he had met South, a short, chunky little man with eyes much too big for his tiny head and ridiculously long lashes that gave him, in combination, the appearance of a cartoon character. He had been walking with his mother outside 101 Collins Street when they bumped into him. He remembered the incident clearly. Even above the city din, his memory had managed to record the words between his mother and this stumpy little man and he now replayed the scene in his mind.

"Not a word from you, Horace, just smile," she instructed under her breath as they had approached. Then she walked up to this short little bloke wearing a look of feigned surprise...

"Well, well, well. My, my, my! Long time no see, Bill South." "Gidday, Clara, how yer goin' love?"

South possessed a bushman's drawl and an accent you would expect to find west of the Great Dividing Range.[106]

"Top of the world, Bill, and you?" "Whatch yer up to these days, Clara?"

"Oh, a little bit of this and a little bit of that."

Bill then looked up at Horace. Even at 14, he was the taller of the two. "This yer boy?"

"Say good morning to Mr South," Clara commanded, even though moments earlier she had told Horace to keep his mouth shut.

Bill was a popular identity with the public in the idiom of a leg-spin bowler or an opera star. Journalists were always writing him up for something. On the one hand, he was successful; on the other, he was a spectacular failure. A year ago he was forced to settle a negligence action brought by a trapeze artist: to wit, failing to replace a faulty rope resulting in a nasty fall. The artist still looked like a china doll that had been picked up and thrown against a brick wall. Six months earlier an old lion had mauled his trainer. These temporary setbacks, as South called them, were newsworthy; his capacity to rise like a Phoenix from the ashes, legendary.

Recently, however, he had fallen foul of the editor of the *City News*. The tiff, rift, call it what you will, was over the coverage the paper was giving to his greatest adversary. Smith was at a complete loss to understand the editor's obsession with Bullen and his amphibious giants and scraggy-haired sword swallowers; the "Bullen this" and "Bullen that" got up his nose.

"You've had that cove on the front page for the last six weeks," he screamed down the telephone.

Bumping into Clara was South's lucky break, or should I say it was Horace's? That singular event plucked Horace from the shadows and took him from ironing billiard tables in his grandfather's billiard room to the front pages of newspapers around the country. Although his star might have been on the ascendant, it took the experience of 12 months with the circus to move the story of his career rise from the lead page of the sports section at the back of the paper to the news stories at the front of the paper.

Clara took her favourite seat at the Windsor while South went to make a phone call. He promised to be five minutes. Clara knew that meant 15 minutes, so she ordered afternoon tea from Arthur, the lanky waiter from Toorak. An assortment of finger sandwiches – egg and mayonnaise, cucumber, celery and walnut, smoked salmon and cream cheese – half a dozen *petits fours* and two English breakfast teas.

---

[106] A series of plateaus and low ranges, the Great Dividing Range, Australia's most substantial mountain range and the third-longest land-based range in the world, spans 3,500 kilometres from Dauan Island off the northeastern tip of Queensland; the range runs the length of the NSW coast and finally fades into the central plain of the Grampians in wester Victoria

Arthur returned to dress the table. Clara watched his every move, her ear to Tommy tinkling the ivories. Tommy was playing a favourite, Jolson's "Climb upon my knee, Sonny Boy".[107] South accepted tea, although he would have preferred a stiff drink, and, greedily eyeing the *petit fours*, squeezed his sizable bottom onto the leather lounge.

"Bit Flemington, isn't it?" He commented. Bill was admiring the pretty young fillies dotted around the room.

"Now, to business, we've known each other a long time and I know you didn't ask me to tea for nothing. What can I do for you, Clara?"

Clara picked up her handbag and propped it on her lap.

"It's not what you can do for me, old boy, it is what I can do for you. You could do with a helping hand. Engage young Horace, Billy my boy and we'll have those Yankees on the next boat."

South hid his amusement behind a linen serviette. Standing proudly in his knickerbockers and gripping his cue case, Horace was smiling up at him, as if he were sharing the joke.

"Come and see him, Bill. He'll wipe the smile off your face."

"Well, if looks count for anything, he's a looker, I'll give you that, but has he got the talent?"

This time it was Clara who was choking on the words.

"Has he got the talent! I know you don't believe what they write in the newspapers but when they write about Horace I am telling you they are writing the truth."

Three days later South's curiosity got the better of him and he turned up at the billiard room.

"I never would have believed it if I hadn't seen it for meself," he said to the journalist standing next to him.

"Brilliant! The boy is bloody brilliant!" Oake agreed.

"When I watch this boy doing smooth quiet positional shots with a beautiful cue rhythm it makes me think of velvet."

South moved a little closer to the action.

Horace was now dancing around the table, potting balls faster than the referee could get them out of the pockets.

"Well?" asked Clara, sidling alongside and timing her move to perfection. "That's the century," called the referee.

A broad smile spread across South's face. Jack, Queen, King, Ace!

Two months later, while Bullen's circus and three other great circuses, in the style of Stardust, Ashtons and Loritz, were preparing for an almighty challenge in the Haymarket, South's bread-and-potatoes operation was on the road. Four hours sleep, a cup of tar and inland to Grafton the City of Jacarandas, across country to Glen Innes, down to Armidale and along Fossikers Way to Thunderbolt territory[108] where the spirit of Australian poet Henry Lawson still roams the downs.

A week in Tamworth then across the Great Dividing Range to Wauchope and on to Port Macquarie. A few days at the mouth of the Hastings before travelling north to Kempsey, a fish chase on the Nambucca, then up the Jack Perkins track to Bellingen and through the Promised Land to Dorrigo. A swim in the shadow of Mutton Bird Island, a stroll up Royal Poinciana Way, then south-west to Gunnedah, Coonabarabran, Dubbo, Orange and Bathurst.

---

[107] "Sonny Boy" was written by Ray Henderson, Bud De Sylva and Len Brown and first performed in the talkie motion picture *The Singing Fool* in 1928. Al Jolson's recording of "Sonny Boy" was a big hit

[108] Thunderbolt territory (Tamworth), where the spirit of Australian poet Henry Lawson still roams the downs

A few days in Bathurst, back to Orange and on to Parkes, Forbes, Cowra, Young, Cootamundra and west to Temora.

Whizzing along at a cracking pace through corridors of ancient gums, ferns and red-tipped eucalypts, purple weeds sprouting from their roots. Beside banks of rusty-coloured native grasses curtained by undulating hills, purple in hue. Across paddocks blanketed in yellow daisies, sprinkled with wattle and dotted with clumps of geranium. Past parklands, bakeries, antique shops, vineyards, churches, pubs and corner stores.

Town to town Landscape continuously changing. Past farming staions, snapping dogs, sheep and stock horses grazing, blue-breasted water birds pecking for worms, Lyre birds dancing on clumps of sticks, king parrots and rainbow lorikeets foraging for seeds and fruit, wallabies lounging in the sun.

Beside creeks, waterfalls and rivers muddied by rainfall, flocks of sulphur-crested cockatoos screeching overhead. Lumbering into gullies of broken and bleached logs, low-set lantana and piles of burnt timbers lying idle against trees wrapped in long-fingered vines, their spindly arms playing host to chestnut-coloured babblers singing loudly from their nests.

The countryside, a blue forest canvas, layer upon layer of cobweb paintings lit at the corners by tiny triangles of sunshine, textured with dew and insects and scented with smoke and eucalyptus. The smell pungent, sharp, hitting at the nostrils.

Kookaburras, laughing. Flocks of raucous yellow-tailed black cockatoos cawing. Swifts soaring and swirling. Currawongs flying down from the mountains bringing bad weather and forcing South and his circus to battle the elements and cope with the continuous bump of wagons over muddy flats.

Horace thrived on the circus experience. His diary is alive with the reflections of an Australian excited by what was happening around him in a country so thrilling I want to reach out and touch it back into existence. It was an Australia of pioneers and adventurers who understood the hot, gold hush of noon and who saw the sunlit plains extended and the wondrous glory of the everlasting stars in a searing light projected onto an ancient landscape. Sadly for us, we can but look from a great distance and imagine what it must have been like to travel from one country town to another on horseback, living as they lived and encountering what they encountered.

"I need some help to get rid of my nerves," he confided to Sebastian, an aerialist known as the Flying Fox. "I need to become a man of confidence."

"You'll never get rid of the nerves. Nerves are part of your personality. Very few men have nerves of steel and nerves of steel are no good to the artist. What you need to learn is how to manage your nerves. Breathing helps and a smile and a wink go a long way towards winning an audience. Your bigger hurdle will be learning how to combat the adoration."

"Adoration?"

"Nobody can prepare you for the attention you get when you become a big star. You're already being promoted as the Great Lindrum and how old are you! You're headed for the sort of greatness that some men never see. You'll no longer belong to yourself."

"I am not sure I understand."

"Well, you will, young 'Orace, all in good time."

In the meantime, Jack, Queen, King, three Aces and a Joker!

Days passed. Months passed. Brewarrina to Bourke to Parkes. A week before Christmas, South's circus arrived in Wagga Wagga. Once they were perched on the outskirts of the town, a small group of well-toned muscle men set about pasting lithographs while trainers groomed their animals, performers rehearsed their routines and South carried out the usual equipment checks to ensure everything "wizzed, banged and popped". Bewildering pandemonium broke out an hour before the parade. That was when South took up his pistol. One shot to shut up.

Two shots for the church blessing.

Blessing over, dollies and follies pulled on their wigs, donned their makeup and shimmied into sequins and mirrored corsets of the kind that only Gaultier[109] could conjure today.

Musicians tuned their instruments; trick riders, some of whom looked like Peck's Bad Boy and others like Little Johnny Jones,[110] readied their cavalcade of exotic but imaginary boxing elephants for the plodding down the main street.

At midday, South, dressed as a town crier and ringing a large bell, led the highly coloured circus wagons into town. "Hurry, hurry, hurry, the great Lindrum is coming."

Children, dressed in their Sunday best, sucking humbugs and chomping on apple quarters appeared from nowhere, clinging to their mothers' skirts, riding on their fathers' shoulders and dreaming of everything from Uncle Tom's licorice to endless rides on the carousel.

South, sweating profusely and mopping his brow with a large spotted handkerchief headed straight for the town hall. The mayor, a Goliath of a man, stood astride a dais, the welcoming committee on the one side, the Country Women's Association on the other. Raising his eyes to the heavens and tugging at his collar, he muttered, "God, it looks like they're going to lynch me!"

Dribbling with anticipation, the children whinged and whined through the speeches extruding a collective sigh of relief when little Lucy Atkins (an oversized clone of a toe-tapping Shirley Temple [111]) stepped forward to present the keys to the city. Politely accepting the posy of wattle and gum leaves in one hand and the keys in the other, South bowed, winked at the ladies, put a whistle between his lips, pushed the oxygen out of his lungs and signalled:

"Let the games begin!"

Up went the candy-striped tents, spreading their tentacles like giant octopi and out came the ice-cream stand as the Mayor and official party sipped pink lemonade and gasped in horror at the bearded lady.

"Buy your tickets here. Over here!" called a contortionist bent and twisted and walking on his hands.

"Ride the carousel, play the hoop la!" he called again, pulling his head through his legs and waving to a copycat Grimaldi[112] doing the highland fling.

Mothers scrounged in their purses, fathers dug deep into their pockets and children exchanged their piggy-bank savings for tickets while half a dozen pretty young things, one or two courting Fascinators, crowded around the strong man in the gold spandex.

Clutching their tickets, the people of Wagga Wagga filed inside the tent. It was a few minutes after two o'clock when South, dressed in white top hat and tails entered the ring to introduce the grand parade.

In the red ring, floats of pretty girls in spectacular bird of paradise costumes, hoofers in the style of Fred[113] and Ginger[114] and acrobats in royal purple tutus and pink ballet pumps

---

[109] Reference to French haute couture and prêt-a-porter fashion designer, Jean Paul Gaultier (1952–). Before going into business for himself Gaultier worked for Hermes and Pierre Cardin. His sculptured costumes are considered playful, creative, decadent, masterful and irreverent. He designed the infamous cone bra for Madonna's 1990 "Blond Ambition Tour" and has designed costumes for many motion pictures, including Luc Besson's *The Fifth Element (1997:France)*

[110] Reference to the motion picture *Yankee Doodle Dandy* and, more particularly, to the performance of James Cagney in the role of George M Cohan and to Cohan's early on-stage vaudeville performances with his mother, father and sister as "The Four Cohans"

[111] Shirley Temple (1928–2014), was an American-born film and television actress, singer and dancer who, in her later years, became US Ambassador to Ghana and later Czechoslovakia and acted as Chief of Protocol of the United States. Temple was the biggest motion picture box-office success during the period 1935–1938 and, after her performances in the motion pictures *Curly Top* and *Heidi* the Academy of Motion Picture Arts and Sciences awarded her a special juvenile Academy Award

[112] Joseph Grimaldi (1778–1837) English actor, comedienne, dancer. In the early 1880s Grimaldi expanded the role of CLOWN in the harlequinade that formed part of British pantomimes notably at the Theatre Royal in Drury Lane and at Sadler's Wells and the theatres of Covent Garden. The CLOWN became known as "Joey" and he wore white face makeup

[113] American-born Frederick Austerlitz (1899–1987), who performed as Fred Astaire, was a famous star of stage and screen; he was a

springing on and off cream-coloured ponies with the agility of the famously athletic performer known as "the little Nugget".[115]

In the blue ring, a man inside a giant silver ring spinning like Plushenko[116], clowns in the style of Popov and Saluto[117] riding up and down a slippery slope with the precision of the sweetheart of Canada[118] and Merlin prancing like Tati[119] on his imaginary horse, every so often stopping to extract a coin from a child's ear.

Thirty-five feet above the ground, the Flying Foxes exchange swings in mid-air and Blondin,[120] hero of the Niagara, stands on one leg, balancing a pole and eating an omelette. The feat so daring that many in the audience believe him to have been "hit by a windmill."[121]

Below, the band sits on an elevated platform playing Sousa's "Washington Post".[122] Dressed in green suits with shiny brass buttons down the front of their jackets and epaulettes of metallic gold, they court scarlet plumes in caps perched forward on their heads. The conductor, a white-gloved man with a neatly-trimmed beard is the spitting image of the March King.

Ah, the magic of it all.

---

dancer (especially tap and ballroom), choreographer, singer, musician and actor. His most famous dancing partner was Ginger Rogers. Tragically, despite his extraordinary performances on screen, particularly in the film *Top Hat*, Fred Astaire never won an Oscar

[114] American-born actress, dancer, singer of stage, radio, television and film, Virginia Katherine McMath (1911–1995) performed as Ginger Rogers; she collaborated on 73 films with Fred Astaire. She won an Oscar for her performance in *Kitty Foyle* (1940

[115] Born near Dubbo in the state of New South Wales, William Billy Jones (1842–1906) was a famous Aboriginal acrobat who was known as "a manly fellow of exquisite proportions" who could walk a tight rope, dance a hornpipe and perform incredible feats on horseback

[116] Evgeni Plushenko (1982–) Russian figure skater, Olympic medallist and world champio

[117] Oleg Konstantinovich Popov (1930–) famous Russian society clown. Frankie Saluto began clowning in 1928. He was a leading clown with Ringling Bros and Barnum & Bailey circuses

[118] Canadian-born Christin Elizabeth Cooper (1959–) was a World Cup alpine ski racer whose ski run in here hometown resort of Sun Valley was named "The Silver Fox" in her honour. She was considered to be a "sweetheart of a person

[119] Jacques Tati (born Jacques Tatischeff) on 9 October 1907 at Le Pecq, Yvelines, France. Comic actor, writer, director and filmmaker. Academy Award (1958) for best foreign language film, *Mon Oncle*

[120] Charles Blondin was a famous circus performer with the Ravel Troupe. In 1858 the troupe performed at Niagara Falls, a famous tourist destination on the border of New York State and Canada. Blondin convinced the local authorities to permit him to walk a tight rope across the falls. He completed the feat in June 1859

[121] A common saying in Holland to describe someone who is more than a little crazy

[122] "Washington Post" is a march composed by John Philip Sousa in 1889. It remains today as one of his most popular marches throughout the USA. Sousa was known as the March King

Horace waited for the applause to taper off. Then, reaching into his pocket, he withdrew an egg.

"It's a Cooker Billy, Daddy!"

Enthralled, the audience watched as Horace held the egg between his thumb and second finger and then set it spinning along the cushion.

Like a train heading for the station, the egg travelled, unaided, the full length of the table, cannoning off the ball positioned at the top right hand corner and knocking it into the pocket before zipping along the top cushion to pot the ball waiting at the left.

This brought the house down! "Bravo, Horace."

The audience was on its feet.

Mavis, the Turkish Delight in the pink corset, cleared the pockets, sending the balls running back down the table.

Olive, a fair-haired Mata Hari[123] produced a wicker basket resembling a Greek vase, strutted her stuff, turning the basket every way so that the audience could see clearly that all was as it seemed. No more, no less than a wicker basket with a neck opening just slightly wider than the diameter of a snooker ball (52.5mm – 2 1/5 inches). Horace wasted no time. Repositioning the balls, he reached for his cue and took aim.

"Did you see what I just saw?" the mayor asked his wife.

The red ball flew into the basket's narrow neck, the force of its entry spinning the basket around in the opposite direction.

Walking to the baulk end of the table, Horace stopped the white ball, positioned it and took aim.

Later, the local priest told a reporter at the local newspaper.

"First he shot the red ball into the wicker basket and then the white ball went in and the red ball came out. The neck was only this big. Amazing! Absolutely bloody amazing! And what about that shot at the end! He called it the steeplechase. Goodness gracious, that was really somethin'. Jesus, Mary and Joseph, if someone had told me it was possible to do those things, I'd have told 'em they'd b'en kissin' the Blarney stone[124]. The balls there one minute, gone the next. He pots 'em as if the pocket has some hidden magnetic force drawing them into it. As for the tricks with his hands, oh dear Lord! Why, I will be sharing this memory with my congregation for years to come."

The boy from down under took it all in his stride and, as he strolled back to his wagon, listening to little Nell singing: "He flies through the air with the greatest of ease that daring young man on his flying trapeze,"[125] he asked himself, "Where to from here?"

But you never have to ponder the future for long. The pork pies and jellied eels are often much closer than you think. That was what Horace was saying to himself as he stared out

---

[123] Mata Hari (Margaretha Geertruida "Margreet" MacLeod (nee Zelle), born in Leeuwarden, the Netherlands (1842–1891). Matt Hari, a Frisian exotic dancer and courtesan, was convicted of espionage and executed by firing squad in France under charges of spying for Germany during World War I

[124] "The Stone of Eloquence". For over 200 years, world statesmen, literary giants, and legends of the silver screen have joined millions of pilgrims climbing the steps to kiss the Blarney Stone and gain the gift of eloquence. Its powers are unquestioned but its story still creates debate. Once upon a time, visitors had to be held by the ankles and lowered head first over the battlements. Today, management at Blarney Castle and Gardens are more cautious of the safety of their visitors. The Stone itself is still set in the wall below the battlements. To kiss it, one has to lean backwards (holding on to an iron railing) from a parapet walk....Some say the Blarney Stone was Jacob's pillow, brought to Ireland by the prophet Jeremiah. Here it became the Lia Fail or "Fatal Stone", used as an oracular throne of Irish Kings –a kind of Harry Potter-like "sorting hat" for kings. It was also said to be the deathbed pillow of St Columba on the island of Iona. Legend says it was then removed to mainland Scotland, where it served as the prophetic power of royal succession, the Stone of Destiny. When Cormac MacCarthy, King of Munster, sent 5000 men to support Robert the Bruce in his defeat of the English at Bannockburn in 1314, a portion of the historic Stone was given by the Scots in gratitude – and returned to Ireland. Others say it might be a stone brought back to Ireland from the Crusades – the "Stone of Ezel" behind which David hid on Jonathan's advice when he fled from his enemy, Saul. A few claim it was the stone that gushed water when struck by Moses. Reference: Blarney Castle & Gardens, "The Home of the Blarney Stone"

[125] Originally published as "The Flying Trapeze" in 1867, the song was inspired by trapeze artist Jules Leotard. The lyrics to the song were written by George Leybourne, music by Gaston Lyle and arrangement by Alfred Lee. Publication of the song inspired dramatist William Saroyan's short story "The Daring Young Man on the Flying Trapeze" (1934) which first appeared in *Story* magazine. A motion picture, *Man on the Flying Trapeze* starring W C Fields and Mary Brian was released in 1935

the window of the tiny plane winging its way through the thick cloud bank shrouding the jungles and coffee plantations of the Southern Highlands of New Guinea.

"I have no idea what to expect," he told the dashing young man sitting next to him. "All I know is, I love a good adventure."

Errol Flynn agreed and it is more than fair to say that Lindrum and the Tassie-born Flynn took to the adventures of New Guinea as ducks take to water.

Flynn: the playboy, the lady chaser, the swashbuckling hero – waving a sword above his head and leaping from galleon to galleon on a film set.

Lindrum: the young man who had pledged, "not to become a lady chaser", wielding his cue and leaping from break to break on a billiard table.

Horace made his first international trip to New Guinea because Clara saw opportunity there. So did fellow Australian Michael (Mick) Leahy and his mate Mick Dwyer.

Leahy and Dwyer believed New Guinea was not simply a continuation of jungles and precipitous mountains but a land of untapped potential; Leahy's trek to the interior of New Guinea created enormous excitement, although not quite as much excitement as his row with the explorer Jack Hides.

Hides claimed to be the first man to discover and climb Mount Giluwe. Leahy said, "Bullshit" and, like a pit-bull, went on the attack.

"I was the first to have an encounter with that bloody mountain, you lousy phoney," he crowed, storming into the offices of the Royal Geographical Society in London. The very public donnybrook thrust New Guinea into the international spotlight.

"Hurray, Mick has done all the hard work for me," Clara said to herself. "He's even installed a billiard table in his house in the Highlands. I'll write to him and ask him to organise a tour. The tour will generate a heap of publicity and provide Horace with the playing experience he needs before he takes on the Brits. The New Guinea experience will also toughen him up."

Was securing for Horace a seat on the plane next to Errol Flynn part of the plan? We will never know the answer to that question.

After learning to play billiards by the light of a kerosene lamp and how to pot balls into boots, Horace returned home with a princely sum in his pocket. Not quite enough to get him to the Mother Country but more than enough for a ticket to the opening of Garbo and Barrymore's *Grand Hotel*.[126]

It was a beautiful day in Sydney as Empire Airlines flight 002 came in to land at Rose Bay, a gloved hand assisting passengers through the doorway and into a boat bobbing up and down on the harbour. Fifteen minutes later, the boat was scooting around Bennelong Point for the drop-off at Circular Quay.

"Wow! Look at the crowds!" Horace exclaimed to a man standing next to him. The people of Sydney had come out to greet the new addition to the P & O fleet. The *Strathaird* was certainly a beauty.

Horace finally managed to pull his tired body from the ship's rail.

"First the Circus, then New Guinea, now London is calling.

God Bless you, Mum."

---

[126] Released in 1932, the motion picture *Grand Hotel* was inspired by the 1929 novel *Menschen in Hotel* by Vicki Baum. Directed by Edmund Goulding and staring John Barrymore, Greta Garbo and Joan Crawford, the picture won an Academy Award without the film or its participants being nominated in any category

12 October 1935

In a letter to his mother Horace exclaimed:

"Hot dog! If someone had said to me six months ago:

'Horace, you will be in London in October, on the way over, you'll meet and make friends with Prince Farouk and, when you land, you will stand on the same spot where the great Walt Disney was mobbed by children a few months earlier', Mum, I'd have thought them plain crazy! Life is so unpredictable. You never know what it has in store."

The Prince and his entourage, including the Prince's personal tutor, Ahmed Bey Hassenein, joined the ship in Aden. The Prince was *en-route* to the Military Academy in Woolwich. Strikingly handsome and fabulously wealthy, the Descendant of the Terrible Turk oozed charm from the lapels of his Chester Barrie suit to the points of his shiny and magnificently crafted Italian patent leather shoes.

Thousands lined the dock at Tawahi for the vessel's departure and a flotilla of flower-bedecked boats of all shapes and sizes accompanied the liner into the Red Sea. Only the man who saw the spectacle could paint the picture.

> Bit-tawfi in a'Allah.
> May God be with you.
> Rabbena ywaffa 'ak.
> Good luck in your exams.
> All praise to the All Merciful.
> May God make it easy for you.
>
> Goodbye, dear Prince.

The first officer introduced Horace to the Prince at the captain's table and the two hit it off immediately. Six months later Prince Farouk was featured on the cover of *Time* magazine. He had become the tenth ruler of the Muhammad Ali Dynasty, King of Egypt and the Sudan. Horace thought his friend looked uncomfortable on his father's throne. The lean to the right said: "Ma sa'Allah," "God has willed it," rather than "I am happy," but Horace knew only too well that taking responsibility came with a price. The following month journalists at *The News of the World*[127] informed their readers:

> Horace Lindrum of Australia has been invited by the BBC to play Willie Smith of Darlington in the first of an experimental series aimed at putting cue sports onto television.[128]

Fifteen years later, in 1952, Horace was world professional snooker champion and his friend King Farouk was living in exile. Overthrown by his people, Farouk had been removed from his father's throne via a plan crafted by CIA operative Kermit Roosevelt Junior. The plan was code-named "Project (unprintable)". Legend has it that Farouk spent the remainder of his life contemplating the fate of kings, a notebook and a copy of the

---

[127] *The News of the World* was first established by John Browne Bell in 1843. Bell sold to Henry Lascelles Carr in 1891 and Carr to News Limited in 1969. At one time it was the biggest selling English language newspaper in the world with a circulation of eight million in the 1950s. Closure in 2011 was a direct consequence of the hacking scandal

[128] The beginnings of mechanical television can be traced to the discovery of photoconductivity of the element of selenium by William Willoughby Smith in 1873, the invention of the scanning disk by Paul Gottliev Nipkow in 1884 and John Logie Baird's demonstration of televised moving images in 1926

works of William Shakespeare by his side, the bookmark strategically placed at *Richard II*, Act 3, Scene 2, Lines 151–166.

> For God's sake, let us sit upon the ground
> And tell sad stories of the death of kings…

On the notepad he scrawled the words:

> The whole world is in revolt.
> Soon there will be only five kings left.
> King of England, King of Spades, King of Clubs,
> King of Hearts and King of Diamonds.

With the rasping sound of brakes and the shushing of steam, the boat-train pulled into Waterloo station. Bursting with excitement, Horace looked out the window. He was surprised to see so many people on the platform. He never dreamed they might be waiting for him. He woke up to the reality when flash bulbs started exploding.

The British champion, Tom Newman, winked at Jake Bisset. "The boy is all personality. The public is going to love this guy." Newman was right and, when centuries started rolling off Horace's cue faster than marbles off a breadboard, the press proclaimed: "Horace Lindrum of Australia has arrived."

> Horace Lindrum of Australia is proving to be an overnight success. His enjoyment of the game of snooker is especially catching. Why he can hardly take his next shot for laughing. He never pretends with his audience, which – apart from his beautiful style – is one reason among several why he is such an attraction. Try as you may, you won't get a seat for any of his performances .
>
> The Royal Aquarium in Westminster, the St James Hall in Piccadilly, The Union Club in Soho, Saville House in Leicester Square …

ALL SOLD OUT!

My great-uncle Walter and batsman Sir Donald Bradman came along during the Depression era. Horace's star was in the ascendancy in 1928, the year in which Mickey Mouse made his debut in *Steamboat Willie;* D H Lawrence's *Lady Chatterley's Lover* was banned; Duke Ellington and his Cotton Club Orchestra[129] recorded "Diga Diga Doo"; Amelia Earhart became the first woman to fly an aircraft across the Atlantic; Phar Lap arrived on Australian soil; ever increasing numbers of Australians were looking for ways and means to broaden their horizons and the Golden Age of Flight[130] was no longer around the corner but had well and truly arrived.

---

[129] Established by heavy weight boxing champion Jack Johnson in 1920 in Harlem, the 'whites-only' night club was taken over by gangster Owney Madden in 1923 at the height of the prohibition era. Despite the fact that the Cotton Club was a whites-only establishment it featured black entertainers and jazz musicians, including Billie Holiday, Lena Horne, Louis Armstrong and Count Basie. The club moved to the midtown theatre district in New York in 1936 where it was known for its celebrity nights featuring Jimmy Durante, George Gershwin, Al Jolson, Richard Rodgers, Eddie Cantor, Irving Berlin, Sophie Tucker, Judy Garland and many other stars of the era. Duke Ellington took over the resident orchestra at the club in 1927

Billiards was still enjoying popularity in 1928 but by 1936 interest had waned and falling box-office receipts led to British champion Joe Davis's announcement to the London Press Club that "Billiards is as dead as mutton". That statement opened the doorway to the Golden Age of Snooker.[131] Six months later Horace made his debut at the Noble House of Thurston.

Remembering the advice the great Sebastian had given, to always arrive early, Horace agreed to meet Joe Davis at noon so the pair could get some practice in before the match. A good idea in theory. Not so in practice. On their arrival they found the entrance to Thurston's completely blocked by a massive queue of people hoping for tickets. Horace looked at Joe. Joe looked at Horace. "What to do?"

They tried a number of times to explain who they were and why they needed to get through but nobody seemed to want to listen to what they had to say so they tried to edge their way along the walls. Well, this behaviour was not to be tolerated.

"Hey! What do you think you're doing? You take your turn same as everybody else."

"Here! Here!" murmured those around the objector. "But we're playing," Joe responded. "My name is Davis."

"Oh, yeah, and mine is Napoleon Bonaparte and my friend here, well, he's Horace Lindrum!" retorted the sceptic.

At that, Horace jumped upon a ledge and cried out:

Folks, if you want to see Lindrum play tonight, you had better let him through because he's a little fellow about my size."

"Oh he is, is he?"

It was the sceptic again. But the scepticism did not last. Horace's broad grin gave the game away.

"He's telling you the truth. Look at that smile. He is Horace Lindrum."

The crowd started laughing and the sceptic and his friends picked Horace up and passed him over their shoulders to the box office. No mean feat as people along the way were clamouring for autographs.

"You'll be needing this." Up came the cue case.

The crowd then parted to permit Joe to walk up the stairs.

"Ladies and Gentlemen, it is my great privilege to present to you all the way from Sydney, Australia – Australian Professional Billiards and Snooker Champion – Horace Lindrum." Tom Newman's voice was clear and strong, and ear-shattering applause delivered a hearty welcome to the Australian champion.

Thrilled by his showmanship, the British people could not get enough of him and it was the spectacle Horace created, which he had perfected during his time with Bill South's circus, that turned snooker into a box-office sell-out.

Wherever he went after his debut at Thurston's, Horace received a royal reception and he got to know the words to "Waltzing Matilda"[132] extremely well for Banjo's song was played every time he put in an appearance.

In his first attempt at the world snooker crown (1936), which came only months after his arrival, Horace was runner-up to Joe Davis in what was, without a shadow of a doubt, a nail-biting final. Horace needed only one frame to win, but nerves got the better of him.

---

[130] A 20-year period from World War I to World War II known as an era of elegant aircraft and in-flight service and rapid advances in aviation
[131] The period from 1936–1952, interrupted by World War II
[132] A widely-known Australian bush ballad written by poet and nationalist Banjo Paterson at Dagworth Homestead near Winton, a town in the central west of Queensland in 1895. Christina Rutherford Macpherson is credited with the manuscript which was transcribed from a song she heard, in about 1895, played by a band at the Warrnambool races in western Victoria. The song was first published in 1903 and recorded as performed by John Collinson and Russell Callon in 1926

Later in life, he openly admitted that this was the final he should have won. Horace was also runner-up to Joe Davis the following year.

Leicester Square Hall, the famous home of World Snooker

27 February 1937

In *The Referee* of that date, Jack Oake had this to say:

Horace Lindrum achieves fame

In a handicap snooker tournament played in England between six of the world's leading exponents, Horace Lindrum, the young Australian snooker and billiards champion, has gained further fame. Of the six competitors, Lindrum had to concede points to all but Joe Davis. He did not win the event (Joe Davis emerged the victor) but finished a splendid second and set a new world record with a break of 114. When it is remembered that each of his opponents, bar Davis, received between fourteen and 35 points in every set, some idea of the regard in which Horace's play was viewed by the handicappers can be gained. This was easily the biggest snooker tournament ever played in the United Kingdom. It took fifteen weeks to complete and, of this period, twelve weeks was given to play at Thurston's Exhibition Hall in the heart of London and, after the 1936–37 final, the British players came to use the word "Crikey!" on a regular basis.

19 December 1936

A journalist in *The Mirror* wrote:

"Horace Lindrum sets up time snooker record."

"Crikey!" says Davis.

Brilliantly as Joe Davis played again at Thurston's yesterday afternoon, in the last *Daily Mail* Gold Cue snooker heat, he was outplayed by the young Australian. Lindrum was in his most inspired mood.

"Spectacular, daring, brilliant."

"Will you look at that one," Davis muttered.

That "one" was a cut, nearly square, up the cushion into the top pocket at the cracking pace of a Hammond cut to the rails.

Lindrum took a turn at trying to smash the world record of 133 – the record recently made by Sidney Smith – and very nearly did so. He did create a record by winning the third frame by 101 to 31 in six minutes.

Spectators were crouching in their seats, holding their breath and taking penalty kicks at the unfortunates in front as Horace streaked along in the third game, starting with a blue, then all pinks and blacks. The century approached, all going well, then…at 94…Ah, tragedy! Pink had to be potted in the middle pocket. Last red needed touching out from the cushion over the top. Horace concentrated on that red and missed potting the pink by the smallest margin possible. Had he got it the rest were on, amounting to 135.

Horace had all the essential characteristics of a champion. The firm, business-like bridge with fingers well apart. The piston-like cue action. The head well down to the table with chin to the right of the cue. Head perfectly still during and for some time after the stroke. I have a photograph taken of him making a stroke during a match in 1935. Not taken by flash-light, the time of exposure was one second. The cue and cue-hand are obviously in motion. The ball has disappeared, but the profile is sharp and the head has not moved a fraction. Still, no matter how hard Horace tried, there was no "hey presto" for the Showman. Toppling Joe Davis was not written in the stars. Davis had age and experience on his side and Horace always played on Joe's turf, by Joe's rules, and on Joe's tables.

This said, there were other possible reasons for Horace's loss to Davis in those early world championships. The Showman's artistic streak is one reason; his commitment to the ninth commandment of sport is another ("The game is the thing"). Entertaining people was more important to him than winning. It was, however, the combination of Horace Lindrum's youth, good looks, artistic streak and technical skill and Davis's age, experience and technical skill that turned the Lindrum–Davis partnership into a great and marketable team. Scores always terrifyingly close. They are to the history of snooker what Federer, Nadal, Djokovic and Murray are to the history of tennis.

According to the Black Poker:

> "They were the greatest snooker partnership the game has ever seen.
>
> Joe Davis with his grim, determined play. Horace with his smiling face. The temperaments were balanced and, with both players giving of their best, the lucky spectators saw snooker being pushed right to the top as a spectacle with record after record being made and broken in a golden era the likes of which we will never see again."

My mother, the Black Poker, met Joe Davis before she met Horace. The meeting took place during World War II at a small country pub known as The Dog & Pheasant. The pub in the village of Brook in Surrey was run by a cherub of a man by the name of Stan Platt. His watering hole was popular with the armed services and, being the genial host that he was, Platt made a point of introducing his guests to the locals.

According to the Black Poker, Joe was a rotund, jovial clown who fitted his caricature as the Sultan of Snooker[133] and the Emperor of Pot perfectly but there was no fun in the man she met across the desk in the Dickensian offices of the governing body after the war. That man was focused on one thing only, winning the professional snooker title.

The clown in the man had been put to bed.

From 1935 onwards Horace was forever on the move[134] and it was during those early years that he got to know England better than he knew his own country. He covered every main highway from Land's End to John O'Groats, along the way playing celebrity appearances with the Tottenham Hotspurs and great individual legends like Leeds United's Jack Milburn,[135] as he had done at home with great legends like Australian boxing champion Tommy Burns. A photo of Horace and Tommy is inscribed in Tommy's hand,

"Look at our braces. Weren't we something! I was only 22."

The only record I could find of a holiday from the table was a trip to Germany with Melbourne Inman and his wife at the end of July 1936.

The trip coincided with Hitler's Olympics.

---

[133] The great cartoonist, Tom Webster, depicted Joe Davis as "The Sultan of Snooker" and "The Emperor of Pot
[134] During the Golden Age of Flight the route was Darwin, Singapore, Calcutta, Karachi, Cairo and Tripoli; or Darwin, Singapore, Bangkok, Allahabad (India), Rangoon (Burma) and Habbaniya (Iraq
[135] Jack Milburn, nickname "Wor Jackie", played 408 games for Leeds United

Jan Lindrum

<u>Telegram</u>:

1 August 1936
Germany is back in the fold of nations.

Frederick Birchall
Reporter *The New York Times*

Hitler's Olympics were hailed by American officials as the greatest and most glorious athletic festival of all time. Fifty-one nations and 5000 athletes took part. Years later Horace talked of this experience and, on occasion, expressed his admiration for Hitler's oratorical skills. This created an argument in the house as our mother, who had lived through the Blitz (lightning air raids on London) and the Battle of Britain (the battle in the skies to save the nation), appreciated none of Hitler's redeeming features.

Of course, Horace did not like Hitler. He thought Hitler was a monster and he felt great compassion for the Jewish refugees who arrived in Australia after the war with very little money in their pockets. He agreed with the view expressed at the Nuremberg Trials by German-Swiss Psychiatrist Karl Theodor Jaspers (1883–1969) that when it came to events like the Holocaust, no humans on earth could shirk their responsibility.

Horace also frequently talked about and reflected on his friendship with Melbourne "The Nose" Inman and expressed gratitude to the man who had played such a huge role in championing his career.

They say timing is everything and Horace's arrival on the snooker scene in London coincided with Inman's retirement. The thought of becoming somebody else's manager had never crossed Inman's mind. It was his nose[136] for talent that got him thinking about that possibility. He was so enchanted by Horace's play that the performer in him came to accept the need to surrender the stage. After putting his cue in the rack Inman entered an exciting new chapter of his life, becoming a highly successful promoter of the billiards art.

There were several keys to Inman's success as a promoter. First and foremost, he held to the Greek ideal, believing a sportsperson's ultimate goal is to develop artistic and intellectual excellence. Secondly, he possessed an impeccable record of personal bests and his distinguished career as a proponent of the billiards art had earned him the admiration and respect of the billiards fraternity, not just in his own country, but across the globe. Thirdly, he was well travelled, well connected, doggedly determined, financial and, above all else, the possessor of a fabulous sense of humour. The following tit-bit from Horace's diary says something of the spirit of the man:

> Melbourne and I gave an exhibition in Brighton. It was an excellent evening with a most appreciative audience followed by a delicious supper and we were in fine spirits by the end of it, that is until we reached part of the main London to Brighton highway. Under repair, there were red lamps everywhere, all of them strung from a somewhat roughly constructed fence down the centre of the road.
>
> Mel was at the wheel and misjudged the distance of the left mudguard from the lamps and, as we drove through, he caught a post and went into a light skid which caused the car to whip off the lamps, one after the other. At the end of the obstruction, the night watchman was waiting for us.
>
> "Eer, what's your game?" the Yorkshireman asked.
>
> Mel, who was well known for his dry humour, replied:

---

[136] Melbourne Inman was known for his bountiful proboscis. His other nickname was "The Twickenham Terrier" (so-named because of his dogged determination).

"My game is snooker, sir. I have taken all the reds, where are the colours?"

Underneath this entry is a photograph of Inman lounging in a boat. A regular Noel Coward,[137] he has a sandwich in one hand and a glass of Bollinger in the other. There is a marvellous tile on his head, a kind of cross between a panama and a straw. The caption reads: "Inman coaching his friend, Tom Reece, on his long swim through London from Richmond Lock to His Majesty's ship *HMS Buzzard* which lay anchored about a mile below Waterloo Bridge." There were 36 starters in the race that year. Among the more famous was the world-champion long-distance swimmer JH Jarvis. Not all went to plan Reece experienced what he called two pieces of curious bad luck. The first, right at the start of the race, came when another swimmer gave him a terrific kick in the ribs. The kick winded him and the injury caused him a lot of pain during the last few miles. A worse misfortune occurred in the first half-hour when he swam off-course.

"'You're going the wrong way,'" Inman screamed, rocking the boat so hard it nearly landed him in the drink.

"Pull your head out of the water, man."

Reece could hear the noise but he thought the crowd was cheering him on.

"I must have gone some hundred yards up the backwater before I realised that I was horribly, wretchedly alone. Making the best of a bad job, I turned around and swam back to the main stream. By that time, of course, I was completely tailed off. The rest of the race was out of sight.

Notwithstanding, I carried on, swimming steadily and at a fair pace. I caught up with the stragglers before long and, after another mile or two, I was in the race again.

One by one I kept dropping them behind me until I drew level with a giant of a man who was the champion of Denmark. I couldn't pass him. Perhaps, psychologically, I didn't want to pass him. To be brutally honest I think I wanted to make him my friend so he would one day invite me to a place I had always wanted to visit. Anyway, whatever the reason, every time I tried to spurt he spurted with me, and so we swam, shoulder to shoulder and stroke for stroke, for the better part of two hours. I got the Dane in the end, but only just. I finished eighth, he finished ninth."

Six months later Reece made easy work of the English Channel. But it was treading water from one side to another in an effort to get Queen Kellerman to Calais that catapulted him to hero status. *En-route* he proposed three times in an attempt to get Kellerman to focus on something other than the excruciating pain in her muscles. As flattered as she may have been, she declined the offer, quit the Channel swim and took herself off to America where, in 1907, she performed the first balletic swim in a water tank at the New York Hippodrome. In the same year, Reece recorded the highest break at billiards in human history in a marathon event against Joe Chapman who was champion of the Midlands.

The event took place at the Burroughs & Watts Billiard Room in Soho Square on Monday and Tuesday, 3 and 4 June 1907.

---

[137] English playwright, composer, director, actor and singer, Sir Noel Peirce Coward (1899–1973), known for his wit, flamboyance and what Time called "a sense of personal style, a combination of cheek and chic, pose and poise." Famous album: "Mad Dogs and Englishmen Go Out in the Midday Sun"

Spectacular Billiards

> Reece gained position in the first session and never lost it.
> He went on playing the same stroke for five solid weeks and,
> as admission was free to the public, there was a large
> gathering on every occasion, both afternoons and evenings.[138]

One of the spectators finally got up the courage to ask Chapman how he liked the billiard table. He responded curtly: "How the hell should I know. I haven't had a shot for a month!"

Thirty years later the sport was headed for the living room.

---

[138] During this competition Tom Reece used the Anchor stroke. In *Billiards and Snooker for Amateurs* (1948) by Horace Lindrum, Melbourne Inman wrote, "Wisely, this stroke was barred, and a new rule introduced that, after 30 such cannons, the player must hit a cushion before scoring another cannon. Reece then adopted a new stroke called the 'Pendulum'; the Pendulum stroke was later barred" 3, 4

14 April 1937, 3.10 pm

The exhibition played at the Alexandra Palace, London was televised: "Good evening, Ladies and Gentlemen." Elizabeth Cowell's voice was warm and friendly. "We are coming to you live from the Alexandra Palace. Tonight we are making history. Our cameramen are about to look down their lenses at a billiard table for the very first time. With me in the studio are Horace Lindrum of Australia and Willie Smith of Darlington. Horace and Willie are going to give us a demonstration."

In the beginning, lighting was a problem. The lights were so strong that the cushion rails on the table became uncomfortably hot, burning the players' hands and curling the Formica at the joints. But it was the two-year-old tantrums that really turned up the heat. Willie Smith was known for his spectacular McEnroe[139] style tantrums, screaming at the referee, "You can't be serious!"

In front of the cameras, he turned into a proper Orson Wells.[140]

"You touched the white, Mr Smith, before it stopped rolling." "I did not," Smith retorted turning on the spectators.

"Don't sit there like dummies. Did you see me touch the white? Yes or no?" Horace retired to a quiet corner, leaving Willie to fight it out with the referee whilst the journalists rushed to report:

"Our Willie is in the wars again!"

"Australia's Horace Lindrum waits patiently for the umpire's decision."

Tantrums were not the exclusive property of Willie Smith. Melbourne Inman and Tom Reece were fierce combatants. If Reece was responsible for the venue, Inman would tell the press:

"Bloody place is like an opium den. The cloth is in a terrible state and the cushions are as dead as the mouse in that trap over there."

If Inman selected the balls, Reece would ask: "Where did he get these balls? They're the wrong weight and just look at their colour."

Tremendous draw cards, they played to the gallery right to the bitter end. When Inman died, Reece gave a brief interview to the press. In the course of the interview he told a journalist:

"There's no way I'm sending flowers. If I send anything, it will be an iron cross to keep the blighter down."

He then buried himself in a hill of pebbles on Brighton Beach, where he spent the night howling his eyes out, which is what we all do when we lose someone we deeply love. Mac also knew how to throw a temper tantrum. He stopped twice in the final of the 1951–52 world championship to reprimand the audience. During the first frame, he told a fellow:

---

[139] John Patrick McEnroe Junior (1959–), American-born former World No. 1 professional tennis player, often rated among the greatest of all time in the sport, especially for his touch on the volley

[140] American actor, writer, director and producer known for his spectacular tantrums. One of Welles's more famous tantrums inspired the script for the motion picture *Citizen Kane* (1941), considered by some critics to be the greatest movie of all time. The film reflects on the life and legacy of Charles Foster Kane and is based on the life of newspaper mogul William Randolph Hearst. Welles took the lead, directed, produced and co-wrote the screenplay with Herman Mankiewicz with whom he argued violently over the plot. Nominated for nine Academy Awards, the film won the award for best original screenplay

"Sir, if you move again, I'll have you put out!"

In the tenth frame, he had a go at a woman.

"Madam, you obviously didn't hear me when I spoke to that gentleman over there. If you want to riffle in your handbag or unwrap the cellophane on your Iced Mint, for Pete's sake, go outside and do it."

At the conclusion of the 1936–37 playing season, Horace was on the road again on a tour promoted on the back of his incredible firsts. (world-record snooker breaks of 104, 109, 114, 116, 124, 131, 135, 139 and 141). But his greatest thrill turned out to be his greatest disappointment. The governing body refused to recognise his world-record snooker break of 141.

Horace wrote of this event in his diary:

> "Joe Davis and I were playing at Manchester in 1937 before a packed house of two and a half thousand people. The balls broke well for me at the start of the run and as the balls went down, one by one, and my score rose, I could feel the growing tension in the audience. As I neared the century, there was the kind of silence you hear when you know something is about to happen, followed by a murmur as I passed the mark.
>
> When only the pink and black remained, I began to feel the strain. Not a soul moved and I was telling myself to remain calm. The pink went down and there was only one shot left. A straightforward potting black.
>
> I took careful aim for the pocket and, as the ball went in, the entire audience leapt to their feet, cheering, clapping and throwing their hats in the air and all I – the nearly twenty-five year old Australian – could do was feverishly mop my brow."

The bad news arrived a week later.

The governing body rejected Horace's application for break recognition.

> Dear Horace,
>
> It is with regret that we must reject your application for recognition. The billiard table manufacturers and installers of the table, G H Lupton & Co., forgot to measure the table with a Control Council template prior to the commencement of play.
>
> Yours sincerely,
>
> James C Bisset
> Chairman

An 11-year battle ensued.

Dear Mr Bisset,

G H Lupton & Co. have very kindly presented me with a trophy acknowledging the break, assuring me they are completely satisfied that their table conformed to the standard requirements and are extremely distressed that the Control Council has rejected the original application for recognition on the grounds of a technicality. Accordingly, I respectfully ask that the matter be reviewed.

Yours sincerely,

Horace Lindrum

But the governing body was not for turning, a decision which brought condemnation from the media all over the world, including the British press, who asserted that the governing body wilfully delayed recognising Horace Lindrum's big breaks to give their own players an opportunity to write those breaks into history.

Trophy presented to Horace Lindrum by G H Lupton & Co. in recognition of the world-record break of 141.

18 February 1937

Mirror

"England jealous of its records"

Some English Press Officials are becoming impatient regarding the British Control Council withholding the certificate of recognition from Horace Lindrum for his world's snooker record of 141.

The Australian has broken the record three times but his name has not yet appeared on the record list. He lifted Davis's figures of 114 to 116 but the effort was not recognised owing to a "technicality".

On December 11 he made a 131 but a night or two later Sidney Smith got busy and rattled up a 133. Then came Lindrum's 141.

After dilly-dallying, officialdom has intimated it will "consider" the record if Lindrum can satisfy the committee the table was to standard.

Daily Mail (London) of January 14 is wrathful at the idea that a special table erected for an important match is not being accepted as *"standard"*.

Inman was so outraged by the Council's decision, he funded and promoted Horace's 1937 world tour out of his own pocket, proclaiming in the marketing material:

"Horace Lindrum of Australia is the greatest snooker player I have ever seen."

Inman was not the only one to make reference to Horace's extraordinary prowess at the table. At the foot of the last page of his book *Lindrum Billiards* published in 1937, Walter Lindrum states:

'The World Snooker Record stands at 141, made by Horace Lindrum in Manchester.'

On that note Horace must surely have thought:

"Everything's going to be bonza!"

Chapter 5
Everything's going to be bonza!

During the Golden Age of Flight, flying was anything but golden. Flying was extremely dangerous. Poor weather conditions. Unreliable navigational equipment. Aviation pioneers, the moneyed, the entrepreneur with a special gift or talent – artists, writers, performers, scientists, billiardists – are counted among the one per cent of Australians who travelled outside the nation and most of them travelled by ship.

Nevertheless, as Mark Clayton wrote:

> "For millions of Australians aviation had become a way of life by the 1930s, affecting even the most routine aspects of their daily lives. The food they ate, the magazines they read, the clothes they wore, and even the music which they listened to were all influenced by the revolution that was taking place overhead. There also emerged in Australia at that time a cult of the aviatrix, which was sustained, in large measure, by popular women's magazines such as *The Australian Women's Weekly* and *The Home*. Although there were fewer women pilots than men, the public was groomed to accept the aviatrix as an appropriate role model.
>
> For every Kingsford Smith there was a "Chubbie" Miller, for every Bert Hinkler there was a Lores Bonney, and for every Charles Ulm there was a Freda Thompson.
>
> Overseas influences were also important in helping to shape public attitudes at that time. Movies such as *Christopher Strong* (1933), in which
>
> Katherine Hepburn immortalised the aerial achievements of Lady Cynthia Darrington and flying visits by Amy Johnson (1930), Elli Beinhorn (1932) and Jean Batten (1934), all helped to condition an otherwise conservative society."[141]

In the beginning, much of Horace's overseas travel was by seaplane; a mode of travel known as the luxurious Empire class.[142] Service aboard the Empire class was superb and French wines, cheese, roast chicken with baked potatoes and a variety of puddings featured on the menu.

The seaplane took 12 days to fly from Australia to Britain, thus "pilots who represented the nation in international air races and sportsmen such as Horace Lindrum who represented the nation in international competitions became living symbols of the new nation, of the Australian identity and of Australian masculinity."[143]

---

[141] Mark Clayton, *Taking Flight*, Canberra: Australia Post Philatelic Group, 35
[142] Seaplanes, which were specifically designed to strengthen ties with the Mother Country, played a critical role in keeping Australia connected during World War II and became the targets of Japanese attacks on Australian soil
[143] Paul Ashton in Examiner's Report, *The Uncrowned King*, 4 May 2015

That reality might offer one explanation of why many of their stories have been lost to us. Rather than see them as the stories of individual lives, we have viewed them as representations of something bigger than themselves. Only in recent times, for example, have we become interested in the individual lives of the Anzacs.

Of course, even when we capture the life per se of a globetrotting pioneer, no story can ever be expected to contain all of that man or woman's amazing feats and adventures. As Sir Richard Attenborough pointed out in his biographical film *Gandhi*:

> No man's life can be encompassed in one telling. There is no way to give each year its allocated weight, include each event, each person who helped to shape a lifetime. What can be done is to be faithful in spirit to the record and try to find one's way to the heart of the man.[144]

This is what I have tried to do here and why the record should contain the following snippets of Horace Lindrum before the history of his life slips into the sands of time and those snippets are lost to us forever.

---

[144] Richard Attenborough's biographical film *Gandhi*, Columbia Pictures in association with Gold Crest Films and National Film Development Corporation of India and Indo-British Films, starring Ben Kingsley (1982

Ken Shaw, the Secretary of the Transvaal Billiards and Snooker Association for 33 years[145] wrote:

> "The thrill of meeting this dapper little Australian whenever he arrived by air to undertake his playing tours of South Africa will forever live with me.
>
> Also the excitement of the audiences as he made his entrance can only be attributed to the special qualities he possessed, a personality all of his own and which, along with his Magic Wand – that shortened cue – leave memories and admiration of one of the Greatest Cue Ball Entertainers of all time.
>
> Apart from his cueing ability that drew record audiences in South Africa, there was that special brand of humour and cheer which aided in establishing him as one of the most popular sportsmen of his time and, above all, one of Australia's Greatest Ambassadors. He was a gentleman admired and respected for the consideration he had for his fellow man. Horace played many matches and exhibitions for the under-privileged donating the entire proceeds to assist in aiding their plight.
>
> As one who had the good fortune to witness numerous century breaks and which I must add, were compiled under playing conditions that were not always conducive to sizeable breaks, a performance that must be written into history is the one that took place at the German Club in Pretoria on 16 May 1955. Horace compiled his 500th snooker century against the Northern Province champion Doug Lombard, clearing the table with a fast scoring 137. In the following two frames he made breaks of 100 and 103. What makes this feat so remarkable is the fact that it was achieved with the old heavy 'Bonzoline' balls and with such speed."[146]

T. Eng Chwan, chairman of the Union of Burma Billiards & Control Council had this to say:

> "You have distinguished yourself as one of the all-time masters of the game. Your great ability, your equally great showmanship and your easy, affable manner, have made you a notable ambassador for billiards and snooker and for your country, Australia. No less than the other great members of the Lindrum family preceding you, you have exemplified all that is best in professionalism and, wherever billiards and snooker are played the name of Horace Lindrum is an honoured one."[147]

Suzanne Johnson of the Australian Billiards & Snooker Association dubbed Horace, a credit to the sport of his choice and a most successful roving ambassador for Australia.

> "Horace has, of course, visual evidence of this in the many goodwill presentations he has received throughout the world. I recall the occasion when the Prime Minister of New Zealand, the Right Honourable Mr Peter Fraser, and members of the New Zealand Parliament, commissioned the making of a special cue case with an inscribed silver plate affixed. I was present at Parliament House in Wellington when the Prime Minister made the presentation, the theme being not only Horace's tremendous contribution to Australia–New Zealand relations but also to the favourable publicity he generated in the old world for our two countries down under.

---

[145] Ken Shaw also undertook the promotion of professional snooker and billiards competition matches and exhibitions by visiting players in South Africa and Zimbabwe. His letter forms part of the family archive. It is addressed to Suzanne, secretary of the Australian Billiards and Snooker Association

[146] Letter written to Suzanne Johnson, secretary of the Australian Billiards & Snooker Association in support of an application for recognition of Horace Lindrum's achievements. The letter forms a part of the family archive. The Honours system was under review at the time and the Order of Australia was introduced on 14 February 1975, seven months after Horace's death

[147] Letter written to Suzanne Johnson

Horace never hesitated to cheerfully display his great skill and entertainment ability for charitable purposes. He constantly visited hospitals giving exhibitions and, indeed, on the last occasion, met a snooker challenge with New Zealand's leading jockeys captained by Bill Skelton in aid of the well known charity 'Birthright' for crippled and deserving children. The last surviving billiard playing member of the greatest billiard playing family the world has ever seen; a family who, through an incredible five generations, has kept the Australian flag flying high in a global sense; [Horace Lindrum] would gladly be claimed in Great Britain, New Zealand, India and South Africa, as one of their own."[148]

Horace Lindrum played an important role in breaking down the crude racism, sexism, anti-Semitism and class struggle that lay at the heart of amateurism which "is now happily vanishing."[149] He believed, for example, that amateur players were frequently as capable as professionals. The difference was opportunity to practise, play and compete against players better than themselves. He encouraged women, children (especially disadvantaged children) and disabled people to pick up their cues; he deemed himself fortunate to have had the opportunity to travel, expand his horizons and broaden his perspective on life and saw human beings as equal regardless of sex, race, religion and background. It could be argued that he absorbed the Slutzkin "Love Thy Neighbour"and "Share Thy Talent" principles as a boy in Flinders Lane as the record shows that he befriended the workers and they shared their lunch and morning tea with him.

Back to Horace's travels. 1937

First ports of call were Malta and Colombo, then it was on to Bombay and a week of exhibitions at the Taj Mahal Hotel.

"What's the Taj like?" Horace asked Inman.

"What's she like! What's she like! Why, my dear boy, she's the playground of Princes. You haven't stayed anywhere until you have stayed at the Taj Mahal Palace Hotel. If you stand at the ship's rail, you will see her swim into view." Excited, Horace raced to the rail.

"Before the Taj one stayed at Watson's."

Inman stopped to reflect on fond memories of his stays at Watson's and the hours spent sitting in a vintage wicker lounge chair on the terrace, sipping a Whiskey Sour, reading Somerset Maugham, enjoying the cool air flowing from the overhead fans onto the faces of the pink orchids potted in decorative ceramic pots.

"Good times. They were good times."

"Do you think there is truth to the saying, people become people through people?" Horace asked. Inman showed surprise. It was a question from left field.

"Yes, I do, Horace. No question about it, the developer of the *Taj* – Jamsetji Tata – found his artistic soul through Robert Knight the editor of *The Times of India*.

Whilst the Taj is Tata's great legacy, the legacy belongs just as much to the man with the dream as it does to the man who turned the dream into a reality. Not that I want to take anything away from Tata. Poor man hit a wall of opposition when he announced his intention to go into the hotel business. His partners called him a lunatic. His sisters pleaded with him to re-think. Nobody understood his desire to make the grand leap from industry to craftsmanship. From Science Institute in Bangalore to 'Boarding House' in Bombay. Of course, the Taj is not a boarding house. It is an architectural masterpiece. Fortunately, Tata

---

[148] Letter written by Suzanne Johnson in her capacity as secretary of the Australian Billiards & Snooker Association to the Prime Minister, the Right Honourable Edward Gough Whitlam, with a copy to the Right Honourable the Premier of the State of New South Wales, Sir Robert Askin, seeking recognition for Horace Lindrum's achievements. The letter forms part of the family archive along with other letters in support. Around the same time, the Association presented Horace with a trophy recognising that he had held the title of Australian professional billiards and snooker champion for over 33 years; they presented Joy Lindrum with a brooch in the shape of a triangle, the triangle is set in rubies, with one diamond, in recognition of her services to the cue sports

[149] Douglas Booth, Examiner's Report, *The Uncrowned King*, 5 June 2015

enjoyed negotiating with smart thinkers rather than those who thought they could think and put 'vision' (long-term thinking) before 'bottom line' (short-term thinking)."

Horace stretched his imagination about as far as he could stretch it but no stretching of the imagination could have prepared him for his first glimpses of India. As for the Taj Mahal Palace Hotel, here was a conceptual design intelligence far beyond any he had seen before. Stupendous. Iconic. Bold. Adjectives all apt, yet somehow insufficient. There was something – he did not know what – just something – that set the building apart. A SPARK.[150] A perfect star in a fragment-filled universe. He tried hard to pin-point the something. Was it the onion-shaped domes? The pointed arches? The ribbed spires? The rich earthy colours of the stonework? If you looked at those attributes in isolation the answer was No. He spent time wondering what feature impressed the most, but even this studied contemplation failed to provide him with an answer.

Whatever the elusive quality was, the Taj hotel represented a refined sense of beauty rarely found in bricks-and-mortar. It was the kind of beauty one sees in the rear vision mirror from a future at least a century away. Horace's eyes floated upwards to the underbellies of the structure. Inlaid with gold leaf, the sun was beating down on them, projecting great shards of light onto a blue-curtained Ganges.

"It was the first building in Bombay to be lit by electricity," Inman added. "The Grand Ballroom – which is where you will be giving your exhibitions – is supported by the original 10 pillars of shorn iron."

Observing the intensity of expression on Horace's face, Inman smiled.

"What did I tell you!" he exclaimed waving the point of his cane at the Taj. "Come along, my boy. The playground of Maharajahs awaits."

He strode off in the direction of the gangplank, his stunning proboscis leading the way.

English butlers with Yorkshire reserve. Turkish baths. Ceiling fans, Victorian round-backs. Priceless antiques in lavishly carved cabinets singing through the lacquer of old man time. The Taj was certainly the palace of princes.

Horace and Inman were greeted on arrival by the hotel manager who advised them that their visit had created great excitement.

"The exhibitions are a sell-out. Princes and their wives, diplomats, dignitaries and officials will be seated in the first rows. Some 600 hundred guests behind them. The hotel is now offering standing room only."

All truly great performances are born out of adversity. On this occasion the fire from the diamond-studded jackets and bejewelled Mumtaj saris exploded in Horace's lenses and the overhead fans stirred the moisture in the humid air, steaming up the contact lenses he was wearing underneath his spectacles. Fortunately, little obstacles like this were nowhere near the distraction to the Maestro as the pieces of eight later were to the Black Poker's needlecraft. Some years after the exhibition, the Black Poker was darning socks.

"Do you know anything of these, Horace?"

Cuff links and shirt studs – platinum on onyx – each with 13 diamonds. She had found them wrapped in a tissue parcel inside the toe of one of Horace's socks. He told her the story.

"On my first visit to India in 1937, I was invited to play for the Maharajah of Jaipur. At the end of the exhibition, the Maharajah gave me a standing ovation, removed his cuff links and shirt studs, bowed and placed them in my hand. He said:

"Mr Lindrum, that was the most brilliant exhibition I have ever seen, please accept these as a token of my appreciation. Now, if you will excuse me, I must go and change my shirt."

After Bombay, Horace and Inman travelled to Calcutta where Horace had the unique experience of playing on a floating pier. Here, I can boast quite confidently that Horace

---

[150] Reference to the world-renowned architectural firm SPARK of Singapore, established by the visionary architect Stephen Pimbley. The writer enjoys the enormous honour and privilege that flows from collaboration with Stephen and his co-director Wenhui Lim

was one of a handful of sportsmen in the history of sport who was capable of performing under most unusual conditions.

The following letter published in the British magazine *Snooker Scene*[151] is one of many pieces of evidence to that effect.

> Dear Sir,
>
> I have been following snooker since 1947 and I would like to tell you a little about it. Over the years I was privileged to see in action some of the greats such as Joe Davis, Horace Lindrum, Rex Williams and Ray Reardon when they were on tour. I was also privileged to see each of them make century breaks.
>
> On one occasion in 1952 Horace Lindrum played at the Modderfontein Club where the table Lights were hung from a sprung wooden floor above the ceiling.
>
> A lively dance was in progress upstairs causing the ceiling lights to sway backwards and forwards and the shuffling and stamping made the audience in the billiard room feel as if they were sitting beneath a stage during a production of the tap dancing musical *42nd Street*.
>
> Hugging his cue – as if it were his dance partner – Horace expertly waltzed around the table to record a 133.
>
> Amazing! Something never to be seen again.

Next port of call, Rangoon, and a packed house in the billiard room at the Strand Hotel.

The Chinese champion strode into the room with all the majesty of the mythological Emperor Zhuanxu.[152] Fastidiously dressed, right hand clamped to the handle of his cue case, determination written into the tiny muscles of his face, bright eyes surveying the table. The look told Horace he had a fight on his hands. He was right. His opponent was fast around the table and played with accuracy and precision. A number of times during the match he screwed his ball three-quarters along the length of the cushion and into an end pocket without causing the object ball to cross the table. Only the great possess the know-how to execute shots of that ilk.

While Horace was battling the Chinese Knight of the Cue, Inman was tucking into the rainbow trout and raspberry and padang meringues at the Captain's table; his vessel was wending its way across a stormy Indian Ocean towards Singapore. When the vessel arrived, Horace was waiting to greet the ship and share the news of his win.

If I could hear Horace talking to me about his first visit to Singapore I envisage him telling me that he was captivated by the many junks on the waterways hawking their goods to visiting ocean liners and the architecture of the city. The city had good bones. I say this because he was the possessor of a sixth sense. He could see the promise of things to come. My guess is he would also have been captivated by the marketplace where, in those days, mysterious oriental spices, shrimp stock, lard and noodles bubbled away in giant woks; street vendors peddled brightly coloured wax paper parasols, coolie hats, fried spiders, antelope horns and bouquets of up-side-down chickens; and old women sat in doorways juggling dice in tortoise shells.

Penny for your fortune. Sixpence to wake the dead.

"I feel at home here," Horace told Inman as they rode along in a Jinrickshaw manned by a leather-footed man with a smile broader than Glen Lim's *Smiley Canine*.

"I knew you would, my boy. I knew you would."

---

[151] A magazine founded by Clive Everton (1937–), Welsh veteran and former BBC snooker commentator (1978–2010), journalist, author and editor

[152] Zhuanxu is credited with composing the earliest piece of music, "The Answer to the Clouds"

Exhibitions at Raffles and the Fullerton Hotel, then it was off to the Philippines. I had no idea what a Filipino Tinikling dance was so I went to *Memoirs of a Raffles Original*,[153] the work of long-term front-of-house manager at the Raffles Hotel, Leslie Danker. The Tinikling apparently involves two people hitting two parallel bamboo poles on the ground and against each other, in rhythmic co-ordination, with dancers who step over and in-between the poles. I thought it sounded positively dangerous. I was right. There is an element of danger if one steps wrongly and a foot is caught between the poles as they clash against each other.

Between swipes with the pole, Inman confided:'

"We're going to give the audience some real excitement in Manila, Horace."

Unbeknown to his protégé, Inman had reached an agreement for the competition matches to be played under the Continental rules of billiards as well as under the English rules.

"You've done what!" Horace could not believe what he was hearing.

"Don't worry, old boy, with a few hours practice, you'll be fine. Best keep your eyes on the pole."

Miraculously, Horace managed to retain his good humour and hold his own on the dance floor and at the table. That was no mean feat. Continental billiards is a very different game from English billiards. It is played on a much smaller, pocketless table and, although carom or carombole is a member of the billiards family, the sports are far apart, requiring radically different skills.

In billiards, the general object of the player is to score points by striking one ball against another with the aim of either propelling one or both of them into a pocket; or, with one ball, to strike two others successively, that is to "cannon". In carom, the object is to bounce one's cue-ball off the opponent's cue-ball and the object-ball, in a single shot.

To be proficient at either billiards or carom requires the cultivation of touch and the quality required for the two games is best compared with the touch required to play an upright piano versus the touch needed on a grand.

The touch for the "Boogie Woogie Bugle Boy of Company B"[154] is different from the touch for "The Moonlight Sonata".[155] The shape of the hand is different. The lift of the arms is different. The fingers play differently on the keys. The Filipino champion did not take too kindly to the British rules.

"British bloody madness!" That's how he described it to the press but, madness or no, like Peppy playing at the Bijou, Inman's idea captured the imagination and – for the artist – capturing the imagination of the audience is all that ever matters.

Final engagements in the region were at the fabulous Eastern & Oriental hotel in Penang and in Ipoh and Kuala Lumpur. The exhibition in Kuala Lumpur included a performance for His Royal Highness the Sultan of Malaysia, a billiards buff so fascinated by the science and exquisite technicalities of the sport that his eyes remained glued to the table. Horace recorded the event, describing how resplendent the Sultan looked in his Muskat (traditional costume).

> On his head, the Sultan wore the Tengkolok (headdress). Embroidered with gold thread, a diamond-studded crescent-shaped ornament and fourteen-point star was affixed at the front. At the centre of the star, the crest of Malaysia. Attached to a ruby-studded waist buckle, the Royal Keris

---

[153] Leslie Danker, *Memoirs of a Raffles Original,* (Raffles Hotel, Singapore: Angsana Books, 2010), 86

[154] Closely based upon an earlier song "Beat me Daddy, Eight to the Bar" by Don Raye , "Boogie, Woogie, Bugle Boy from Company B" by Don Raye and Hughie Prince was first recorded at Decca's Hollywood studios on 2 January 1941 by The Andrew Sisters. In the same year, The Andrew Sisters introduced the song in the Abbott and Costello motion picture *Buck Privates*

[155] Piano Sonata Number 14 in C-sharp minor Opus 27, No. 2, "Quasi una fantasia" more commonly known as "The Moonlight Sonata", composed by Ludwig van Beethoven and dedicated to his pupil, Countess Giulietta Guicciardi (1802

(short sword) with gold decorated sheath and the Keris Panjang (long sword) with ivory hilt.

From Australia through New Zealand, Vancouver and Toronto, and then across country to New York, our travellers arrived on the eve of the World Baseball series. Newsstands hummed with stories of the Clipper and the Invisible Ray, crowded horse cars pushed along roadways between Sunshine cabs, Dodge humpbacks (panel trucks with flip up windshields and duck tail back ends), and Ford cabriolets (sleek roadsters) and, writ large across the skyline of this fascinating urban landscape, neon signs flashing ads for Ballantine's Beer, Camels and "The Great Ziegfeld".

Horace said the time they would have to wait for table service at the popular Naples Clam Bar was more than an hour, and the queue was about as long at the 25-cent spaghetti diner around the corner, but nobody seemed to mind. People chatted and laughed and tried not to succumb to the delicious smells of doughnut, pretzel, whole hogs with Carolina mustard, fried goats cheese with jalapeno and Polish dog in freshly-baked bread roll doused in hot sauce, pickle and sauerkraut.

"When the Clipper made his first home run there was one almighty roar and I reckon you could hear that roar on the other side of the Atlantic." The excitement with which Horace relayed his memories of the New York experience made me think if he had been born in the USA he would have played baseball not billiards. He would have made a bloody good Lou Gehrig.[156]

Next highlight, a marvellous trick-shot display by the famous and talented, Willie Hoppe,[157] one of Horace's childhood heroes. He was also the subject of many a university thesis. A group of Princeton professors believed Hoppe's incredible skill was due to his eyes having a peculiar faculty for measuring angles with mathematical precision.

>Not all went to plan.
>
>Hoppe was caught telling a common fly to "Bugger off".
>
>In the middle of a swerving masse shot,[158] a fly landed on his cue ball.

Hoppe paused, hoping to God the damn thing would just leave. When it refused to budge the referee shooed it with his silk handkerchief. Alas, the moment Hoppe's cue went up in the air, down came the fly.

---

[156] Lou Gehrig (1903–1941), "Buster Gehrig", American baseball player who played first baseman for 17 seasons of major league baseball for the New York Yankees and earned the nickname "The Iron Horse". Gehrig was the ultimate professional who conducted himself, throughout his career, with dignity

[157] Eighteen-year-old Willie Hoppe defeated the great French billiardist Maurice Vignaux in a world record-breaking billiards final in the ballroom of the Grand Hotel in Paris on 15 January 1906. The purse was 1000 dollars, an absolute fortune in those days

[158] An extreme form of swerve played with an almost vertical strike, usually used to avoid a snooker by cannoning around obstructing balls to pot the ball being struck into a pocket

Horace demonstrating a masse shot

Once again, the referee intervened and the fly returned. This time, it circled repeatedly around before coming in for a landing.

The spectators, joining in on the fun, wielded hats, score-cards and newspapers in a series of threatening gestures that might have scared an elephant but did absolutely nothing to scare the fly.

No less than 18 times the cue went up until Dickey of the Bronx Bombers gave the fly an almighty whack.

"Ladies and gentlemen, I give you, the Yankee fly," he proclaimed, a big grin on his cheeky face.

Marcel Camp – hallowed champion of Detroit – was Horace's next opponent then it was George Chenier, champion of Canada.

"You know why I love the billiard room, Horace?" Chenier asked. "Let me tell you why I love the billiard room. The billiard room is like a hotel. Both excellent destinations for the study of human nature."

"You can learn a lot from watching people," Horace agreed.

"It don't matter where the room is – city, province, north, south, east, west," Chenier continued. "You'll find the same generous impulses or petty meannesses or the same business-like keenness or happy-go-lucky disregard. You'll see the quick thinker whose mind is made up as he walks toward his ball or the slow thinker who gets his ball, then chalks his cue, has a look around the room, chalks his cue, has another look around the room, chalks his cue – you know the kind. Then, when he finally gets down to his stroke – just as the audience and his opponent are breathing a huge sigh of relief – he gets up and goes through the whole process again – ultimately playing the shot you had arranged for him in your mind before he went down the first time.

You see the workman, a plain ball striker, steady and difficult to beat and the man who never goes straight to his objective. You see the university student– the little storehouse of knowledge ready to button-hole his professors. You see the old codger courting his medals from Ashanti and Tel-El-Kehir. 'I cannot play a stroke these days,' he tells you. 'I never get any practice. My right arm is semi-paralysed and I can't see the length of the table.' You take pity on him, give him a start whereupon he thrashes you within an inch of your life."

The conversation moved to the profile of the cue sports.

"Let's consider, for a moment, Horace, the bad publicity the games get at times. I don't want to sound as if I'm preaching the Gospel but I think the cue sports are a reflection of the schizophrenic personality of man. No fault lies with the Sports, for they are highly intelligent and demanding arts. No, the fault lies in man. Shakespeare got that one right. The fault lies with the player who regards the table as something purchased at a sixpenny store. Cocky, this fellow bounces the balls, drags his sticky fingers along the cloth, over-chalks his cue. Uses enough chalk to chalk every cue in town. Calls for a cigarette. (Now we have chalk and ash on the cloth). Later stubs out his cigarette on the floor, bangs down his cue, natters to spectators and brags about his imaginary conquests." Horace made no comment. He did not need to. Chenier was simply describing a reality that could be applied to every sector of human life.

The trip home was first class aboard the *Bremen*. Built to delight Kaiser and King, *Bremen*[159] was renowned for its spectacularly opulent hospitality, barber shop and first-ever mail service. The vessel ended up at the epicentre of a major controversy when anti-Nazi protestors boarded her and ripped the Nazi flag from the jackstaff. Hitler did not take kindly to the assault, proclaiming the flag to be the 'official' flag of Germany.

Back in the UK, Horace kicked off the winter season with a week of snooker at the Albert Institute in Leeds. His opponent was a leading British professional snooker champion Sidney Smith, the first player in history to make a total clearance in snooker competition with a break of 136 recorded in a final against Joe Davis in 1939. There was some pretty exciting match play over this period and a rather fancy prize for the highest break. Lord Milton, later Earl Fitzwilliam, donated a personal cigarette case, quite something in the days when audiences went gooey over Bogart puffing on a Black Cat[160] in movies such as *The Maltese Falcon*.[161]

At the first session, Sidney Smith completed a break of 120 and it seemed he had the prize in the bag. Then, at the last session, Horace took several reds and, when the remaining balls split nicely, he realised there was a chance of a higher break. The points began to mount, as did the tension. Horace did not always find it easy to remain cool. He did not like the pressure of competition.

However, on this occasion, he found himself very much in control finally clearing the table with a break of 130.

The prize is an important piece of family memorabilia. It was donated by Peter Wentworth Fitzwilliam (the 8th Earl Fitzwilliam) who was romantically linked to Kathleen "Kick" Cavendish, one of President John F Kennedy's sisters. Unable to escape the "Kennedy curse", Cavendish, along with the Earl, was killed in an air crash in France in 1948.

"Australia's Horace Lindrum reaches another final with our Joe."

It was months before the Big Broadcaster slipped in any mention of the storm clouds building on the horizon and, when they eventually wrote a tit-bit into history, nobody took much notice. Not at the beginning. Why would they take any notice? The smiles and the handshakes were saying:

"No worries, mate. Everything is going to be bonza!"

On that note, Horace and Inman set out on another tour of the Continent, landing in Bergen and picking up a Rolls-Royce Phantom II[162] for the drive to Oslo. In Oslo they were guests of the Texaco Oil Company and gave the first of a series of exhibitions for the

---

[159] Constructed from 7000 tons of high-strength steel, *SS Bremen* was built by the German company Deutsche Schiffund Maschinenbau for the Norddeutscher Lloyd line to work on the trans-Atlantic sea route

[160] Named after a black cat that sat regularly on the window-sill of the Carreras' Wardour street shop, Black Cat cigarettes were introduced into the United Kingdom by Carrera Ltd. in 1904. The Wardour Street premises came to be known as the "Black Cat shop

[161] A detective novel written by Dashiell Hammett originally serialised in the September issue of the *Black Mask magazine, The Maltese Falcon* (1929) inspired a cinematic masterpiece by the same name. Released in 1941, director John Huston's directorial debut classic was nominated for three Academy Awards. Dubbed the first major film noir by Panorama du film noir, the film starred actors Humphrey Bogart, Mary Astor, Sydney Greenstreet, Peter Lorre and Elisha Cook Junior

[162] The "Continental" model or "Phantom II" was designed by Ivan Evenden but, at first, the design did not capture the imagination of the Rolls-Royce sales department. Attitudes changed when the department learned of Evenden's Grand Prix d'Honneur win at the "Biarritz Grand Concours d'Elegance" (1930). On his return to the factory he found the sales brochure ready to go. Featured in the motion pictures *The Yellow Rolls-Royce* (1964), *Indiana Jones and the Last Crusade* (1989) and *The Sorcerer's Apprentice* (2010), the distinguishing features of this model were the short wheelbase and stiffer, five-leaf springs

company's employees before driving on to Gothenburg, Stockholm, Copenhagen, Hamburg and Bremen. By the time the Phantom reached Essen it was flying a spectacular array of flags and pennants; the Southern Cross and Union Jack were strategically placed on either side of Syke's "Spirit of Ecstasy"[163]

The boys had stayed with Inman's old friend, Herr Berlingroahdt at 3 Hans Niemeyer Strasse a number of times but this time Berlingroahdt was not his usual jovial self. He kept telling them how things had changed. He did not want to worry them but they should be mindful. "It seems we have swapped the clockwork turning of the German National dance for the thud, thud, thud of army boots."

En-route from Dresden to Munich, Herr Berlingroahdt's words took on real meaning. Beer houses once filled with the music of Romberg's *Student Prince*[164] were by then overflowing with poker-faced men dressed in brown dungarees shouting "Heil Hitler!".

"Something must be done about this," Horace said to himself, but those in power rarely listen to the thoughts of extraordinary men and women. Not until it is too late.

In Berlin the Phantom was vandalised. The pennants were ripped off, torn, shredded and thrown in the gutter, the flags, burned, gigantic swastikas painted on the doors.

"I say! This is rather unpleasant. Not what I'd call Fair Play. What shall we do, young Horace?"

"Roll up our sleeves and get on with it, Mel," Horace responded.

They cleaned down the doors – restoring the Phantom to its former glory – pulled spare flags and pennants from the boot, redecorated the vehicle and drove to refugee camps where they picked up their cues and performed for intellectuals like the historian, Fernand Braudel, who wrote the first draft of his masterpiece, *The Mediterranean and the Mediterranean World in the Age of Philip II*, in a war camp. At each exhibition, Horace and Inman raised the Union Jack and the Southern Cross and sang "God Save the King" and "Waltzing Matilda". Neither could sing particularly well. Both received an electrifying rendition of: Ich habe einen kameraden. *("The Good Comrade"*, a traditional song of the German armed forces – "I had a buddy, you could never find a better one"[165]).

Braudel was right when he wrote:

> "The historian can never get away from the question of time in history. Time sticks to his thinking like soil to a gardener's spade."

---

[163]Designed by British sculptor, Charles Robinson, and, originally, dubbed "The Whisperer", "The Spirit of Ecstasy" carries with it the story of a secret love affair between John Walter Edward Douglas-Scott-Montagu (the second Baron Montagu of Beaulieu from 1905) – a pioneer of the motor vehicle industry – and Eleanor Velasco, the editor of *The Car Illustrated* magazine (from 1902), who was the model for the work. "The Spirit of Ecstasy" is also known as "The Flying Lady" and "The Silver Lady". The artefact features a woman leaning forwards with her arms outstretched behind her, the billowing cloth flowing from her arms to her back resembles wings. Eleanor Velasco died on 30 December 1915. A passenger aboard the *SS Persia* and the vessel was torpedoed by a German U-boat. The love affair between Douglas-Scott-Montagu and Velasco was kept secret for over a decade due to Velasco's poor financial circumstances
[164]*The Student Prince* is an operetta in four acts based upon the play *Old Heidelberg*, written by Wilhelm Meyer-Forster with music by Sigmund Romberg and lyrics by Dorothy Donnelly. The work was first performed at Jolson's 59th Street Theatre on Broadway on 2 December 1924
[165]Text written by poet Ludwig Upland in 1809

Six weeks later Neville Chamberlain went on his most important mission to meet Hitler. The mission failed. After that, Kahal and Fain's "I'll be seeing you in all the old familiar places"[166] topped the charts and Horace and Inman found themselves on the last train out of Germany.

"Heil Hitler! Ausweis bitte" (Passports please).

Checking the documents, the officer looked first at the faces, then at the photos. He repeated this action three times, which was somewhat nerve racking, before returning the passports.

"Danke schon" (Thank you)

"Excuse me, officer, how many miles is it to the next station?" Horace asked. "Thirty-two kilometres," he replied. "From now on you will speak only in kilometres. Heil Hitler".

He clicked his heels and moved to the next carriage. "Where does the world go from here?" Mel asked. Horace knew the answer.

Language had shifted from Art to Science.[167]

Photos of Horace with members of the Armed Services during World War II

---

[166] Music by Sammy Fain and lyrics by Irving Kahal, "I'll be seeing you" was first published in 1938. The song became an anthem for British and American soldiers serving abroad

[167] Language needs to be art and science as the combination of these two concepts provides nourishment for body and soul

Horace used his talent with the cue to raise money for the Comforts Fund

The Uncrowned King

> *Though you might like this photo of mine at Mawson Base Antarctica as you can see the dogs are interested in the game of snooker — I have this in colour — the dogs are not allowed in the huts — but some one felt sorry for the — Today no huskies exist in Antarctica mores the pity — it's called progress — the tables were supplied by the Lindrum family — we were grateful — I am going ok — did a full medical, my surgeon said I will not get feeling back in the left toes where gangrene set it — but wished me well in the Olympic Torch Relay day 98 — Rooty Hill N.S.W. Wed., 13th Sept, 2000*
>
> *Happy Easter 2000*
> *Anzac 2000*
> *Warm Regards*
> *Pat Lee*

A letter to our mother from World War II veteran and explorer of Antarctica, Pat Lee. The first paragraph is omitted to conceal the address. Pat Lee says:

"I am one of the Stolen Generations. Someone stole my youth. Yet another Anzac Day I will march again. For how long, I don't know. Today, no huskies exist in Antarctica. Mores the pity. It's called progress. The tables were supplied by the Lindrum Family......

We were grateful."

Lindrum's Pitt Street Sydney was opened to the Armed Services during World War II for recreational purposes. Horace established a competition and donated a trophy for the event. Today the trophy is held in the Officers' Mess at Victoria Barracks, Paddington, New South Wales. In the photograph above, Horace is presenting the trophy to the winner of the event.

While Horace and Inman were making their way home, a British teenager was contemplating her future. She had been born into one world and had come to inherit another which seems to be the "Way of the World".

Chapter 6
Joy's Journey

The White family purchased a compact radio in 1938. They were huddled around that radio on 3 September 1939. Neville Chamberlain's words sent shock-waves through their household and through nations across the globe. In Australia, Prime Minister Robert Menzies delivered the call to arms and Australia's finest responded. One of those was Horace Lindrum.

Rozemai raised her eyebrows and glanced across at Arthur who was slumped in his chair, hands locked. "The Great War. The Great Depression. You and I have been looking down the barrel of financial ruin for I don't know how long. Will there ever be an end to it?"

Strange as it might seem their youngest was thrilled at the prospect of a full-frontal attack on Hitler. There had been talk of it for months and there was something euphoric in the reality. The euphoria was short-lived. Rozemai was frank. She had seen it all before. She knew what to expect or she thought she did. "Survival is dependent upon being prepared. If the war is not settled quickly, your father and I will find ourselves out of work. Within six to twelve months everything will be rationed. Meat, eggs, fats, cheese, bacon, sugar, milk, sweets, soap, toothpaste, rice, bananas and oranges will be considered luxuries and will be in very short supply. Fruit and rice supplies that become available to us will be passed to you, Dorrie, for my grandchildren. Rice builds bone and we cannot have the children growing up not knowing what a banana or orange looks like. I want you to start using things sparingly. Every ounce of toothpaste is to be squeezed from the tube. We cannot afford to waste anything."

She turned to Joy.

"I know how much you love your dramatic studies, my darling. However, we now need to watch every penny."

Reality kicked in after the family had gone to bed.

"I wonder what the future has in store?" Joy asked herself as she lay looking up at the ceiling. She told Jesus she did not want to give up her drama lessons. She did not think that was fair.

Self reliant. Optimistic. A desire to impress. The lines on her palm showed she was philosophical and reflective, with depth of feeling. She tended to ponder maturely, but was often introverted. The shape of her hand indicated: The Far East would play an important part in any plans for travel.

Before she went to sleep her mind travelled to the place where the seeds of her love of drama were planted. Fortescue Primary school on the opening night of *The Mad Hatter's Tea Party*. The Dormouse failed to show. Where do you get a Dormouse at short notice. "Joy White is small enough to fit the costume." That performance turned into a burning passion to tread the boards but the opportunity to do so was cut dead. Writing came to fill the void. In the beginning she wrote feverishly in a diary. Later she wrote short stories, articles and collections of anecdotes. Her work has served a great purpose and her pieces of wisdom represent a meticulous record of a truly remarkable life. Without her work I would not be telling you this story.

When Joy woke the following morning, all she could think was:

Damn you, Mr Hitler!

Before the declaration of war, Joy worked part-time in her mother's beauty salon. The appointment book was always pretty full, particularly during holiday periods, so the extra hands were welcome. Joy's step-sister Dorris Fry was the apprentice. Dorris was the daughter of Rozemai's first husband, Private Frederick William Fry of the Middlesex Regiment. Private Fry was killed in a desert flank attack. Legend has it he was flung from his horse. Rozemai knew Frederick was dead before the Scroll arrived. Like Caesar's wife, she had a premonition. Later, there was a knock at the door. The chaplain and notifying officer were invited into the front room where the officer delivered the news. The chaplain did his best to provide emotional and spiritual support but how do you mend a broken heart?

Tuesday 1 June 1915

The Regimental Command could not say where Frederick was buried. They just could not be sure. They thought it was one place, then, some time later, said it was another.

From that time forward the sweetheart brooch became a permanent fixture and the photo album was locked in the dresser drawer. Rozemai wore the key to the repository of memory around her neck.

Gone were the days of sitting in the bath till the scum glued itself to the outer rim. Gone were the days of Pears Soap and Christopher Robin and Nanny's dressing-gown hanging on the peg behind the bathroom door. Gone was the young man whose spirit lay at the heart and soul of her being.

> Memories, memories, dreams of love so true,
> O'er the sea of memory,
> I'm drifting back to you…

Memories of Christmas, the whole family together.

My great-grandmother slicing sponge, iced with vanilla, sprinkled with coconut – this way, that way – 50 small pieces.

Memories of great-grandpa watching. He never said much. His ancestral line were graduates of Woolwich. They did a lot of thinking and knew the value of silence. Great-grandmother made up for the both of them. Good gypsy stock, she was the life of the party. They loved Frederick as they loved their own. He was such a sweet natured boy.

He was not made for war.

He was not made for charging at an enemy.

When the Scroll arrived Rozemai wept until there were no more tears. When the tears dried up, she put the six-inch, 15.24-centimetre cylinder on the mantelpiece. It was still sitting on the mantelpiece 60 years later.

Hairdressing took her mind away from her broken heart but she nursed the wound until the day of her death. She married Arthur Puxley White a year before Joy was born.

Joy's father –Arthur Puxley White –
Gunner 931031 with his brother during World War I

Returning to Joy's story.

Joy's school chums envied her. They saw their friend as a "New Age woman" and thought her lucky to work in her mother's salon. Joy liked the idea of going to work but she did not see anything New Age in mixing white henna[168] and pasting it on somebody's head. (Hairdressing was a lot different from how it is today. The Eugene machine baked the hair so the customer came out looking like Medusa and the Marcel wave; pinched waves across the head to the nape of the neck; was a tedious and time-consuming process. Products used in the salon were not purchased from corporations but prepared from the hairdresser's own set of secret recipes).

For Joy there was only one thing worse than mixing and pasting and that was getting cups of tea and coffee for snotty-nosed customers who complained if you dribbled milk in the saucer.

The last straw was the sniggering over her father's dug-out (air-raid shelter).

"It's taking up half their garden. Concrete this thick. What can the man be thinking! I'm pleased we don't live next door. Imagine waking up in the morning and pulling your curtains to a view of that monstrosity." Rozemai jumped to Arthur's defence:

"Hitler is not going to stop at Czechoslovakia."

"Rubbish, my dear. Look at this photo of Edward and Adolf. The lovely smiles on their faces." The customer pointed to the picture of the Duke of Windsor[169] and Hitler, front and centre, shaking hands.

Joy bit her tongue and disappeared into the storeroom with a copy of *The Mitcham News and Mercury*.

"Wanted: Junior clerk for a business house in Streatham Vale."

"I could do that," she said to herself. "I'll ask Mum for the time off to go to the pictures with my friends."

Later that day she searched through her sister's wardrobe looking for something suitable to wear for the interview. Dorrie was a lot taller than Joy so the sleeves of the jacket she selected needed to be turned at the cuff and the skirt needed to be hoisted at the waistband.

Mr Leach thought she was a nice, polite little girl. He quizzed her on her age. "You are fourteen?" Joy crossed her fingers behind her back. "Yes, sir." It was only a little lie.

In less than a twinkle, she closed the chapter entitled "childhood", crossed the bridge and embarked on the first of two pathways that would teach her the art and importance of preserving history.

---

[168] Magnesia, sodium perborate and peroxide
[169] By the time the former King Edward met Hitler in October 1937, he had abdicated and had been made Duke of Windsor

Above photo of Joy in school uniform

Group, Joy is fourth from left, holding the bench with her hands.

"Last days at school"

On her return home she found her father relaxed over a cup of tea. "You're home early, love."

"Mum gave me the day off to go to the pictures. I didn't go to the pictures, Daddy, I went for a job interview."

"You did what?" "I got a job."

"Job! What sort of job?"

"Office work at Marco Refrigerators. You have to understand, Daddy, hairdressing is not for me. I start at 9.00 am Monday morning. The salary is sufficient to help you and Mummy and pay for my drama lessons."

"You're not yet fourteen. What about your schooling? And, what on earth will your mother say! You better think seriously about what you are going to say to your mother and you owe her an apology for not telling her the truth. Best set the table for dinner then run upstairs and remove that make-up."

Rozemai and Dorrie arrived home at 6.30 pm.

From the laughter at the gate Arthur could tell they were in good humour. "Thank the Lord," he said to himself.

"We're home, love."

"Sherry in the parlour, my dear.'" Arthur waited for Rozemai to relax.

"I, ah, today, well, you know there comes a time, when…" Rozemai couldn't stop laughing.

"Did you hear that, Dorrie? Joy has got herself a job for the August holidays." Joy wanted to explain that the position was permanent but her father stopped her with a look that said: "Be quiet. Your mother will find out soon enough." On Monday morning, Joy waited until her mother and sister had left the house before she came downstairs to say goodbye. In her peplum skirt and cloche hat, she looked a tad too grown-up. But Arthur did not say anything. He accepted his daughter's fierce ambition to go places. A year later, Joy stepped up the ladder into a secretarial position in the offices of Mr Stephen Chart the Town Clerk at the Mitcham Council[170] and, after business hours, she was making a name for herself in the theatre.

---

[170] Originally fertile farmlands, Mitcham is located 11.6 kilometres south-west of Charing Cross in the district of south London within the borough of Merton bounded by the London boroughs of Wandsworth, Croydon, Lambeth and Sutton. The Wandle river bounds the town to the south-west. The name "Mitcham" is old English for "big settlement" and evidence of a Celtic settlement was found in the area. The poet John Donne, the brilliant scholar and explorer, Sir Walter Raleigh – famous, among other things, for his chivalry – laying his expensive cape over a puddle to ensure Queen Elizabeth I's shoes were not sullied – and Vice Admiral Horatio Lord Nelson and Lady Hamilton all owned property in Surrey.

Variety magazine: 16-year-old Joyce White, is a youngster the film magnates are bound to snap up...

That headline hit the front page of *Variety* the day Horace and Inman boarded the last train out of Germany. The Declaration of War came 48 hours after their arrival in Aden. Inman got on the phone and made immediate arrangements for a return to the United Kingdom. Horace purchased a seat on the first available flight home to Sydney. Days after his arrival he set to work raising money for the war effort.

On Tuesday 1 October 1940, *The Manilla Express* reported:

> A very large number of billiards enthusiasts gathered at the Mechanics' Institute on Friday night to witness an artistic display of billiards and snooker by Horace Lindrum. Possibly of all the champions in action today none can delight the billiard public better than Horace Lindrum. His game is simplicity itself, and his general mastery of strength and touch in all-round play commands a host of admirers from across the globe.
>
> Horace Lindrum, who is still on the youthful side of 30, was a quiet unassuming young man. His worldwide fame and success against the best of players had not swayed his mental balance. To all he was just Horace Lindrum, the billiard champion.

Jan Lindrum

6 January 1942

Lindrum enlists...

> Twenty-nine-year-old Sapper Lindrum enlisted in the Royal Australian Engineers at Millers Point, Sydney yesterday and was allocated Army Number N181304. Sometime around midday he was dispatched to Tamworth.

18 months later...

> Honourably discharged on medical grounds, Lindrum will serve out the war raising money for disabled servicemen and women.
>
> What did Horace have to say of his time in the Army?

"Against those six-footers, I was far better with a cue than a screwdriver! But boxer Tommy Burns and I did our bit peeling potatoes in the mess and, when the chance presented, we took our relaxation in the billiard room."

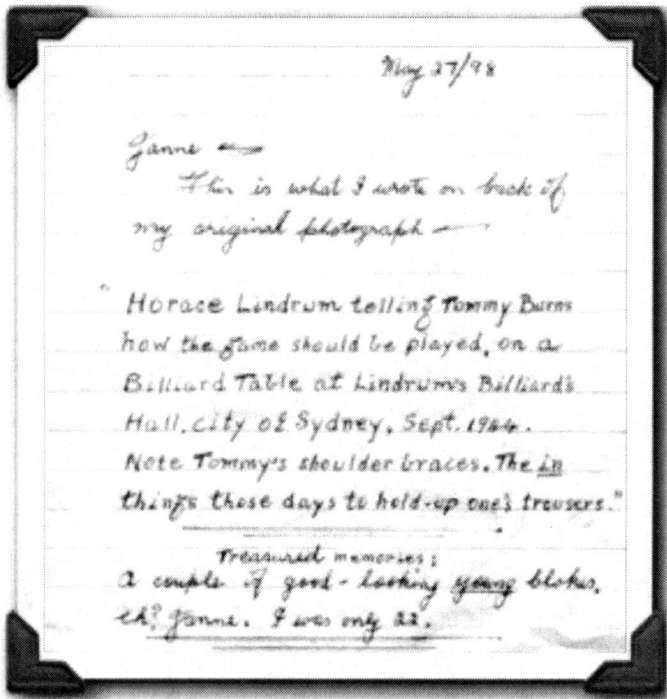

Above letter written to Janne Lindrum 27 May 1998 by Tommy Burns.

"Horace Lindrum telling Tommy Burns how the game should be played, on a Billiard Table at Lindrum's Billiard's Hall, city of Sydney, September 1944. Note Tommy's shoulder braces. The "in" things those days to hold-up one's trousers."

Treasured memories:

"A couple of good—looking young blokes, eh? Janne. I was only 22."

In the United Kingdom, worlds were blown apart before anybody picked up a Springfield gun. Lack of customers saw Rozemai close the doors to the hairdressing salon. A few weeks later, Arthur boarded up the butcher shop. Three incomes wiped out overnight. Arthur applied for a government job and was appointed meat inspector at the Smithfield markets.[171] In the photograph below, Arthur is the man in the white coat and black hat standing with his hands in his pockets observing the scene. He is thinking about how to solve a problem. The men have gone out on strike.

Hanging and lying behind Arthur is the meat that needs shifting.

Off-cuts from the market carried the family through the war years and Joy's position at the Council put her in the ballot for two 10-yard allotments (market gardens). Such allotments offered families the only opportunity to put fresh fruit and vegetables on the table. The White family were lucky enough to have their name pulled out. Establishing the allotments was blistering work.

You needed to dig down two spits through soil that was rock-hard and devoid of all nourishment. But, despite the poor condition of the soil, many of these gardens still bear fruit and vegetables.

Aside from establishing allotments, hoarding food and practising survival plans, not a great deal happened in the first few months following Chamberlain's announcement. Parroting "Have you got your gas mask" was about the extent of it. A year later the bill-posters came along and slapped up the warnings. "Beware in a Blackout" was the first to go up, alerting the man in the street that things were getting serious.

Inside households, family members were delegated specific tasks. In the White household Joy was responsible for the dug-out clothing; Dorrie took care of the first-aid kit, the portable radio, candles, matches and torches; Rozemai managed the food supply. Rations

---

[171] In the ward of Farringdon at the City of London's north-west in central London, land use for market purposes can be traced to rights granted under Charter by King Edward III in 1327. Buildings were commissioned by the City architect, Sir Horace Jones, in 1866 and completed in 1868. Ten lives were lost and massive damage occasioned to the buildings when a V-2 rocket struck in 1945. During the war years secret scientific experiments were conducted in a refrigerated meat locker in the butcher's basement. Led by Dr. Max Perutz, the experiments were on Pykrete – a mixture of ice and wood pulp – which was believed to be tougher than steel. The experiments were later abandoned

were lean: bread and dripping, Marie biscuits, a flask of tea and lemon barley water. Arthur was the keeper of the metal box containing important documents, ration books and national identity cards.

Horace's ration book

A the first sound of the sirens, the family went straight to the bomb shelter. Sirens at 6.00 pm meant hours of sitting on concrete or lying on a straw mattress (a straw mattress was known as a "palliasse"), breathing stale air and praying for it all to end. Yet, frighteningly real as it was, the experience bonded people. Men shared their Great War stories. Women exchanged recipes for sponge cakes made with the smallest amount of butter and dried egg. Children played tiddlywinks.[172] All learned to laugh.

Meat was strictly rationed. Arthur managed a leg of lamb once a fortnight and Rozemai learned to spread that lamb like butter. When there was no lamb, there was spam, liver, ox tongue, tripe and pig's trotter washed down with a cup of Nestlé condensed milk. Rozemai tried to vary the diet. She even experimented with whale meat but the smell of it proved too much for her. It also proved too much for the golden-haired spaniel Joy won in the "Funds for Warship Week" raffle.

How they all laughed about the spaniel with the big feet. Joy had never won anything in a raffle. Then she went and won another mouth to feed the day after the strict rationing announcement! He was Munch by name and munch by nature; or was his name Merlin? Whatever he was called, the family managed the extra mouth. God knows how they did it. Some say it was good old Cockney humour. Whatever the truth, spring came without blossom, it took Munch and it made young men old before their time.

By the summer of 1941 "You know the procedure" was rolling off the English tongue like a Gracie Field's melody. A sort of "Wish me Luck as you wave me goodbye"[173] between the clanging bells of ambulances and later the zoom and bang of V1 buzz bombs. Defence installations were prime targets, as were the industrial towns. Coventry and the Midlands took a real bashing. Hitler's order was to break morale

On 7 September, a shelf cloud formed on the horizon.

Behind the shelf, 348 bombers and 617 fighter planes. At high noon, a terrible silence. At 4.00 pm, a deafening drone.

"Luftwaffe, Luftwaffe overhead."

---

[172] Tiddlywinks is a game of skill. The aim of the game is two-fold; to land small plastic discs in a pot using what is known as a squidger (disc) and to prevent your opponents discs from reaching the pot
[173] A song by Harry Parr-Davies performed by Gracie Fields in the motion picture *Shipyard Sally* (1939)

In the half-light children clambered atop bomb shelters and yelled: "Go that way! Go that way!"

"Come down this minute, don't you realise you are wishing bombs on others!" Hour after hour of bombs screaming and thumping down until, finally, raid over, the all-clear sounded and people poked their heads out like hedgehogs emerging from winter hibernation.

"St Paul's is still standing. Christopher Wren's masterpiece has survived to live another day." Their astonishment plucked as one might pluck a ripe pineapple or strum a string on an imaginary violin. London, the Pina colada of Europe, was as it was and as it had always been, a bastion of freedom teetering on the brink of an ice ledge. A city corralled by a ring of fire, frill-necked lights, lace curtains, tin kettles, Mum's favourite tea caddy, Dad's model ship– a home – a lifetime – Ker-put!

The US journalist Edward R Murrow stood on the steps of St Martin-in-the-Fields in Trafalgar Square near the entrance of an air-raid shelter. This is how he described the scene the night before the drop

"This is London and tonight, as on every other night, the rooftop watchers are peering out across the fantastic forest of London's chimney pots. The anti-aircraft gunners at the ready.

I've been walking tonight Down Regent Street to Shaftesbury Avenue (the theatre district) to Tin Pan Alley and on to Trafalgar Square where I am standing and speaking to you now. At the present, London is a beautiful and lonesome city where men, women and children are trying to snatch a few hours sleep. You can hear in the background, an air-raid siren. A singular searchlight scans Big Ben and the Houses of Parliament. Lord Nelson stands on a column in front of me. Red buses pass like ships in the night; the odd soul peering out windows that look more like portholes. Occasionally, a fellow passes. Stands for a time. Lights a cigarette. Puffs away. Stubbs out. Disappears underground."

As the scene changed, so did the reporting. Talk of billowing black smoke, burnt eyes, lifeless bodies, razor blade suicides and unwanted pregnancies became par for the course and, although Churchill's "We will fight them in the streets and on the beaches and we will never surrender" raised spirits, the words did nothing to assuage the underlying fear.

Call-up time

Volunteer or be drafted

Rozemai could not bear the thought of Joy's joining the WAFS and being posted overseas so she pleaded with her daughter to volunteer for the Land Army

Joy still wearing her trademark smile. British pluck they called it and I believe British pluck underpinned the story of her life.

"There's the paperwork, love."

The sergeant directed Joy to a small desk near the window. She fumbled with the forms. Lodging the papers would be the highlight of what had started as a bad day. The alarm did not ring. It was freezing outside. The taps had frozen in the bathroom. Snow had started to fall. Before the day was out, sleet would set in. Back at the Council, Stephen Chart was arguing with someone on the telephone. "Look, damn you!" Joy heard him scream into the mouthpiece. "I've received instructions to turn Mitcham Common into an agricultural area. I need Miss White's help to execute this plan." His pleadings and protestations failed.

> Dear Miss White,
>> Please be advised that, immediately after the Mitcham Fair, you will proceed post haste to Plumpton Agricultural College, where you will learn how to milk a cow and drive a tractor and, from there you will be taken to the Estate of Sir John Leigh at Witley Park near Godalming in Surrey.

Friday 28 August 1942
The Mitcham News and Mercury

"Jolly time at Woodlands"

If you were not present at 'Woodlands', Commonside East, last Saturday, I feel sorry for you because the event was a treat. The sideshows were particularly well-patronised. "Dunk the Mayor" and the Lovely Ankle Competition were the top money-spinners.

Joy White is to be congratulated.

Oh – by the way – Happy nineteenth, Officer White.

Fete over, Joy followed orders. Shortly after arriving at Sir John Leigh's estate she had a chance meeting with a man who played a pivotal role in her life. Her diary set it out:

> Mr. Bisset is a regular visitor to the Estate. He gets up early each morning to observe the bird life. The Egyptian Goose[174] and the Goldeneye[175] are his particular favourites. His observations are recorded in the *Field* magazine.
>
> 'There are three things I can't pass up,' he told me.
>
> 'The first is studying bird life. The second is a game of cricket on the Village Green. The third is a game of billiards.' He is the chairman of the British Billiards Association & Control Council.

New set of orders

> Dear Miss White,
>
> > You will leave Sir John Leigh's estate at the end of the week. You are now required to attend for night duty at the Foreign Office on the Thames Embankment.

Arthur and Rozemai were not happy. The most dangerous times were at night and they feared for their daughter's safety but Joy was pragmatic. Sir Robert Helpmann and Dame Margot Fonteyn had danced through the Blitz, so she was not going to show any fear in the face of Hitler. To the contrary, the former secretary of the Junior Imperial League and Entertainment Officer of the Girls' Training Corp was prepared to lay down her life to ensure freedom from tyranny.

Excerpts from Joy's diary 'The Foreign Office experience'

Night One

> I sat on a lounge, drinking tea and staring out the window. It was raining. Over the past few weeks it had rained continuously. Grey clouds. Grey chatter. Ear to the ground. "Beware! Beware!"
>
> "Silk stockings, Miss? Five coupons for the fully-fashioned type."
>
> "I'll take five pairs."
>
> I succumbed to the salesmanship of the Oxford Street black marketeer only to discover the stockings had a beautiful seam up the front!
>
> "Would you like to read a book? There's a copy of Neville Shute's *What Happened to the Corbetts*[176] in the cabinet over there and, if you spin the dial on the radio, you will catch *ITMA* with Tommy Handley."[177]
>
> I went to open my mouth but the passer-by scurried away.

---

[174] A member of the duck, goose and swan family. Considered sacred by the ancient Egyptians
[175] A medium-sized sea duck
[176] Written in 1938 and published by William Heinemann the following year, the novel is a critique on the effect of bombing raids on the British maritime city of Southampton
[177] British comedian Thomas Reginald "Tommy" Handley (1892–1949), best remembered for the BBC comedy series *ITMA* which inspired a film of the same name (1942)

Jan Lindrum

Night two

"Who are the?" I asked the secretary, nodding towards the fellows standing in the back office. I could see the men clearly through the glass and they could see me watching them. In their dark suits and heavy-framed spectacles they looked pretty scary. The secretary mumbled something but I could not hear what she said and before I could say "I beg your pardon" she had picked up her notepad and disappeared.

Night three

The interrogation started.
What do you do in your spare time?
Do you belong to any organisations?
What do you think about the war?
Do you have many friends?
Who are your friends?
What do your friends do?
Where do your friends live?
Where was your mother born?
Tell us about your father and your sister's husband?

None of it made sense, but Joy was young and it is sometimes easier to understand the cloak-and-dagger later in life. What was the reality? If you believe reality exists, the reality was that the Government needed people it could trust and the fact that Joy's great-uncle was Field Marshal Sir George White, the defender of Ladysmith[178], probably said she was prepared to tackle the enemy.

Two weeks later Joy received her orders:

"Miss White, we are sending you to Bletchley Park. You will need to take clothing and personal belongings. Don't expect to go home every weekend. You will receive the rest of your orders on your arrival. Good luck."

Joy followed orders and boarded the Northampton train from Euston.
To Bletchley Park via Milton Keynes and Leighton Buzzard. When the train arrived at Bletchley Park she alighted to an empty platform. She had been told to walk up and over

---

[178] The Battle of Ladysmith was one of the early engagements of the Second Boer War. Field Marshall Sir George White (1835–1912) was awarded the Victoria Cross for conspicuous bravery during the engagement at Charasiah on 6 October 1879, when, finding that the artillery and rifle fire failed to dislodge the enemy from a fortified hill which it was necessary to capture, Major White led an attack upon it in person. Advancing with two companies of his regiment; and climbing from one steep ledge to another he came upon a body of the enemy strongly posted, and outnumbering his force by about 8 to 1. His men being much exhausted, and immediate action being necessary, Major White (aged 44) took a rifle, and, going on by himself, shot the leader of the enemy. This act so intimidated the rest that they fled round the side of the hill, and the position was won. Again, on 1 September 1880, at the battle of Candahar, Major White, in leading the final charge, under a heavy fire from the enemy, who held a strong position and were supported by two guns, rode straight up within a few yards of them, and seeing the guns, dashed forward and secured one, immediately after which the enemy retired. At Ladysmith he took command of the garrison during the Siege of Ladysmith with his aide-de-camp Clive Dixon: when his position there became untenable he was instructed by General Sir Redvers Buller to destroy the guns and surrender the garrison the best terms he could White responded "I hold Ladysmith for the Queen" and held out for another four months before being relieved in February 1900. For this he was appointed a Knight Grand Cross of the Order of St Michael and St George. White's Victoria Cross is displayed at the Gordon Highlanders Museum, Aberdeen, Scotland

the pedestrian bridge to the front entrance of the station and through the car park where she would find a small dwelling surrounded by a paling fence with a brass plaque inset into the red brick and engraved with the words, **"Stationmaster's cottage"**.

The shades were drawn and there were no lights on inside the house, not that Joy could see. She opened the gate, walked to the front door and knocked. No answer. She knocked again. A little louder this time. The door opened and an elderly man materialized holding a lantern with the tiniest of candles burning inside it.

"Can you direct me to Blet............"

"Shush!" he said pussyfooting around the door. "Name?"

"Joyce White."

"Wait over there." He pointed to a crate then raced back inside the house and shut the door behind him.

Ten minutes later, two vehicles arrived. A civilian Jeep and a Maudslay Standard 12 four-door saloon. "Station X", the stationmaster directed. On arrival, the driver of the Jeep flashed his lights and two metal gates opened revealing a long driveway with huts on either side. A walled community, the estate had the ambience of a mental asylum.

"What do they do here?" Joy wondered.

The vehicles came to a stop inside a turning circle in front of a Gothic-style mansion surrounded by rockeries and rose gardens, two stone gargoyles guarding the entrance.

Admiral Sinclair had purchased the mansion at Bletchley in the spring of 1938. As with Arthur and his dug-out, Sinclair had been publicly ridiculed for expressing his concerns about Hitler. He had fought his way up the chain of command at the Foreign Office, arguing that Britain needed an intelligence base and that Bletchley Park was ideal for the purpose. He faced a wall of opposition.

"The War Office is responsible for war. Go ask the General."

"Look, old chap, as a former director of naval intelligence, you should know to go to the Admiral."

"I say, Sinclair, you are a part of the Foreign Office. I suggest you go ask the Mandarins."

Churchill was right:

"It would be a great reform if wisdom could be made to spread as rapidly as folly!"

"Miss White, welcome to Bletchley Park, I am Captain Bradshaw, pleased to meet you. Follow me, please. John will look after your luggage."

Joy climbed out of the car and followed Bradshaw through a veranda arch and into a hallway of timbered-panelled walls and ceilings, leading down to an elaborate staircase lit by a mullion-and-transom window.

"Wait here," he ordered, disappearing into a room on the left, only to reappear seconds later in the company of Commander Edward Travis.

"Miss White, I am pleased to meet you. I am Commander Travis. Now, if you will come with us, we will get the formalities out of the way. Would you like a cup of tea?"

"No, thank you, Commander."

"Righto, then, down to business. We have arranged for you to stay with Kittie Hearne in the village. Kittie has kindly made available a nice single room. There is only one bathroom. I am sure you can manage. Everything is there for you to use, so make yourself as comfortable as possible.

There are only a few of us at present. Around 200 hundred. We are expected to grow to around 3500. Sixty WRENS recently moved into Woburn Abbey. They are a great bunch. Word of advice: they are very good dart players so if you are going to take them on, be prepared. The Chintz wallpaper in their quarters is already looking a bit the worse for wear.

No mail is delivered here. Letters to and from your family are delivered and/or collected by the Military."

He paused for a moment before continuing.

"This is a top-secret mission. There can be no talking, on or off the job. The sinking of *HMS Hood* is an example of Enigma Cypher compromise. Fifteen hundred lost. Only three survivors.

You and your colleagues have been hand-picked. Your record and the credentials you come with tell us we can trust you. If we've got that right, you will be one of the geese that gets to lay the golden egg but you must never cackle. Do we understand each other? Nothing you say or do must pass to anyone other than Number One."

"Who is Number One, sir?" "Number One is Number One." None of it made any sense.

What did Enigma Cyphers have to do with geese laying golden eggs? And who the hell was Number One?

"What exactly do I have to do, sir?" Joy asked trepidatiously.

"I'm coming to that." Travis's eyes moved as swiftly as those of a leopard stalking his prey.

"First I must have your assurance you will speak to no one." "Yes, sir."

"Righto, now we understand each other, you need to read and sign these papers. We will leave you to digest the content."

"What am I getting myself into?" Joy asked herself.

Twenty minutes later the papers were in the hands of the Military and on their way back to the Foreign Office in London.

"One small thing, Miss White, before I take you through your duties." The chief-of-staff turned to look out the window.

"At the end of each shift, you will report to Commander Denistone's office for a debriefing session. These sessions will help to clear your mind."

He paused half-expecting a question, but no question came; only in recent times did Joy break her silence, pulling back her hair to show the scars from the burns she received. They were caused by the twirling heat ray that was used to erase her memory of the day's activity. How cleverly she had learned to cover those scars with her make-up.

"You are assigned to Hut number 4. Morse code messages will be handed to you. You are to translate those messages from German into English. From time to time you will be asked to run errands. You can ride a bicycle?" "Yes, sir."

"Good. Wear your gas mask at all times and remember the locals think you are a wealthy 'odd bod'."

Joy's imagination kicked in. "Why are you here?" "Depression."

"And you?"

"Obsessive compulsive disorder."

A tall man, fortyish, entered, brief case in one hand, plastic bag in the other. "You're back early, John. Now, what you have you got there? Do you mind if I take look in your bag?"

Half-eaten Humbugs, an overripe banana, an egg sandwich, wrapped, rewrapped, rewrapped, rewrapped..."

"Okay, you're through. You've just time to clean up before dinner. I think the choice tonight is cod and mash or corn beef with onion sauce."

The Commander's voice lifted two or three decibels and Joy shivered out of her daydream.

"From time to time, you will work alongside Job Cooper and Kit Fox. Job and Kit are Hinsley people. Job is an Oxford Don. Kit graduated from Cambridge. They thrive on the boring and laborious, but will always make time for a chat, the occasional Charlie's Aunt [farcical play] and a good sing-song around the piano in the common-room. Best learn the

Bletchley anthem, Miss White." (The so-called Bletchley anthem was sung to the tune of Alfred Kilmer's "I think that I shall never see a poem lovely as a tree".[179])

The Anthem

If you can keep yourself from going crackers at all
the things that you are told to do when Hitler sends
along his air attackers with squibs and bombs and tries
to frighten you.

If you can hear the hellish banshee warning without that
sinking feeling in your breast; or you can sleep in dug-outs
till the morning and never feel you ought to have more rest;

If you can laugh at every blackout stumble or murmur when
you cannot find a pub. If you can eat your rations and not
grumble about the wicked price you pay for grub.

If you can keep depression down to zero and view it all as just
a bit of fun then, Sir, you'll be a bloody hero and, what is more,
you'll be the only one!

That's all for now, we'll see you bright and early in the morning. Get a good night's rest. John will drop you off at your digs. Good night." As he disappeared through the panel in the wall, Joy reflected on her day dream and it crossed her mind that she might, indeed, have landed herself in the nut house

Half-way between Oxford and Cambridge, the Hell-hole Bomb Room and the 180-trillion-character Colossus worked a treat. Outsiders had no idea what was going on inside the gates.

---

[179] Born Alfred Joyce Kilmer (1886–1918), Kilmer was an American writer, journalist, critic, editor and prolific poet whose works celebrate beauty, nature, faith and spirituality. He is best remembered for the short poem "Trees". Kilmer was killed by a sniper's bullet at the Second Battle of the Marne in 1918

In her diary Joy described her daily life at Bletchley Park:

> On my first day, I was given the tour. Lecture rooms, tele-printer room, radio room, mess room and so on. Whilst on the tour, I stopped to admire the Jacobean-style oak chimney piece in the dining room and imagined what living in the house would be like outside of war times.
>
> It was a sort of miss-mash in some ways. Past owners had simply had no single aesthetic approach. All the special rooms, like the ballroom and billiard room, had been converted for the war, notwithstanding, the house was, strangely, a work of art.
>
> Later in the day, some of the 'bright sparks' (boffins) invited me to the Beer hut. I'd never tasted beer. Initiation meant joining in on a game called Cardinal Puff Puff. Vera Lynn was singing "There'll be Blue Bird over the White Cliffs of Dover"[180] on the radio and a couple of lads on the other side of the room were mimicking *Tokyo Rose*...[181]
>
> "If you let this racket distract you, girlie, you'll miss the runway. If you miss the runway, you'll drink it down."
>
> I failed the initiation and woke with a pounding headache. The headache was so bad I never took the liquid amber again. A week later, the Japanese bombed Pearl Harbour.

After the attack on Pearl Harbour, I was ordered to organise some tea dances to take minds off the bad news. You could not go anywhere without hearing a radio playing George M Cohan's "Over there"[182] and a great sense of relief prevailed, that the Americans had finally decided to come to England's aid.

Invitation prepared and dispatched by Officer White
Held in the Assembly Hall, Wilton Avenue, Bletchley,
Friday 22 December 1944.
RSVP: Miss J. White, Secretary, Room 10 A, Block E

---

[180] One of the most popular songs of World War II. Composed by Walter Kent (1941) with lyrics by Nat Burton, the song was written to lift the spirits of the Allied troops at a time when Nazi troops had conquered much of Europe and were bombing Britain

[181] A generic name given by Allied troops in the South Pacific during World War II to English-speaking female broadcasters of Japanese propaganda who taunted the troops in an effort to lower morale. One of the most famous personas was Iva Toguri. Native to Los Angeles, Toguri was stranded in Japan at the outbreak of the War. Evidence suggests, however, she was not a Japanese sympathiser. The story of Tokyo (Tokio) Rose is reflected in the book *Flags of Our Fathers* (1945) authored by James Bradley and Ron Powers. *Flags of Our Fathers* tells the story of the Battle of Iwo Jima. The book inspired a film by the same name directed, co-produced and scored by Clint Eastwood (2006)

[182] Written in April 1917, "Over There" was used in World War I and World War II to persuade young Americans to join the fight against "the Hun", as soldiers dubbed the German enemy in those times

I met Ken of Lavender Lane at the Christmas tea dance and went on to break Ken's heart. Not intentionally. You see, Ken fell in love with me but I was in love with a man I had only ever seen in a newspaper.

Inside my mother's diary, a letter carefully folded in four parts and pressed with a flower.

>Dearest Joy,
>
>It is not my intention to telephone you any more – nor to seek to take you out again. I feel that by taking this course I shall be doing the right thing. I can assure you that deep down – in the heart – I love you very much. This love has come to me slowly but steadily and it has blossomed out in such a way that I know it will be everlasting.
>
>Joy – whosoever you choose as your companion for life is bound to go through hell in later years should you not be very sure of your love for him. If – after most profound and earnest consideration – you are guided to make another man your partner for life, I shall be able to take it. I shall be consoled by knowing that your future happiness has been secured.
>
>My love for always, Ken

Joy spent the remainder of the war years, save the last two months, behind closed doors working for Alan Turing, the genius who broke the Nazi codes. Tragically, Turing never received his dues for reeling in the fish and smashing the Secret Writer. Why? A homosexual incident and a suicide.

On 9 September 2009, British Prime Minister Gordon Brown issued a posthumous apology.

A couple of months before the end of the war Colonel Dickinson arrived. His job was to tie up an avalanche of loose ends. The real work was over. On 30 April Hitler shot himself in the head, German troops surrendered to Field Marshal Montgomery and allied troops started coming home.

On hearing the good news, Jake Bisset took a stroll to the post office.

A telegram arrived for Joy:

> Miss White, I should be most grateful if you would call me urgently. We have a position for you at the Control Council STOP
>
> Yours sincerely,
> James C Bisset
> Chairman

War over, the White family took stock.

A resilient lot, they had escaped the bombs but there was no escaping the crippling arthritis and the lemon-peel poverty.

Youth gone, old age was now on the doorstep."

Copy of Certificate of gratitude awarded to Joyce Doreen (White) Lindrum by British Prime Minister David Cameron MP, May 2010

Chapter 7
It's all in the stars...

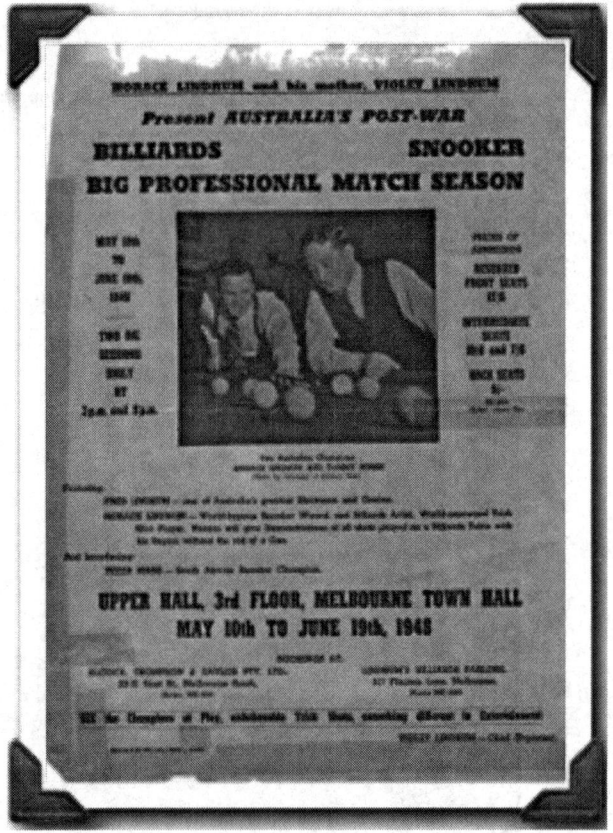

Promotional flyer for post-war event featuring Tommy Burns (left) and Horace Lindrum (right)

Popular potter of snooker balls, Horace Lindrum the Australian champion is coming back for another shot at the world title. He is due sometime next month.

Front cover of Program created by Joy White for the inaugural Snooker Ball at the Victoria Halls London. Joe Davis and Horace Lindrum will head the list of over a dozen players who will take part in an exhibition in a large lounge between the two dance halls. Sid Field, the comedian, has said that he will attend. Among the other players who will take part in exhibition play will be Alec Brown, Sydney Lee, Herbert Holt, Arthur Groundsill, the one-armed player, John Barrie, John Pulman and Sidney Smith.

Painting by Joy White depicting the carnival atmosphere she wanted to create at the ball.

On New Year's Day, Joy was working to complete the program for the year and finalise the guest list for the inaugural Snooker Ball[183] when she received an unexpected visitor.

"Good...ay!"

"Oh, you startled me."

"Sorry about that. You must be Miss White? Horace Lindrum from Australia." He presented his business card.

His handshake was strong. The smile warm.

"Pleased to meet you, Mr Lindrum. You must be looking forward to the season. What can I do for you today?"

"Oh, nothing, I just popped in to see if anyone was at home." "How are you enjoying London?"

Well, Miss White, it is good to be back but it's a little chilly, isn't it!" "I suppose it is pretty hot in Australia at this time of year?"

"A little warmer than London." "Only a little warmer, Mr Lindrum?"

"You may not need that coat." He pointed to the fur-lined hooded overcoat hanging on the hook and they both burst out laughing.

"You look very busy."

"I am. There's a lot to be done to organise the year ahead."

"Well, I am sure it will be a tremendous success with you at the helm. I've heard you are pretty damn good at your job."

"Is he making a pass?" she wondered. "Mr Lindrum..."

"Call me Horace."

"Alright." A little uncomfortably.

"Horace, Mr Bisset will be in touch with you some time next week to go through the program. We've all been looking forward to your return to the UK. You've got a big fan base over here. There are a few sacks of mail for you to answer out back. You might like to borrow a desk after next week's meeting with Mr. Bisset. It will probably take you four or five hours to respond." "How is old Bisset?"

---

[183] After the Ball, Mac presented Joy with her first cue. Later, he weighted the butt of the cue down with a billiard ball to stop her raising her elbow when she took a shot. Sadly, the cue was stolen from a club in Tooting.

"See for yourself."

Joy pointed to the painting on the wall.

James C Bisset
Chairman

"Why the old fox hasn't changed one iota. Is he still as sharp as a tack?" Joy nodded.

"Well, my meeting with him may take as long as it will take me to answer that mail."

"Why is that, Mr...Horace?"

"I need to raise certification of my world record break of 141."

"Oh, I see," Joy changed the subject. She was never keen on the politics of sport. "May I have your autograph?"

"Sure." He took out his pen.

Thank you so much. Now, if you will excuse me, I'd better get cracking."

"I hope you won't think me too forward but it is lunchtime. Would you like to have a bite of lunch with me?"

Joy flushed a brilliant shade of red and moved to the filing cabinet in a desperate attempt to avoid eye contact. All the while the thought "He's far better looking in real life" whirring in and around in her head.

"That is really nice of you. However, I feel I must decline on this occasion." Do not ask me why my mother knocked him back. Perhaps she did not want to appear too keen. It was two years before he asked her again. They were still going to Maxim's Chinese restaurant after I was born and I know it disappointed them that I did not like the famous three-Michelin-star pineapple. I can still hear them telling the Maitre D:

"'Don't worry, she will grow into it", which I did.

Menu cover MAXIM'S Chinese Restaurant London

"We could go to the Palm Court Lounge at Claridges. I don't know whether you have been there. The green velvet lounges are remarkably comfortable."

Goodness, you Australians are persistent. A tempting offer. Maybe next time." Her heart thumping hard against her rib cage.

"Okay. I get the message. Down under we call it the brush-off." He looked disappointed.

"Oh, no, I am..."

"Not another word. I will think of you whilst I'm sitting on my Jack Jones. See you next week." With those words he disappeared as quickly as he had appeared.

Bisset picked up the vibe early in the piece. He knew instinctively that the Council's most valuable commodity had fallen head-over-heels in love with Australia's Horace Lindrum, the player who held the governing body to account.

Their credibility on the line, they were forced to pass a motion issuing three break certifications. A certificate for the first world-record break at snooker of 141, a certificate for the first world-record break at snooker of 144 and, a short time later, a certificate for the greatest number of snooker centuries recorded in championship play at Melbourne Town Hall against Peter Mans of South Africa. Two centuries to Mans. Ten centuries to Lindrum. (Horace Lindrum recorded the following snooker breaks: 100, 101, 102, 102, 103, 105, 112, 123, 135 and 141).

Photograph taken in London at the conclusion of Horace Lindrum's world-record snooker break of 141 (1937). In a radio interview Horace stated that he considered this episode to be the most exciting event of his entire career. To quote: "I was so excited, so thrilled, so overcome with emotion, when I next went to the table I could not hit a ball!"

Bisset was cordial.

"Congratulations, Horace, old chap, a very fine effort. Sorry it has taken us so long. You will be pleased to know the arrangements for the world championship are now well underway."

Four weeks later, lithographs promoting the championship were plastered all over the City of London. Horace and Joe insured themselves for 3000 pounds against non-appearance (a huge sum of money in those days). The tall and attractive Joyce Gardner, (seven times women's billiards champion) signed a contract to compere the event for an undisclosed amount and the governing body issued a press release announcing a ground breaking technological advance: technicians had devised a method of attaching microphones to the table lights so as to amplify the click of the balls.

The championship, held at the Royal Horticultural Hall in London in 1946, was a box-office success. Twenty-four sessions sold out within the first two hours. The final was set at 145 frames. The longest final in history. High tribute must be paid to the promoter. Bob Jelks organised and staged the championship with aplomb. Credit is often given to others but Jelks of Holloway was the man who put snooker on the map in London for the very first time.

Before the event the BBC "Big Broadcast," with a wide national audience reported:

> The season is to wind up in a big way as far as professional snooker is concerned. Joe Davis is to meet the Australian champion, Horace Lindrum, in the final of the world professional snooker championship in the Horticultural Hall, Westminster, beginning May 6.
>
> The event will last for two weeks and West End ticket prices will be charged. Over this period we shall see the most spectacular staging of snooker that has ever taken place. We have to go back to the days when

John Roberts and William Cook played for the billiard championship in the presence of that great sportsman, the Prince of Wales, later, King Edward VII, to find anything comparable with it.

Who will win? It's anybody's guess, but, if I am to proffer an opinion, I will have to put my money on Davis. I say this for one reason and one reason only. Davis is the more experienced of the two in competition play. However, I was wrong in picking Arthur Spencer for the amateur billiard title and Albert Brown for the amateur snooker title, so, I could be wrong again. Many think Horace Lindrum has an excellent chance and, indeed, none can deny that he is a wonderful player.

Insofar as the century race, Davis's record now stands at 196 and Lindrum's at 182. Not much in it and, remember, Davis got an earlier start. He was born in 1901 and Lindrum in 1912

Davis, I imagine, will have the advantage as far as the mental and the physical strain is concerned. (Davis has the nervous system of a fighter pilot.)

Lindrum has shown no weakness in this direction, but this will be no free-and-easy exhibition match. In this regard Davis is the veteran with the veteran's advantage. Notwithstanding, both are great sportsmen and very popular and each will be as ready to congratulate his victor as any man among the spectators. It is an Empire Championship in one sense and if Horace Lindrum happens to win, his victory will be as sincerely popular here in the Empire as it will be in his native land.

World title final 1946

Horace Lindrum (left) and Joe Davis (right) shake hands before the final

Photograph of the audience World title final 1946

Above: Front cover of the souvenir program for the World title final 1946

At the conclusion of the event the "Big Broadcast" reported the results.

Horace lost but the report noted his skill at the game and graciousness in defeat:

> Last season ended with a spectacular flourish in the Horticultural Hall, Westminster, when Joe Davis successfully defended his title of world professional snooker champion against Horace Lindrum of Australia.
>
> The match was wonderfully stage managed by W. Jelks and, by an ingenious system of microphone adjustment, the referee's voice, though he spoke in a quiet conversational tone, could easily be heard by every spectator.
>
> As most "knowing ones" expected, Davis (with his uncanny skill of getting on to the second object ball) emerged the victor though I must say Lindrum (with his incredible long pots) put up a bloody good show and nearly took him out. I saw several of the sessions, all of them thrilling. During the match, both players made multiple centuries, but, hard as he tried, Davis couldn't match Lindrum's 141 nor, might I tell you, do I think he could match Lindrum's generosity of spirit for I don't think I have seen a more elegant runner-up.

Horace, quick around the table, with his great sense of theatre, his humour and Peter-Pan grin, turned the green-shaded, hushed and cathedral-like atmosphere and the occasionally monotonous, "click, click, click" of the balls into a sparkling environ of polished execution. But Horace never managed to take the title from Davis. Notwithstanding, he was Joe's greatest adversary.

Testament to this fact is the prized gift still in our family's possession: Joe Davis's billiard table ring. The ring is solid gold with a billiard table delicately etched on the outside. Davis's signature appears on the inside. Davis recognised that, even though Horace succumbed to his superior tactics and greater confidence, not a final was won without one hell of a bloody fight.

Press shot – Horace Lindrum (left) watching Joe Davis poised for the shot

A year later Horace was on tour in Australia and New Zealand. On 23 September 1947, his mother wrote to Joy on Horace's letterhead:

> HORACE LINDRUM Under Vice-Regal Patronage
> Billiards and world renowned Snooker Champion
> Proprietor: Billiard Parlours and Match Hall
> 236 Pitt Street, Sydney (Between Market & Park Streets)
> Over the Liberty Theatre.

My Dear Joy,

First of all, I do hope you are keeping very well, also your lovely Mother and Father... I am going along very well with all my new ventures, but of course everything takes time and there is lots of hard work to be done.

We landed in Auckland last Monday week, and two days after that, Horace had one hundred and eleven engagements.

Well, Joy, I must say I was impressed with the organisation in London. You are certainly a very wonderful girl at your job, and I will never forget how hard I saw you working. Let me know if you ever decide to come to Australia. I feel quite certain that you and I and my one and only sweetheart Horace could do a thorough job in Australia, and be the greatest representatives in the world for our game.

Give our regards to your lovely Father, and accept a tone of love to your Mother and your lovely self, from both of us. Write to me when you can and let me know how you are getting on.

Your sincere friend, Violet xxx

(Mrs) Violet Lindrum

In recent times I became curious and asked the Black Poker a lot of questions about her magic carpet ride and I have done my best to share some of her adventures with you. What a woman! Aside from her role as wife and mother, she dipped her toes into show business, politics, foreign affairs, history and diplomacy and her exceptional organisational skills, coaching, cajoling and firm hand have left us an enduring legacy.

I was curious to hear first-hand of her relationship with her mother-in-law and she told me that Clara found it very difficult to let go of her son. I was also curious to hear her eye-witness account of Horace's final battle against his fiercest rival, Joe Davis, and about Tommy Leng who refereed the championship in 1946. Sporting referees play such an important role.

"Aside from Leng's kindness towards you, if you could write about Tommy Leng, what would you write?" I asked.

"I'd write about the night he performed blindfolded at a London Club shortly after the war. That was really something. Tommy knew how to entertain an audience. Of course, I could also write at length about how things have changed...."

There was sadness in her voice.

Below: Front cover Sports ILLUSTRATED featuring Horace Lindrum "Wizard of Snooker"

Press shot – Horace Lindrum (right) watches Joe Davis (left) poised for the shot.

Boy, oh boy, they can play snooker but they can't swim the channel!
Philip Mickman (schoolboy Channel Swimmer) takes lessons from two champions

Horace Lindrum depicted as "Happy". Joe Davis depicted as "Snow White".

Chapter 8
The eyes have it...

Where have you come from?
The other side of time to find you.
How long will you stay?
Till the end of time.

Korda's Thief of Bagdad

Joy wearing Scarlett O'Hara hat, London 1949

Radio on the boil, Joy was belting out "The Trolley Song".[184]

"Well, aren't we a happy little vegemite." Tommy Bradlaugh Leng called up the stairwell.

"Good morning to you, Tommy. Come on up."

Joy leaned over the balustrade and looked down at him.

"How is my favourite referee this morning?"

Ready to take you to St Ermin's."

'Fantastic. Two ticks, Tommy, I've just got to sign off on the artwork for the Women's Handbook."

---

[184] "The Trolley Song" was composed by Hugh Martin and Ralph Blane and made famous by Judy Garland in the motion picture *Meet Me in St Louis* (1944).

Born Babette Valerie Louise Hobson (1917_1998), 'Valerie Hobson' was a famous British actress who appeared in a number of successful motion pictures in the 1930s, 40s and 50s, including *Bride of Frankenstein, Kind Hearts and Coronets* and *Great Expectations*. Joy was the driving force behind securing Hobson as Patron of the Women's game. The slogan – "You can't keep women out"

Bessie Wright (left), Valerie Hobson (centre), Joy White (right)

Tommy frequently popped in to take Joy for a morning cuppa or an early lunch at St Ermin's.

A fine establishment, St Ermin's enjoyed a superlative reputation for serving pasture-fed English meat and Tommy had a penchant for a juicy rump. Reaching the landing, he stopped to draw breath. A big man, he was not one for stairs. Tommy made himself comfortable and surveyed the room. "That's some hat, my dear." He was pointing at a hand-made straw.

"Very Scarlett O'Hara."[185]

"A present." "A present!"

"The boy has got taste." Tommy grinned.

"Received an invitation to Ascot have we? The Queen's box, perhaps?"

"No, Tommy, but I do have this."

She flashed the solitaire on the fourth finger of her left hand. "Now, that's a rock. Garrard[186] no less!"

It was a clear-cut diamond.

Lucky girl! This is a turn-up for the books. If my memory serves me correctly, a week or so ago you told him to go to buggery. This isn't someone new is it? Someone I don't know about?"

"Of course not," Joy retorted.

"Well, you can't blame me for asking the question. You were pretty angry with Horace."

"I was cross with him for going on to the reception after his last exhibition without me."

"Cross! That's an understatement. You were fuming."

"I was being fragile. Guess I've got to get used to sharing him with the world."

"I'm afraid you do, my dear. You do. The sooner you come to grips with that reality the better. Anyway, the good news is, he has finally popped the question. I must say it's about bloody time."

"Tommy, I'm so happy. Mrs Horace Lindrum. It has a nice ring to it. We are going to tie the knot at the Registry Office in a couple of weeks."

Tommy swung on his heel.

"Oh, no, you're not. If he wants to marry you, Ding Dong (Tommy called the Black Poker "Ding Dong" because of her beautiful singing voice) he's going to do it proper like. You're having a wedding with all the trimmings, my little love." He looked away. "I wonder if I can talk Paul Bocuse[187] into crafting a billiard table cake?"

"Tommy, my Mum and Dad don't have that sort of money."

"Not another word from you on this. I am picking up the tab. All Mummy and Daddy have to do is come along and enjoy themselves."

"Have you told the boys in Fleet Street?"

"No, not yet, Tommy."

"My dear, the story is front page news. You better get some rest.

You want to look your best when the press turn up on your doorstep." "Oh, my life!" Joy thought to herself.

"Go get your hair done, have a facial, buy a new dress." Tommy pushed a hundred pounds into her hand.

How quickly life changes.

---

[185] The central character in Margaret Mitchell's epic historical romance *Gone with the Wind* (1939) which inspired a motion picture of the same name directed by Victor Fleming, George Cukor and Sam Wood and starring Vivien Leigh and Clark Gable. At the 12th Academy Awards, the film received 10 Academy Awards, including an outstanding award for the use of colour for the enhancement of dramatic mood

[186] Entering his mark in the Goldsmith's Hall in 1722, George Wickes (1698–1761) established R.& S Garrard & Co. in 1735, Haymarket now headquartered at Albemarle Street in Mayfair, the company has a long, rich and interesting history. In 1843 Queen Victoria appointed Garrard Crown Jewellers. This privilege was revoked on 15 July 2007, but the company still designs and manufactures under warrant of the Prince of Wales. In 2006, the company was acquired by US private equity firm, Yacaipa companies. Prior owners include, Prince Jefri Bolkiah, a younger brother of the Sultan of Brunei, and private investors, Lawrence Stroll and Silas Chou. During its long history, Garrard & Co. has gained a stellar reputation for distinguished craftsmanship, dealing with a number of famous jewels, including the Cullinan diamonds (including, Cullinan 1, "The Great Star of Africa"), recutting the famous Koh-i-Noor into a brilliant and crafting the Imperial Crown of India (1911), Queen Mary's crown for her coronation (1911) and the crown for the coronation of Queen Elizabeth (wife of King George VI and mother of Queen Elizabeth II

[187] Paul Bocuse (1926–) is an internationally acclaimed French chef, renowned for the high quality of his restaurants and his innovative cuisine

One minute, sitting behind a desk at Bletchley Park worrying yourself sick that the bouncing bomb might skid into your hut. The next, meeting the man in the newspaper who you never really believed you would ever get to meet. Joy reflected on a memory close to her heart.

"Joy, I'm giving a party tonight. Please come along. I'll send a car to pick you up around seven."

Horace wasn't going to take no for an answer. Not this time. "Mum! Mum!"

"Up here, Titch." (Rozemai and Arthur had called their daughter "Titch" since she started school because she was the shortest in her class.)

"Mum, I've been asked to a party and you're never going to guess…" "Slow down, slow down."

Joy burst into the box room.

"I am going to a party in the Mayfair Suite at Claridges. Mum, did you hear what I just said?"

"I heard you."

"What on earth am I going to wear and what am

I going to do with my hair?" Rozemai thought for a minute.

"I'll get the curling tongs. You get out your silk dress. I have something that might look very nice with your silk dress. I'll be back in a minute."

Rozemai's jewellery box had pride of place. A gift from her mother on the occasion of her 18th birthday, it sat in the centre of her dressing table next to her ivory brush-and-comb set. Carved in sandalwood, the gift never lost its fragrance.

There was no time now to take the letters out, instead she lifted the bundle to her lips, kissed them lightly and put them back. Frederick was a letter writer. He was the letter writer we would all like to be. His mother had taught him well.

"Ask yourself a question before you put pen to paper or open that mouth of yours," she'd told him.

"Is what you want to write or say mindful of others? Words are important. Words are not something you use carelessly. You don't throw them away. You must think about what you want to say and how you want to say it and you don't want to go to bed regretting what you have written or said during your daylight hours as tomorrow does not come with a guarantee."

To write of the noise and the wet, the severe frosts, spoiled food and almost continuous swoops would have caused distress and that was the last thing Frederick wanted to do because he loved Rozemai with all his being so he wrote poetry and waxed lyrical about the future they were going to have together when he came home.

The future that never came.

Rozemai sighed deeply then made her way back to her daughter's bedroom.

"What do you think?" she asked uncurling the fingers of her right hand. "Oh, Mum, they're beautiful."

Frederick's parting gift.

A pair of cameo earrings worn every day till the Scroll arrived. At 7.00 pm, a Silver Wraith[188] pulled into the kerb.

Rozemai's gasp brought Arthur and Joy to the window. The two women looked at each other, raised their eye-brows, giggled and fell into a hug.

"You'll need this." Rozemai walked to the coat stand and removed the stole they had affectionately nicknamed, "The Bear".

---

[188] The Silver Wraith was the first post-war Rolls-Royce model. It was manufactured at the Crewe factory from 1947 to 1959

"Thanks, Mummy. Don't wait up for me. I love you."

Her father took the stole and wrapped it round his daughter's shoulders. Joy hugged her father and wished her parents, goodnight.

Rozemai made herself a cup of warm milk with Horlicks and curled up by the fire hoping that she would drift off but she was still wide awake an hour later when she made her way to the bedroom. Arthur was in a deep sleep. Careful not to disturb him she climbed in and rolled herself in a ball. Still sleep escaped her and Arthur could feel her rolling first to one side and then to the other. "Go to sleep, Rosie."

"I can't. I am going to make myself another cuppa." "It's cold, love. Try counting sheep."

"I'm going to make myself another cuppa," she repeated firmly, climbing back into her dressing-gown.

She was sitting by the fire in the parlour when her daughter put the key in the lock.

"Mum, what are you doing still up?"

"I was so excited for you, I couldn't sleep. Come on, tell me all about it." "Golly, gosh, Mum, you should see how the other half live! Our whole house would fit in the hallway of the Mayfair Suite."

Many late-night chats ensued as Rozemai and Arthur came to accept that their daughter had lost her heart to a young Australian.

The following entries in Joy's diary relate to their courtship.

Joy's diary – The courting days

> "The Cadbury's chocolate factory"[189]
>
> "Miss White, whilst Mr. Lindrum is giving his exhibition, would you care to inspect our factory?" What an interesting day! I got to sample quite a few chocs on the way through. On the way home Horace asked me to tell him about the factory and he asked me whether I had saved him any chocolate. I felt dreadful because I didn't even think to do that. He saw the look on my face, pulled the car into the kerb and said, "Quick, get out. I have something to show you." He pulled the boot.
>
> "I thought your Mum might like a few boxes." A few boxes!

---

[189] Situated 6.4 kilometres south of Birmingham, the Cadbury Bournville factory was established by Quaker brothers, George and Richard Cadbury. Testament to the brothers' quite extraordinary long-term vision, especially that of George Cadbury who saw the importance of purchasing a large land parcel of 120 acres for future expansion, is the fact that Cadbury remains one of Birmingham's main employers. The Bournville location was selected because of its close proximity to the canal network and planned railway expansion which would aid the delivery of milk products and cocoa. The Cadbury brothers' interest in the manufacture of chocolate flowed from their long-term involvement in the Temperance movement and, in particular, the belief that nurturing a taste for tea, coffee, cocoa and chocolate would deter people from drinking alcohol

"The Corner House"

Every Friday evening at six we'd meet at the Leicester Square Tube station, wrap our arms around each other and make our way to the Corner House. The Corner House was a fascinating place filled with intriguing people. A stone's throw from Thurston's Hall, Joe Lyons founded the establishment on the Harvey principle.

"Ladies and Gentlemen, we must protect our good name. Remember, the customer is always right." Then he would carry out an inspection.

"Jones, there is a spot on your apron. Smith, you need to fix your hair. Brown, when did you last starch your cap? Pratt, remove that nail varnish and, please do try to remember, knife to the right, fork to the left."

Not until all had passed the inspection were the doors opened for business. The clientele never complained about any delay. It was accepted that standards were standards. The florist needed time to change the water and ever so gently clip the stems of the carnations and the fruiterer needed time to discard bruised fruit.

"Another pastry, Madam? Rum-ba-ba perhaps? Or, a portion of English port wine cheese?"

The string quartet was playing "The Railway Song".

(London is not the same without Joe Lyon's Corner House).

Front page news in London

"Aussie Superstar to wed"

Evening News and *The Star* 28 June 1949

"Seen here walking in London's Leicester Square are 36-year-old Australian snooker champion Horace Lindrum and his bride-to-be Miss Joy White of Colliers Wood. Lindrum, who ranks second only to Joe Davis in the World snooker list, came to England in April last, intending to stay here for about 18 months but Cupid has put a stop to that, and now he will make his new home in Britain. The happy pair will be married at St Martin-in-the-Fields on 5 July."

On Tuesday 5 July 1949, Horace did not wire his mother.

He thought about sending a telegram and decided against it. I guess he knew the idea would not appeal to her. She had been telling him for years that there was no place for a wife and family. Family is too much weight for a champion.

Rozemai was not happy either. She turned up at St. Martin-in-the-Fields[190] with a sour look on her face. She had a sneaking suspicion she would lose her daughter to Australia and that idea did not appeal to her one little bit.

The bride was extremely late.

Whispering, Ted Lowe did his utmost to put Horace at ease. "She's not coming, Ted."

"She'll come. There's obviously some sort of problem. I'll go and speak with the Verger and find out if he's got a teapot of brandy in his cupboard to calm your nerves."

A jovial fellow, the Verger had a face like a vintage Anglo-Swiss admiral, its hands stuck on five past ten.

"Don't be concerned, Mr Lowe, this happens from time to time. It's Princess Margaret."

"Princess Margaret?"

---

[190] An Anglican church on the north-east corner of Trafalgar Square in the City of Westminster. The present building was constructed in a Neoclassical design by James Gibbs from 1722 to 1724

"Yes. Princess Margaret often brings London to a stand-still. She loves to go shopping." His cackle was infectious.

Joy wanted to get out of the car and walk. She opened the door of the Silver Dawn[191] and went as far as to place a foot on the roadway but Arthur leaned across and ever so gently pulled her back into the vehicle.

"Dad, he won't wait."

"He'll wait," Arthur responded calmly.

Fighting to calm her anxiety, Joy's mind fell into memory. She was seven or eight. She could not quite remember.

"You naughty, naughty cat," she screamed whacking the tabby with her golliwog."

The feline slunk away.

"Cheer up, darling," her mother comforted, scooping up the remains of Joy's pet bird.

"Chips has gone to heaven. Come, we'll give him a proper burial. Go get your spade."

Joy went to the shed, collected the spade and dragged it back by its great wooden handle. Then she rammed the blade into the soil and started to dig furiously.

"Hey, if you dig any deeper you'll end up in Australia!" cautioned Rozemai. "Australia?" Joy looked puzzled.

"Are there people down there? Do they walk on their heads?"

Joy picked up the bird, placed him in the hole and, ever so gently, covered him over while her mother recited the Lord's Prayer.

Six years later, Arthur struggled through the front door – a bunch of flowers in one hand and a rather large leg of Australian lamb in the other. "Is that you, Arthur?" Rozemai called down the stairwell.

"Hello, Duckey. I've brought you a nice leg of lamb." "Ooooh! Loverly," came the response.

Hearing her father's voice Joy flew into the hallway.

"Let me take that for you, Dad," she offered, relieving him of the lamb. "They're rather nice," she whispered eyeing the flowers he had placed on the bureau. "Are you in trouble?"

Arthur ignored the question. He hung his coat and hat on one of the three hooks on the cloak stand, threw his daughter a very deliberate wink, picked up the bouquet and climbed the stairs two at a time.

Rozemai was pumping on the pedal of her sewing machine as one pumps up a tyre.

"For you," he said, pulling the flowers from behind his back. "I love you."

Joy had returned to the kitchen to ready the dinner and, standing at the bench, potato peelings on one side, leg of lamb on the other, she read the story of a young Australian.

At the end of the story she heard a little voice inside her saying:

"That's the man you're going to marry."

2.00 pm, 2.30, 3.00...Still no bride.

It was 3.30 pm before the Verger summoned groom and best man to the altar. "She's arrived," he whispered tucking the flask of brandy under his cassock. "It will take her a little time to make her way to the front door. There's quite a crowd outside and a veritable gaggle of photographers."

---

[191] Produced at the Rolls-Royce factory at Crewe between 1949 and 1955, the Silver Dawn was the first Rolls-Royce to offer a factory-built body.

At around 4.00 pm, Joy started down the aisle to Handel's "Water Music"[192] Her journey into the Lindrum family had begun.

Joy and her father arriving at the church

Joy and her father making their way through the crowd

---

[192] Composed by George Frideric Handel, "The Water Music" is a collection of orchestral movements often published as three suites. The work premiered on 17 July 1717

Horace with his best man, Whispering Ted Lowe with the BBC outside St Martin-in-the-Fields in Trafalgar Square

St-Martin-in-the-Fields, Trafalgar Square

The Uncrowned King

Above photograph of The Fleet Street Press waiting for a shot of the bride and groom as they emerge after the wedding

Matron of honour, Dorris Webb (nee Fry), page boy nephew Lawrence Webb, flower girl niece Anita Webb

BBC filming the page boy and flower girl on the steps of the church

Horace and Joy making their way through the crowd after the marriage ceremony

The smiling bride and bridegroom on the way to their receptio

Evening News and *The Star*
Photograph Sports & General

FAMOUS AUSTRALIAN WEDS IN LONDON

The wedding between Horace Lindrum, famous Australian snooker star, and Miss Joy White, of Colliers Wood, Surrey, took place at St Martin-in-the-Fields, London today…

The Albany Club   Reception

The Famous Rolling Pin to keep Horace in check

My maternal grandfather delivering his speech at the reception

My maternal grandmother (Rozemai – Rose May – White) on the left looking wistful. Joe Davis's wife sharing a joke with the newly weds as they cut the cake. Mrs Davis is in the woman in the stunning white hat to the right of the cake

British champion, Joe Davis, has a kiss for the bride

Joe Davis snookered on a billiard table cake Joy watches on

"The Crazy Gang" of London Palladium fame with an arch of cues.

Jan Lindrum

London

The News of the World

"Billiards star visits Jolly Cricketers"

Within a few days of his marriage, billiards star, Horace Lindrum and his beautiful bride were luncheon guests of Mr Percy Calcutt proprietor of "The Jolly Cricketers" in Evendon. The meeting was a private one. Mr Calcutt who has long been keenly interested in the Bishop of Chelmsford's fund for restoration of bombed Essex churches and post-war needs soon found a kindred spirit in Lindrum.

A little birdie tells us that, later in the year, Lindrum will give a series of billiards exhibitions and partake of a little cricket on the Village Green to raise funds. The same little birdie told us, Lindrum is not just a genius at the table, he can bowl like Larwood[193] and bat like Polly Umrigar.[194]

The Bishop of Chelmsford takes aim as Horace looks on

In contemporary terms, Horace, with his movie star looks, was as young and passionate, and as driven and, indeed, as captivating as Indian cricketer Virat Kohli.[195]

[193] Harold Larwood (1904–1995) a professional cricketer for Nottinghamshire and England between 1924 and 1938. A right-arm fast bowler, combining unusual speed with great accuracy, he was the main exponent of the bowling style known as "Bodyline" and found himself at the epicentre of a furore during a tour of Australia by the Marylebone Cricket Club in 1932–33 which brought Anglo-Australian diplomatic relations to the brink of collapse. According to Harold Larwood's biographer Duncan Hamilton: "Larwood was one of the most talented, accurate and intimidating fast bowlers of all time. But he is mainly remembered for his role in the 1932–33 Ashes series, in which the England captain Douglas Jardine ordered him to bowl according to "fast leg theory" to suppress the batting of Don Bradman. Larwood was made a scapegoat – and he never played cricket for England again. Devastated by this betrayal, he eventually emigrated to Australia, where he was accepted by the country that had once despised him." *Harold Larwood* (London: Quercus, 2009)

[194] Pahlan Ratanji "Polly" Umrigar (1926–2006) played first-class cricket for Bombay (Mumbai) and test cricket for the Indian team mainly as a middle-order batsman but also bowling occasional medium pace and off-spin

[195] Virat Kohli (1988-), a right-handed middle-order batsman who captained the Indian team to victory at the 2008 under-19 Cricket World Cup in Malaysia; he is the current Indian Test cricket captain and has received many accolades and awards

[196] Jersey is the largest of the Channel Islands. Officially the Bailiwick of Jersey (Bailliage de Jersey), it is off the coast of Normandy, France

After the visit to The Jolly Cricketers, the newly-weds made their way to Jersey[196] for a brief honeymoon but there was no escaping the press.

Horace and Joy with Nanny

It was during their stay on Jersey that Horace first expressed concern about his eyesight. He had every reason to be concerned. He made his living from his craft and he now had a wife to support. Joy called the hospital at 147 Harley Street.[197] . A week later Horace was declared technically blind. When the British tabloids got wind of it, they got on the phone.

"How on earth do you play billiards and snooker?"

Horace told them that he played by ear. The lenses of his glasses suggest he was telling the truth. The Black Poker believed the eyesight deterioration was the result of non-stop match-play. That was one possibility. The other was the tragic result of Clara's blood test. Syphilis was the scourge of the world in 1912 and untreated congenital syphilis always had the potential to cause blindness in a mother's infant. Curiously, Horace made more centuries in the latter part of his career than he did in the first 25 years when his eyesight was more acute.

Immediately after the consultation, the specialist briefed Karneham Brothers Manufacturing of London to design a super-light, well-constructed frame ensuring clear and unimpaired vision through a swivel lens.

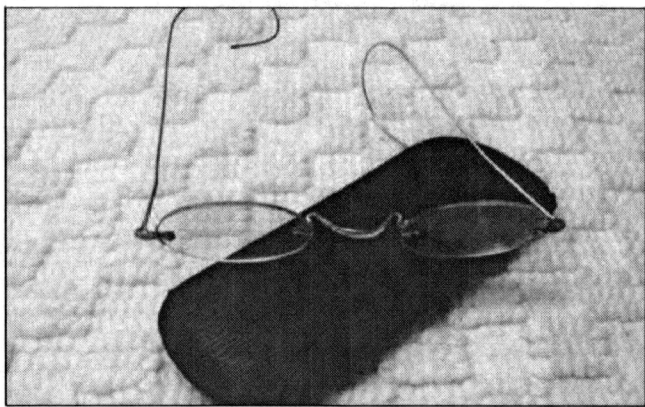

Above a photograph of Horace's spectacles;

---

[197] One of the most prestigious and respected private hospitals in London

I was born on Friday 14 April 1950

Christening St. Martin-in-the-Fields, Trafalgar Square. My godmother watches on

According to Chinese astrology, I am a metal tiger who thrives on a good challenge, pounces when necessary and does whatever it takes to defend the family honour. This is about defending my family honour.

It was a long labour. I am afraid that I gave my mother rather a bad time. In my late teens and early twenties, I gave everybody around me a bad time. I am not going into that now but I may get up the courage down the track. We will have to wait and see.

Not long after my entry into the world I was introduced to the billiard table and to Hillcrest

Below photograph: Joy (left), Horace holding me, taken on a visit to St Martin's Boys' Home.

Hillcrest was the first real home I ever remember and the only home I've ever felt I really had until recently. Now I live in a paradise: sea, sand, majestic gum trees, king parrots, rainbow lorikeets, galahs, wallabies...

Hillcrest at 36 Streatham Common was a white-rendered, two-storey home bordered by poplars and a manicured hedge. If we were to travel back in time, we would see the iron gates, the circular driveway and the apple trees. Today, the house is a memory. The land has surrendered to what we call progress.

Selling Hillcrest was the worst financial decision my parents ever made but I might not have my wonderful family if they had not made that mistake.

It was on this acreage that life began for me in earnest and where I got to see a side of my father that only those who live at the coal-face get to see. The Keystone Kop[198] version of the champion.

"Joy, Joy!" Horace was painting the bathroom.

Joy rolled back the linoleum she had just laid in the toilet and raced down the corridor.

"Oh, my God!"

Pink, pink and more pink! Horace had closed the ladder with the open tin sitting on the top.

After the disaster with the pink paint, he cut through the electrical wire of the Black & Decker hedging implement while attempting to trim the hedge. Next, he pinned a catherine-wheel to the billiard room door and burnt off the brand new paint. Whatever Horace was, he was not a handyman! He was, however, a perfectionist.

In the lead up to the 1951–52 world championship he was practising eight to ten hours a day, appearing in person only at teatime. The billiard table was my father's life.

On 28 August 1951, Alex Brown, the acting chairman of the Professional Players' Association called Horace to inform him that the association's chairman, Joe Davis, had called an extraordinary general meeting of the association at the Albany Club at 2.30 pm the following day.

The British players were getting greedy. They were putting their love of cash before their love of their sport and they had made a decision to boycott the world title in an attempt to pressure the governing body into bowing to their demands for a bigger share of the pie. Journalist Geoffrey Simpson leaked the story of the rift between the players and the governing body in his column in

The Daily Mail.

> Simpson concluded:
>
> The main reason for the break is not to improve playing fees but to undermine the authority of the game's controllers.

Horace and Clark McConachy attended the meeting. Sipping brandy and puffing smoke, the British professionals were hunkered down around a boardroom table. They were trying to work out how to persuade Horace and McConachy to withdraw their entries to the championship. Joe cut to the chase with words and phrases they had never heard him use before but they stood firm. They would not be bought. Not under any circumstances. Rather, they adopted the view that a boycott could potentially damage reputations, threaten long-held traditions, embroil the governing body in controversy and compromise the ethics and integrity of the cue sports. Horace pointed out that they had always played for the honour and prestige of participation and, to that end, they had been well remunerated. Even during the War years they had been able to put bread on the table. He

---

[198] Fictional incompetent policemen who featured in silent films from 1912 to 1917. The films were produced by Mack Sennett for his Keystone Film Company

felt holding the governing body to ransom was the wrong thing to do and both he and McConachy each advised Joe Davis that they would not be withdrawing their entries.

After that they were asked to leave the meeting while the British players took a vote on the matter. McConachy protested, pointing out they were paid-up members who were also entitled to a vote and to have that vote recorded.

But the response was, "I'm sorry boys, you're not British."

The following day the secretary of the Professional Billiard Players' Association served a list of demands on the governing body, which gave a Biblical response telling the players to "Honour thy Sport"!

Upon receipt of the Control Council's response, the secretary of the Professional Player's Association wrote to Horace and McConachy in a further attempt to secure their support for a boycott.

    To: Mr Horavce Lindrum
            Hillcrest, 36 Streatham Common

Dear Horace,

We have now received a reply from the British Association and Control Council to the effect that the conditions for the world professional snooker championship must stand as issued and that the closing date for the championship is July 21, 1951. Only players who have entered by that date will be allowed to compete. It is, nevertheless, the desire of the Professional Billiard Players' Association that ALL members will support the resolution of the Players' meeting by refraining from entering the championship and that anyone who has already entered will take immediate steps to withdraw their entries.

Yours faithfully,

W H Edward, Secretary
c/- Sports Press, 102/5 Shoe Lane, London, EC4

A whiff of a controversy and journalists turn into a whirling mass of bees swarming around a honey-pot. They called my mother to find out what position Horace was going to take. When my mother told them they would have to ask her husband that question they set up camp on the front lawn waiting for Horace to return from the meeting.

Horace told them:

> "I regard myself as a visitor to England and, as such, enter the championship and accept the conditions of the host country. It is my belief that the control of the sport should be independent of the profession and, because that is my belief, I propose to uphold tradition and play by the rules set down by the governing body."

The Fleet Street press reported:

> Full marks, Horace. You will go down in history for taking the ethical pathway and making the right decision. The billiards and snooker loving public will not forget you.

Then on Tuesday 19 February *The Daily Express* published the following article under the heading "Snooker Pros Boycott Title":

> The split in the professional billiards and snooker world is widening. Yesterday the Professional Billiards Players' Association confirmed its decision to boycott the World Snooker Championship staged by the British Association and Control Council. The Bully Boys of Sport are going to run their own world championship for the next three years and "to avoid confusion" have decided to name it "the world match-play snooker championship"…

Journalist Harold May believed the boycott was over money. I do not know whether it was or it was not. I can only speculate. It is also possible, having lost the billiard crown to New Zealand that year, the Brits were not too keen on losing the snooker crown to Australia and there was a real risk of that happening. You see, the Peter Pan of Snooker was at his peak.

There can be no question as to that reality.

Six months later, *The News of the World*, on Sunday 12 August 1951, announced that all was set for the world professional snooker championship between the world professional billiards champion, Clark McConachy of New Zealand, and Horace Lindrum of Australia. The English players were still persisting with their boycott of the event and "the fairytale scene from earlier championships had been put to bed."

Horace and Clark (Mac) played a marathon 145 frames of snooker on a championship table with Kentfield pockets to capacity audiences at the Houldsworth Hall in Manchester over a two-week period. During the event the press hailed them as two of the greatest sporting heroes of all time for upholding the fair play principle. Horace emerged the victor, winning 94 frames to 49, but the Pheidippides of snooker (the only snooker player in history who has run a marathon, notching up 50 years at the table) conceded the battle against McConachy was the toughest of his career[199].

---

[199] The day before the championship Clark McConachy recorded the possible 147 and he entered the championship already holding the title of world professional billiards champion

As Horace wrote in his book *Snooker, Billiards & Pool* published posthumously in 1974:

> "Clark is a very strong deliberate player and a master exponent of the screw shot. I can say with all honesty I didn't feel happy until I had secured the winning lead."[200]

There was great excitement the day Horace drove up the Streatham Hill with the world championship trophy strapped to the top of his car. Sadly, I do not remember that excitement nor do I remember being photographed with the trophy but there is no denying the evidence of the win nor the reality that Horace Lindrum was the first snooker player in history – and the only snooker champion thus far – to record 1000 snooker centuries in public performance on championship tables with Kentfield pockets.

Two-year-old Janne holding the handle of the world championship trophy after Horace's win of the world professional snooker title 1951–1952

Immediately after the final, Horace received a number of oral challenges. News of this brought about a sharp response from Harold May.

Talking Sport
Sunday Empire News
9 March 1952

"They've snookered themselves" Harold May

As with everything else, so in sport: just as soon as there's something you haven't got, and you can't have, you want it. At least, that's the way it looks to be with the billiards professionals.

When they couldn't have their cake and eat it where the world professional snooker championship was concerned, members of the Professional Billiards Players Association decided they weren't interested in the event at all. They even decided to run their own "championship". For once, praise be, the Billiards

---

[200] Horace Lindrum, *Snooker, Billiards & Pool*, Sydney: Paul Hamlyn, first edition, 1974, 85 (*Snooker, Billiards & Pool* became a best-seller in the international market with eight print editions

Association and Control Council went on with their plans for the one and only official event, and so, for the first time, the 40-year-old Australian, Horace Lindrum, is champion of the world.

But, no sooner does he win it, than the fellows who've contested the previous five finals – Fred Davis and Walter Donaldson – trot out five-hundred-pound challenges to him to play one of them anywhere, anytime.

That does just two things.

It proves that the title they tried to "kid didn't mean a thing" unless it could be won on the professionals' own financial terms is worth something after all – in fact, they snookered themselves – and it makes it abundantly clear that if the British Association and Control Council pursue their present strong line they will win the breakaway battle with the professionals as sure as night follows day.

Horace did not receive any official challenges, which needed to be in writing, but he told Harold May that he was prepared to meet any challenges that came provided the challengers were prepared to play by the rules of the sport.

No formal challenges were received and he retired as undefeated world professional snooker champion six years later.

Now, before you go listening to those responsible for Rafferty's Rules, who argue the Professional Players' Association needed to take the reins for the sake of the sport, let me give you one or two pieces of information from the Control Council's annual report.

The first point to make is the Control Council was manned by a team of well-respected and highly successful businessmen who were absolutely committed the growth and development of the cue sports and, through their efforts, the sport of snooker had enjoyed unparalleled popularity from 1936 to the outbreak of World War II. During the war years the council managed to hold the playing leagues together, loaned tables to the armed services across the world and raised thousands of dollars for the war effort. But events before, during and after the war progressively changed the complexion of snooker and, indeed, of sport.

These included, the scratching of Phar Lap in the Caulfield Cup (1930); the poisoning of Phar Lap (1932); the Bodyline controversy (1932–33); the fast leg theory of bowling a cricket ball at the batsman's body so as to cause harm; the mysterious and yet to be explained disappearance of the entries of Horace Lindrum and Frederick III in the world professional billiards championship (1932–33); the nursery cannon controversy (1933); and the bombing of Thurston's Hall (1940), which destroyed valuable billiards antiques.

After the war, the Control Council set out to rebuild the profession but the Gaylord Ravenals (the gambling boys) were not interested in a professional rebuilding program; all they wanted was to make money. That meant finding ways and means to harness the sport and muzzle the players. This set of men did more than "infest the various places of public resort, and live upon the spoils of the unwary"[201], they surgically removed the soul, *the eros and ethos,* of the sports of billiards and snooker. Now very few sports remain untarnished. Performance-enhancing drugs, match-fixing, gambling, alcoholism, drug addiction, domestic violence...

---

[20] E. White, *A Treatise on the Game of Billiards,* (London: W. Bulmer & Co., 1807

Gentlemen,

I have found a man whose business is "publicity".

I think the term is "publicity expert".

He is, at present, doing the publicity for the National Sporting Club, the Wembley Stadium, the Auto Cycle Union (speedway) etc. and is in touch with all those essential to know – if you get my drift.

I have in mind exploitation, real gossip, live news stories. Anything and everything to make the life of the sporting journalist more comfortable.

Poised for a takeover, the gambling boys sank their teeth into the governing body's jugular but the governing body did not fold overnight; the decline was progressive. You could say the body was white-anted, corrupted from within. Bisset was given the golden handshake. The Black Poker was offered a position at Western Pools at twice the salary. She had no option but to take it as her family had been financially decimated by war. However, she might have thought twice had she known her removal from the association was part of an almighty plan to change the complexion of the sport. She might, in fact, have realised this was the case after the event because she left Western Pools to take on the management of Horace's career.

Whatever the case, after Bisset and Joy's departure the Gaylord Ravenals set up a private company to run the sport, bought their way into the trade and worked towards straitjacketing the profession so that only those who would play the game by their rules would be permitted entry to the golden circle. The final break came in the seventies. It coincided with the death of the last member of the billiard-playing Lindrums.

After the boycott, the Gaylords had tried to axe Horace's career by feeding it to a global press the claim that Horace had retired. Colin Duncan, barrister-at-law, on instructions from Messrs. Good, Good, & Good of 1 Southampton Place, High Holborn, London, WC1, stated:

> It is not defamatory to say of a man that he is retiring from his occupation although in the case of a man who gains his livelihood from being known to follow a particular profession or occupation, such a statement is obviously calculated, if untrue, to cause him serious damage.

Horace decided not to take action. He knew that a skilful leader subdues the enemy without fighting. He also knew he would pay a price for defending the governing body. But that did not seem to worry him. He was determined to do the right thing no matter what the personal cost.

To escape the politics of sport and avoid being caught up in match-fixing, Horace chose to become an exhibition player, an artist and, in the second half of his 50-year career, the Press across the world waxed lyrical at his showmanship and achievements and, as you might expect, he received many, many requests to speak. On occasion he took the opportunity to push his views on the changing complexion of sport, which he believed was changing too radically for its own good. As he said at the London Press Club on his retirement from competitive play in 1957:

> "Looking back, I can only have the warmest regard for the profession which made my exciting travels possible.
>
> That same profession is scorned by some as a sign of a misspent youth. This raises the hackles on the back of my neck. For me, for my family, the billiard room was and is our temple. It symbolises respect, discipline, damned hard work and extraordinary and, sometimes, surprising strokes.

> A favourite diversion for men and women like Mozart, Mary Queen of Scots, Napoleon, Rudyard Kipling, Mark Twain, Queen Victoria, Prince Albert, King Edward VII, King George V, Marconi, and many others, Omar Khayyam (1048-1131) wrote of snooker or, a game very like snooker, in one of his epithets and the sport has presented as a sanctuary for convalescence for disabled ex-servicemen and women and as an aid to encourage young people to 'think'.[202] Still, the filmic image of seedy and unsavoury pool rooms threatens to turn the once sacrosanct billiard room into a haunt for juvenile delinquents, gamblers, cheats, drug-pushers and other hardened criminals and the once-dignified sport of ladies and gentlemen into the spiritless recreation of gypsies and thieves.
>
> [There would be] no knowledge or understanding of the "Fair Play" principle. The click, click [would be] within ear-shot of the Ker-chink of the bandit.
>
> Billiards and Snooker are games of science and skill and I ask you to please do what you can to preserve the soul of these sports and the remnants of what has truly been a glorious age."

Horace thus became a hero of ethical sportsmanship. Speaking openly of his concerns might have earned him enemies. He believed that the sports of billiards and snooker would die if transported into the clubs and pubs because that would make them inaccessible to women and children. Furthermore, greed, the need for space to house more poker machines, would dramatically reduce the size of billiard rooms, even obliterate them.

He appreciated the role that pubs and clubs had played over time in building a sense of community, but the installation of coin-operated tables and poker machines would, in his view, bring about a radical change in the complexion of pubs and clubs themselves and certainly, over time, a radical change in the complexion of the sport.

Coin-operated pool tables conjured the image of American gangsters during the Depression era, who were frequently depicted huddled around pool tables. As well, poker machines, by their very nature, were anti-social and contradicted a sense of community and social contact found in pubs and clubs before the introduction of the machines.

The larger impact, of course, would be the impact on community, family and culture by popularising gambling, and somehow making it a normal part of society. Horace was right to express his concerns. This engraving on the psyche or implanting in the brain has insidiously created a massive blight on families and communities across Australia and elsewhere.

It is not always easy to look reality in the face but the reality is, if a person loses money he or she turns to drink and a drunken and broken man or woman is a WMD,[203] harming self and others. Lotteries, for example, originally established to raise money for major infrastructure projects such as the Sydney Opera House, have become pure money-making activities.

Horace did not refer to a "set of men infesting the places of public resort"; rather spoke of "gambling men and big business interests". He knew, from his own experience, that when powerful forces and big business interests come onto the playing field, it becomes a controlled pitch. Participants and consumers become tools for moneymaking ends and the corrupt practice that first appears as a trickle becomes a tsunami.

---

[202] Snooker was the favourite diversion for famous Russian Soviet pilot and cosmonaut Yuri Alekseyevich Gagarin (1934–1968), the first human to journey into outer space. Gagarin's Vostok spacecraft completed an orbit of the Earth on 12 April 1961

[203] Weapon of mass destruction

It is interesting indeed that Horace's retirement from competition play coincided with the premiere on Broadway of American composer Meredith Willson's most famous work *The Music Man* (1957)[204] which features the song "Ya Got Trouble".

The lyrics of this song criticise gambling, alcohol, tobacco and other anti-social behaviours and foreshadow the concerns that Horace was expressing about the corruption of the sports he so loved.

The following is an exert from the song "Ya Got Trouble You":

> Well, either you're closing your eyes to a situation you do not wish to acknowledge or you are not aware of the calibre of disaster indicated by the presence of a pool table in your community...
>
> I consider that the hours I spend with a cue in my hand are golden, help you cultivate horse sense and a cool head and keen eye...It takes judgment, brains and maturity to score in a baulk-line game.
>
> I say that any boob can take and shove a ball in a pocket and they call that sloth. The first big step on the road to the depths of Deg-ra-day...
>
> I say, first medicinal wine from a teaspoon then beer from a bottle
>
> An' the next thing you know your son is...[gambling]...

On reflection, I think Horace felt that "transmutation of the whole social order is necessary."[205] (We needed a "Road to Damascus" transformation). That transformation is long overdue and might or might not now be possible but, at least, as I said at the beginning of this story, we should do what we can to slow the decay.[206]

One of the tragedies, aside from the fact that billiards and snooker are not Olympic sports, is the fact that the governing body founded by John Roberts Senior and Field Marshal Horatio Herbert Kitchener,[207] and the rich history that flowed from the establishment of that enterprise which included the golden days of the Leicester Square Hall, have been totally disregarded or discarded by the new guard.

Then again...

> "Laying that special piece of history to rest with the dignity it so richly deserves is probably far better than seeing it placed in the wrong hands."

Janne Lindrum (28 August 2016)

---

[204] It took composer and lyricist Meredith Willson eight years and 30 revisions to perfect *The Music Man*. Two of his musical scores were nominated for Academy Awards. Another of his works *The Unsinkable Molly Brown* was also a success on Broadway. Both musicals were made into motion picture.
[205] Joseph Campbell, *A Hero of a Thousand Faces*
[206] Many an eminent professor believes that is all we can do
[207] Field Marshal Horatio Herbert Kitchener (1850–1916). Senior British Army Officer and colonial administrator who won fame in 1898 for winning the Battle of Omdurman and securing control of the Sudan after which he was given the title "Lord Kitchener of Khartoum". As Chief-of-Staff (1900-02) in the Second Boer War he played a key role in Lord Roberts' conquest of the Boer Republics then succeeded Roberts as Commander-in-Chief. He went on to play a central role in the early part of World War I

Front cover of the book entitled *The noble game of Billiards* published by Thurstons Leicester Square, London

Chapter 9
Two sides of the same penny

Mr Round managed a "good morning".

Clara responded with the smile of a saint.

Engaged to provide legal advice on the operations of Lindrum's in Pitt Street, Sydney, Round was not looking forward to what he knew would be a tough meeting. He talked generalities until the refreshments arrived then he put his guard up. He began by telling Clara it had taken him some time to scour the journals and ledgers in order to understand how the business worked and to determine the current position. He had also considered the lease. He went on to give her the news she did not want to hear. There was more money going out the door than there was coming in and Clara would need to revisit the business model and secure an injection of capital if she wanted to continue. She would also need to solve the "noise" problem if she wanted to keep her patrons happy. Rights existed under the lease. She could complain to the landlord about the noisy tenants he had installed on the ground floor. If their noise did not cease, she could institute proceedings against them seeking damages for loss of quiet enjoyment. But Round was forced to point out the proceedings would be timely and expensive.

Clara told him what he could do with his advice. There was nothing wrong with her business model. There was something wrong with the drunken hoons downstairs.

"Their 'hoo-hooing and ker-chink' is destroying my business," she told him. "The greedy landlord is a party to the plan. The new tenants have offered him more rent to take over my space and they are trying to get me out by ruining my business."

Mr Parker appeared in the doorway. He had come to say hello. Clara did not give him an opportunity to open his mouth.

"Parker, you and I have known each other for how long? You damn well know there is no way I am going to give up my business. Why the hell didn't you pick up the phone and save me the journey in here today? You're being paid to solve problems. Those ruddy Gaylords (gambling men) are engaged in a wilful act of destruction."

Then she turned on Round.

"Mr Round, life is like a game of football. You can get injured in the scrum and, at the end of a game, there can only be one winner. But the winner is the person with the principles not the person who breaks the rules. Have you read *War of the Worlds?*"[208]

Round nodded.

"Well you obviously didn't understand what Mr Wells was saying. He was issuing a warning to mankind. The Martian invasion was a symbol for World War III. A war between man and the machine. When you pull the handle on a poker machine you surrender body and mind to a *Clubman*.[209] When you play billiards and snooker, the piano,

---

[208] *The War of the Worlds* is a science fiction novel which first appeared in serialised form in 1897 in *Pearson's* magazine in the United Kingdom and *Cosmopolitan* magazine in the United States. The text was published by William Heinemann, London, in 1898. A Halloween performance of the text on 30 October 1938 at the Mercury Theatre (an independent repertory theatre in New York established by Orson Welles and John Houseman in 1937), broadcast by Columbia Broadcasting System radio network, caused mass panic. Orson Welles, who acted in and directed the production, convinced listeners that the Martian invasion was really happening.

[209] A one-armed bandit (poker machine) rolled out in 1953.

a violin you use body and mind. Surrender the mind and you surrender the self. That is the reality."

Clara was vehemently opposed to any activity which she perceived served to destroy the intellect. Rallies, demonstrations, Band of Hope marches, she had participated in them all and, as a member of the Temperance movement, she had fought long and hard to convince the collective consciousness to debunk the six o'clock swills. "Dream of the possibilities don't drink and gamble your life away." That was the underlying philosophy.

She now felt defeated. Yet, something inside of her refused to surrender. The theatrical part of my soul imagines her quoting Mary Queen of Scots:

> Win now, take your triumph now,
>
> But I'll win men's hearts in the end,
>
> Though the sifting takes this hundred years or a thousand.[210]

Parker was sympathetic. He was at a loss to understand why the authorities had allowed the spread of the gambling disease. The only answer he could find was taxes. The state was fuelling itself on the lure of cigarettes, alcohol, spinning reels and clustering illusions. This reality caused him to fall into a great period of reflection on the "influence peddlers": industries that preyed on or played a direct role in preying upon the most vulnerable in society. How easy it was for the uneducated to be sucked into the Monte Carlo fallacy (the popular misunderstanding of the mathematics of chance). He could see the virus spreading. New and more innovative strategies would come into play. People would become obsessed with the mechanical, even addicted to the point where the brain became hypnotised by special effects and the promises of truck loads of cash and dependent upon the operations of the machine rather than the operations of the intellect.

Instead of moving forward, society was going backwards.

A few weeks after her visit to Round, Clara left the business in the hands of a manager and sailed to London on the *Dominion Castle*.[211] The purpose of the voyage was to talk through the problems associated with the business with her son in the hope of finding solutions and making the tough decisions that needed to be taken. Her arrival coincided with the latter stage of the Black Poker's pregnancy, which might explain why Clara decided against raising the issues. Instead she told Horace of her concern that interest in the cue sports was waning in Australia.

This news distressed Horace greatly but he was locked into playing commitments in London and was not sure how he could help. The Black Poker came up with three ideas: writing articles incorporating explanatory diagrams for one of the local newspapers; licensing his name to an Australian billiard table manufacturer; and a Lindrum versus Lindrum challenge.

"Would you play your uncle Walter for the Australian title?" she asked. "Darling, if you can convince my uncle Walter, you've got me."

Walter declined the invitation. Not even the *Mirror's* cheeky, "Walter come down from your Ivory Tower", could get him to the table.

A few weeks after her return to Australia Clara instructed Parker to write to Horace and ask him to transfer three semi-detached cottages in Melbourne into her name. The plan was to sell them to keep the Lindrum name in lights. When Horace refused, Clara declared war. She threw a tantrum the likes of which Parker had never seen before. The tantrum was largely fuelled by Horace's refusal to transfer the properties, but it was also

---

[210] An excerpt from the play Mary Queen of Scots by American journalist, author and playwright James Maxwell Anderson which was turned into a motion picture of the same name in 1936 starring Katharine Hepburn as Queen Mary, Frederic March as the Earl of Bothwell and Florence Eldridge as Elizabeth
[211] A vessel of the Dominion Line founded in 1870 as the Liverpool & Mississippi Steamship Company

fuelled by his decision to get married without consulting her. Displeasure stored in the subconscious detonated a violent emotional outburst, best compared to the explosion of a cellar full of wine bottles bloated by carbon dioxide.

Ihave given my whole life for this boy and what does he do? He goes and gets married without telling me. When do I hear about it? When I see it on the front page. Why didn't he tell me, Parker? I'll tell you why he didn't tell me. He didn't tell me because he damn well knew what I'd say to him. Champions and family don't mix."

Out came the newspaper article.

"Australian Sports Star – Horace Lindrum – marries Joy White, the organising secretary of the British Association and Control Council."

Storming around Parker's desk, she crumpled the paper and threw it into the garbage bin.

"If he won't transfer those properties himself, I'll transfer them for him. Get out the deed box, Parker."

Buddha was right. It is better to travel than to arrive because you never know what might be waiting for you at your destination.

While Clara was getting on with it on one side of the world, her son was doing the same on the other. Within days of winning the World Professional Snooker Title, the Savile Row tailors were fitting Horace out for his official tour.

Horace with the tailors from Savile Row, London

During the official tour he covered a vast territory, including Rhodesia, Botswana, Kenya, Ghana, South Africa, Malta, India, Ceylon, Thailand, Malaya, New Zealand and Australia. He met his mother briefly during the visit to Australia. She said nothing of her intentions.

Part one of the journey
Destination: Bombay

Horace, Janne and Joy on their way to India

Mode of travel, the *SS Chusan*[212], a handsome vessel of the Peninsular and Oriental Steam Navigation Company.

Front cover menu from Gala Dinner on board SS Chusan

---

[212] Built by Vickers Armstrong Limited, Barrow in Furness, United Kingdom for the Peninsular and Oriental Steam Navigation Company, London and launched on 28 June 1949, *SS Chusan* was the first ship to operate a regular mail service between Britain and Australia

Dear Horace,

We have arranged for your wife, Joy, and daughter, Jan to accompany you through the entire itinerary in the South of India but, as it can be very, very cold in the North at this time of year we thought they might prefer to remain in the south of the country? Let me know.

Looking forward most eagerly to seeing you again and I know that, when you leave us, you will take with you more than pounds, shillings and pence. You will have the love, admiration and affection of our people. Sir Razik Fareed and Mr. Husaair have assured me, a wonderful welcome awaits.

Sincerely and with kindest regards,

M M Begg,

Chairman

Billiards Association & Control Council, India

Welcome card

Joy's diary set out just how much fun we had:

> "Jan took easily to shipboard life.
>
> The rougher the seas, the louder she laughed.

Our first Port of call was Port Said.[213] With three hours available to us, we went ashore, hired an open horse-carriage and settled down to some serious sightseeing. We visited the Cathedral of the Virgin Mary with its magnificent stained-glass windows and then went on to the glorious Salaam Mosque. Our guide at the Mosque was a charming gentleman who spoke impeccable English. He described, in perfect detail, the scene before dawn when his brothers came to wash themselves in the troughs of clean water before kneeling to pay homage to God. He then took us to view a copy of the Qu-ran.

"This is the Book," he said "in which there is no doubt since its author is Allah, the Creator of this universe, and Allah possesses complete knowledge. Allah understands it is a long journey to being human. To believe in Allah is to be grateful and of all the bells one can ring in one's life, it is the bell of gratitude that has the greatest ring for it is the bell of gratitude that celebrates our humanity."

At the end of the tour, our guide's curiosity got the better of him. "Sir, how many wives do you have?" he asked Horace.

"One. I have one wife," Horace responded.

"One!" he exclaimed in horror. 'Sir, I have four wives, twenty-six children and ten grandchildren."

After leaving the Mosque we took a brisk walk around the souk where we purchased half-a-dozen balloons for Jan before returning to the ship. Passage through the Suez was dreamy and, at around 7.00 pm, we anchored in the Red Sea. Horace and I took a stroll around the deck and found a place away from the world where we held each other close. I lived for these moments of intimacy with my husband.

We reached Aden in the late afternoon of the following day and escaped to say hello to some friends Horace had met on earlier trips with Melbourne Inman. They were lovely people and we talked and laughed for hours until, seeing I looked weary, (as young mothers often are), they walked us back to the jetty. On arrival at the steps Horace announced he would stay on, walk our friends home and catch the last launch.

---

[213] Port Said is north-east of Egypt, extending 30 kilometres along the Mediterranean Sea, north of the Suez Canal. Rudyard Kipling once said: "If you truly wish to find someone who travels, there are two points on the globe you have but to sit and wait, sooner or later your man will come along. Those two places are the docks of Port Said and the docks of London"

Back on board, I went straight to the cabin where I chatted away to the babysitter until I realised the time.

"Goodness, I wonder where Horace has got to? Would you mind staying with Jan a little longer, Joan, whilst I go look for him?"

Joan kindly agreed and I hared down to the gangway only to discover it had already been pulled away. The seaman-in-charge suggested I try the second gangway so I hot-footed it to the stern of the ship. The second gangway was still in position but, seconds after my arrival, several seamen arrived on the scene to unhook it.

"Excuse me," I said, desperately.

"I am looking for my husband. He doesn't seem to have made it aboard." "When did you last see him, Mrs Lindrum? Are you sure he isn't in one of the lounges? Or back in the cabin? You may have passed each other in the corridors without realising."

That sounded feasible so I raced back to the cabin. No Horace.

The ship was due for departure and I was now frantic, so frantic the purser referred the matter to the captain who ordered the radio room to wire the relevant authorities. Standing at the ship's rail, peering into the darkness, around 10.50 pm, a light appeared. As it drew nearer I could see Horace standing at the bow. He was beaming from ear to ear and appeared totally oblivious to the fact he had held the ship's departure by twenty minutes.

"Darling, do you know you nearly missed the boat?" I asked. He smiled back at me.

"Did I!" he exclaimed. "Jolly good show." "There is a big penalty for holding up a ship." I was cross with him.

Really cross.

The following day we received a request to attend at the purser's office.

"Mmmmm!" I said, looking down at the note. "I wonder how much you have cost us?"

Horace didn't seem to be the slightest bit concerned. In fact, on the way to the purser's office he told me of a prior occasion – during one of his tours with Melbourne Inman – when the pair had been forced to charter a speedboat to catch the ship.

"We had to climb aboard on a rope ladder with our cue cases strapped to our backs. The applause was deafening."

I was not impressed.

"Good morning, Mr and Mrs Lindrum, thank you for coming down. I was just wondering what you would like us to do with all these?" Inside the purser's office was a bundle of beautifully wrapped packages. Gifts from the Yemeni Association.

Glorious sunshine greeted our arrival in Bombay and, within a few minutes of docking, our cabin was a mass of flowers. I was bursting with excitement. I had never been to India before and had no idea what to expect. The experience was far greater than any I could have imagined and the memories of that visit so ingrained in me that, no matter what happens to my mind down the track, my soul will carry the inscriptions.

Shortly after the ship docked, the joint secretary of the Bombay Billiards Association Mr Rafeek Dina came aboard with his entourage to deliver an official welcome. Garlands of flowers and leaves were placed around our necks following which we were escorted down the gangplank, through a guard of honour, and into a waiting car.

Horn blasting, Dina's driver sped through busy streets, past buses and between buses and between buses and 'puck-puck' bicycle carts and across footpaths and on to the Taj Mahal Hotel where Mr Begg and Mr Rutton Adenwalla and his charming wife, a doctor of fine art, were waiting to greet us.

The next ten days were a whirl. Horace was playing three sessions a day. Not very well in the beginning. Within twenty-four hours of our arrival he had come down with a shocking virus and the hot and humid airs of India were sapping his energy. Fortunately, he managed to shake it off.

Wednesday 19 November 1952

National Standard

A FIRST FOR INDIA

Horace Lindrum, world professional snooker champion, showed a glimpse of his class on Tuesday when playing R K Vissanju at the WIAA Club.

Lindrum broke the pyramid and Vissanju sank three reds. The champion then cleared the table, with a spectacular break of 115, the first official snooker century in India.

Horace had recorded snooker centuries on prior visits to India but this century was officially recognised as being the first snooker century recorded under championship conditions. A magnificent silver trophy commemorates the event.

Joy's diary also records the moments away from the table:

> Our suite at the Taj overlooked the gateway to the city of Bombay and, in the evenings, hundreds came to enjoy the cool breezes and stroll between the Umbrella and Palmyrah Trees. From a small table in the window bay we took our somewhat hurried meal between playing sessions admiring the symphony playing out along the waterfront beneath us. Graceful women draped in glorious mirrored saris, turbaned peddlers some in colourful kaftans and others in long silk shirts hawking gay balloons affixed to long broom-like sticks, fishing boats bobbing up and down, ass-drawn carts in strange procession on return from the marketplace, herds of children flying kites – the sun, sizzling like butter in a burning hot pan, sliding ever so slowly into the line between sky and sea, unwillingly surrendering to thousands of twinkling lights – and, beyond the Toddy palms, long laneways of immaculately kept makeshift shops and dilapidated houses.
>
> On one of our few days off, we travelled to Juju beach in Ville Parle, which is approximately 12 miles [18 kilometres] from the City centre. Horace had talked of the beauty of Juju and promised me a visit. It did not disappoint. We strolled around the food market, savouring the local delicacies. I settled on a thick vegetable masala with a great dob of butter and slice of fluffy bread. Horace chose a sizzling kebab and potato patty. The patty had been mashed with garlic, chillies and coriander dipped in chickpea flour, fried until golden and spread with coriander chutney. To say it was mouthwatering would be an understatement.
>
> After lunch we walked down to the beach. I felt I was in Paradise. The sand stretched for miles and the sea was crystal clear, warm and inviting. There was nobody about and we were contemplating stripping down and going for a swim when our plans were interrupted. Hobbling on legs weaker than the trusses under the Bridge over the River Kwai, his left foot dragging behind the right, a one-man circus.
>
> 'Sahib, Sahib," he called as he made his way towards us, the monkey on his shoulder clinging to the tiny fez perched on its head.
>
> "I am Achy. I am named after Achalesvara and Achintya. I am God of the Immovable and beyond comprehension."

He was more Lord of the Seven Seas. I wished for a palette and a canvas for a subject like this one does not come along every day. His coffee-coloured face taut as the hide on a drum. His eyes, black as coal. His teeth whiter than sheets soaked for months in a pot of bleach. He had…Chutzpah. I could have said gall, nerve, effrontery, but how can you pass on a word like "Chutzpah"!

Chutzpah has no equal.

"Sahib. You lovely wife. I give you lovely wife photo. See, look what I have with me."

Like a magician whipping the cover off a birdcage, he whipped off the Cossack-like skirt around his waist revealing a small basket underneath. "Come, lady, look," he coaxed, plonking himself on the sand.

I had a fair idea what he was going to do next and I was happy to keep my distance. Waving a reed with the grace of Daniel Barenboim preparing the Israel Philharmonic Orchestra for a recital of "Tales from the Vienna Woods"[214], Achy lifted the lid. The sound from the reed was hauntingly beautiful.

"You hold?" he asked with a wicked grin. "Oh, God, he's offering me a Cobra!"

With some considerable misgiving, I was persuaded to hold the tail. There were a few little interludes like this one and I remember saying to myself whilst sitting at a table on the terrace at the Brindavan gardens in Bangalore: "I wish it could always be like this" but Horace didn't belong to me. He was the world's property and breaks from the table were regulated by his demanding program of events.

We stayed in Bangalore for two days then Horace travelled on to playing engagements in Madras, Hyderabad, Kakinada, Kolkata (Calcutta), Lucknow, Delhi and Jaipur.

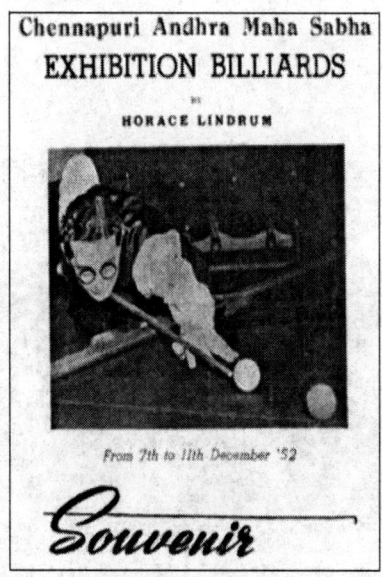

Front cover souvenir program for exhibitions in Andhra

---

[214] "Geschichten aus dem Wienerwald" Opus 325, one of six Vienna waltzes composed by Johann Strauss II in 1868, featuring virtuoso part for zither

There was trouble on the train to Hyderabad.

Potti Sreeramulu, a staunch devotee of Mahatmaji, had fasted to death in a last ditch attempt to force the Government of India to bow to public demands for the separation of the Andrha region from Madras.

Sreeramulu was much admired in India.

After losing his wife and child he had joined Gandhi's ashram and taken an active role in the Indian Independence Movement. In 1930 he was imprisoned for participating in the 1930 Salt Satyagraha. Notwithstanding this horrific ordeal, he was known to walk barefoot for hours in the hot sun, no umbrella, carrying large placards demanding government action. On hearing of his death, hooligans decided to loot the Vijayawada Railway Station.

Horace described the events to me on the telephone. Eighty miles outside Andhra the train was forced to a halt. Men were lying on the tracks and an angry mob, some brandishing long knives, began stoning the carriages. "Hurry, hurry, Horace, we must get off the train." Horace's travelling companion was gesturing wildly. "Horace, no time to wait, follow me."

I can't tell you how relieved I was to hear he was safe.

"What about your luggage?" I asked.

"The only thing I grabbed was my cue case."

Understandably, Horace hadn't given his luggage a second thought and all thirty-four pieces were still on the train. The Indian tailors are craftsmen of the first order. You can choose your material one day and your suit is ready to wear the next. A blessing when you need dress clothes for your appearance in Delhi before President Rahebdra Prasad and his health minister Amrit Kaur.

8.00 am the following day, six tropical whites and a dinner suit arrived at the Great Eastern, Calcutta, for the attention of Mr Lindrum.

Three days after Sreeramulu's death President Jawaharlal Nehru declared Andrha a separate state.

Group press photo Madras. Front row Joy wearing sari and holding onto Janne. Horace in whites.

Front page photo by Joy, Janne and Horace. Sprt and Pastime Magazine

Souvenir program Bombay Official Tour India 1952

Group press photograph Bombay Joy front row centre 305

Special souvenir program from Official visit to India 1952

Left: Horace demonstrates the masse shot

Below Horace (left) with M M Begg chairman (centre)

Group photo Secunderabad 1952

Jan Lindrum

Radio interview, Delhi

This is Ram Singh. Good evening listeners. I have with me this morning world professional snooker champion and professional billiards and snooker champion of Australia, Horace Lindrum.

"Good evening, Mr Lindrum." "Good evening, Mr Singh."

"It is a great pleasure to welcome you to Delhi." "Thank you."

"I would like to ask you a few questions. I hope you won't mind." "Not at all. It will be a pleasure."

"First of all, please tell us what is a good age to start playing billiards." "Twelve. I think twelve is about the right age to get serious about any human enterprise. By age twelve the student is mature enough to take in what is taught by the instructor."

"Ah, Mr. Lindrum, you are an Aristotelian. What does it take to be a champion do you think?"

"Hard work. There is no easy road in any profession." "And how does it feel to be the world snooker champion?" "It is a dream come true."

Horace and New Zealand Champion, Clark McConachy

Whilst Horace was in Delhi, Jan and I went shopping. We purchased a Christmas tree and some really pretty decorations from the Grand Market. I will never forget my husband's face as he came through the door of our hotel room. He hadn't had a great deal of time for Christmas in the past. After Christmas Horace returned to his playing engagements. On the eve of our departure we were guests-of-honour at a dinner party at the Islam Gymkana. Mrs. Adenwala had taught me the essential arts. How to make a curry and how to drape a sari. For this occasion, I selected a cameo pink and rosa quartz sari and an evening bag of red velvet and gold brocade. A beautiful evening, I understood what Monet[215] meant when he wrote: "I haven't managed to capture the colour of this landscape."

---

[215] Claude Monet (1840–1926), French artist and father of French Impressionism

The colour at the Islam Gymkana was beyond descriptors. Canary yellow, cobalt blue, emerald green, fresh, jazzy, iridescent. Aside from the breathtaking fashion, warm greetings and superb hospitality.

Long tables dressed in starched white linen set under a black velvet sky dotted with thousands of stars, hundreds of flickering candles, large pottery vases of champa and cornelians, jugs of sherbet, tureens of curry, an assortment of rices including one with goat and aromatic spices, platters of tiny dumplings filled with mince meat, bowls of condiments, papadums, breads and luscious fruits. We ate and laughed and ate and laughed. After dinner, there was a bit of an incident. A little worse for drink, a rather pompous fellow leaned across at me and, with a smarmy look on his face, asked:

"Ah, Mrs. Lindrum, in all honesty, tell me, what do you think of India? Don't be afraid to say, we are all friends here."

Insolent puppy, he clearly believed himself in some way superior.

I remained silent for a moment contemplating how I should respond. I couldn't smack him in the face but he certainly deserved a slap. Instead I served him a withering stare. Then – summoning the acting skills I inherited from Brian Gwaspari (a distant cousin and actor in many episodes of "The Gentle Touch") – I ever so quietly, told him:

"I am here at the invitation of a Sporting Association and I would not consider it in the best of taste to pass anything but polite comment about India and the Indian people. If you don't like it here, young man, I suggest you hike it back to England."

There was a deadly hush at the table. I am sure my hosts were shocked by my forthright comments. They were also secretly pleased for a quiet smile appeared at the corners of their mouths. The serve was long overdue. The "boy" - for I can only refer to him as such – fiddled with the cuffs of his freshly-ironed shirt for a short time then drained his wine glass, made his excuses and left the party whereupon we set our minds to some vigorous dancing.

We departed Bombay the following day.

Next stop, the famous Falle Face Hotel on the beautiful island of Ceylon, a visit to the Moors Islamic Cultural Council and, from Colombo to Africa.

Jan Lindrum

The Uncrowned King

Below: Horace on one of many visits to African villages where he lent aid

Below: Joy enjoys a day at the magnificent Victoria Falls

Above: Horace and Joy with Ken Shaw
President of the Association for South Africa and the Transvaal for 33 years

Below: Photograph taken on one of many visits to Botswana

Over the next two months we covered 4000 miles. Joy spent most of her time behind the wheel, driving from one destination to another.

The professional snooker challenge took place in Johannesburg. Horace's opponent was the South African Professional Billiards Champion Peter Manns Senior. During the challenge, Horace was asked to make a broadcast. The rehearsal was left in the hands of a young lad who knew absolutely nothing about snooker. The first red went into the middle pocket bringing the cue-ball behind the black and into an excellent position near the top right-hand pocket. The rest was needed for the next shot. Horace called: "Rest, please". The "rest" is a long cue-like instrument used to rest the cue on, in lieu of the hand bridge, when the cue ball cannot be reached. Thinking Horace was asking for a rest from the table, young Jim put down the numerous wires he had been holding on the ground, sniffed and proclaimed loudly:

"My goodness, don't these professionals tire easily," which, naturally, brought the house down.

Wherever Horace went, the press went with him. There was enormous interest in his record-breaking ability. There was also a lot of interest in his wife's magic carpet ride. This is evidenced by the article in *The Sunday Mail*,

12 May 1957: "Globe-Trotting Wife: Billiards Her Magic Carpet"

"The click of billiards and snooker balls in eight countries has meant thousands [of] miles of travelling in the last three years...Mrs Lindrum was aboard the *City of Port Elizabeth* which called at East London Harbour and sailed yesterday. She is on her way to join her husband who is at present making a tour of Natal. She will meet him in Durban and that is "where my driving spell starts" she told me. They will both tour the country with Mr Lindrum playing snooker and billiards and Mrs Lindrum meeting old friends. This is the third time Mrs Lindrum has toured South Africa with her husband, although he has been to the country seven or eight times. Mr Lindrum did not, however, introduce Mrs Lindrum to snooker and billiards. Prior to her marriage to Mr Lindrum, Mrs Lindrum worked for the British Association and Control Council."

Other press articles followed the progress of the tour:

Lindrum "The Ace" – deadly accurate potting

"Australian snooker wizard, Horace Lindrum, has taken the Basutoland snooker title with a break of 139 made at the Memorial Institute in Maserum in the presence of the Resident Commissioner, Mr. A. G. T. Chaplin. That brings his century tally to nineteen this trip.

In total to date, he has notched up six hundred and sixty-six centuries in public performance."

"Maestro" is making his mark

His eyes always seem to be smiling and for good reason. The Australian champion is blitzing it! At the Toristo Hotel in Standerton last night, Horace Lindrum of Australia took the South African snooker record with an outstanding break of 143.

There are many memories from this trip. Escaping the baboons at the Victoria Falls, hunting crocodile on the Zambesi, driving at dusk in the Kruger National Park, a giant bird flying at the windscreen, a herd of elephants stampeding down the side of the roadway, walking into a billiard room for a practice session to find a 10-foot native boy standing on top of the table beating the cloth with a birch broom on instruction to ready it for "The great Lindrum." Then there was the joy flight with Rex Johnson.

Jan Lindrum

Horace had met and played Rex a number of times on his previous visits and secretly hoped that one day Rex would invite him to ride in his plane. When the invitation finally came, he jumped at it. To his surprise, Joy was not too keen and he had to do quite a bit of coaxing.

"The scenery will be visually spectacular, darling," he told her. "Think of all the amazing photographs you will have to show to your Mum and Dad."

She finally agreed and they met Johnson at Mtubatuba airfield.

"Horace, Joy, good to see you, I'm afraid the weather isn't doing us any favours. It will be a bit bumpy. Are you up for it?" They nodded.

Rex strapped them in then climbed into the pilot's seat. Seconds later, the engine roared into life and they taxied onto the runway and took off to the north. Once airborne the craft quickly gained speed.

"If you look to starboard, you'll see the sugar farms and, to port, the swamp-lands. In a short time, we'll reach the St Lucia River. Get your camera ready. There's a few Mick Molloys [sailing craft] to windward. Good day for it."

Rex was clearly at home in the wide blue yonder.

"Ah!" he exclaimed. "There they are." He was tracing a line of footsteps at the water's edge. Frolicking in the surf, a group of happy-go-lucky Africans. Terrific body-surfers, they were propelling themselves forward onto the breakers and riding them into the shoreline.

"Let's give them a stir."

Neither Horace nor Joy knew what a stir meant but they felt the downdraught. The boys knew the game and they played along splendidly. They ran from the water, placed their palms in prayer position and rattled their knees. When the engine kicked into a vertical climb, they hooted and waved and beat their legs with their fists.

"Oh, my goodness, Hello You!"

Flicking the plane away from the beach, Rex directed their attention to a sand bank on the other side. Sunbathing on a huge mound, the largest crocodile imaginable. "He's a killer that one. Shall we take a closer look?"

On the first fly over, the croc did not take any notice. On the second, he opened his jaws so wide that Horace was sure they were going to be swallowed up. Joy turned a terrible shade of green and Horace was forced to hand her a brown paper bag.

"Will you be okay? Can you stick it out, old girl?" he whispered. She nodded. "You can do it," he said reassuringly. "Let's show Rex what we're made of." Loop the loop.

Rex was completely oblivious to the air-sick passenger in the back. "Hippo coming," he yelled.

Reverse Cuban Eight. (Like the Cuban Eight, a Reverse Cuban Eight can be formed by flying two Reverse Half Cuban Eights back to back)

"Rhino over there." Avalanche.

Later, over a hot toddy and a Bunny Chow[216], he confided he was getting his own back on Horace for beating him at billiards.

"Let me make it up to you," Rex offered. "I'll take you and Joy tribal dancing before you go on to Potchefstroom." They needed more than one application of liniment after that little episode.

At Potchefstroom [217], Horace's exhibition captured the imagination of a sweet-faced African named Matuba. After the exhibition Matuba approached him and asked to see the basket. Horace handed him the trick-shot basket and watched as he inspected it closely.

---

[216] Traditional South African dish comprising curry served in a hollowed-out loaf of bread
[217] Potchefstroom is approximately 70 miles from Johannesburg

"Master, you do trick again." Horace executed the shot. "Master, I see basket again?" "Certainly."

He repeated the examination turning the basket every which way. "Master, you Tokoloshe.[218] You basket Tokoloshe."

"Matuba, what does Tokoloshe mean?" Horace asked. "You billiards witch, Master."

The press ran with the headline and the nickname stuck.

En-route to Umbukwe Tobacco Farm, the Billiards Witch was confronted by three obstacles; a flood, most unusual for the time of year; a large floating log that turned out to be a crocodile; and a spot of mechanical bother. Thankfully, the owner of the property where we were staying had met up with us 10 miles back and told us to follow him in. When he failed to see the car in his rear vision mirror, he turned around and came to investigate.

People in the remote areas of Africa learn to be pretty handy. There is no alternative other than to learn to do it yourself. Townsend was a curate's egg who could do just about anything, sometimes well, sometimes not so well. One of his major achievements was a beautiful handcrafted billiard table which he had constructed from fossilised logs found on the banks of the Zambesi. His neighbours admired the table but they did not have a good word to say about his generator and were often overheard grumbling amongst themselves in the local village. "For Pete's sake, what was wrong with the kerosene lamp!"

Leaving the farmhouse, we moved on to Salisbury and from Salisbury to Umtali. Not even the most descriptive words could evoke the landscape of Umtali. In the early morning the depth of beauty on the scenic drive along the winding mountain road to Leopards Rock is unfathomable. At the top is a hotel surrounded by well-laid lawns, a golf course, tennis courts and, as far as the eye can see, mountain ranges of indescribable colour. Here we sat, under a bright sunshade, and forgot the world until the gentle "click, click" from the nearby billiard room reminded Horace that he needed to be somewhere else.

Bulawayo to Jo'burg and...

"Oh, my Lord, I have forgotten my cue case." "You're not serious, my darling?"

"I am afraid I am."

Joy was used to driving long distances, so back she went, a journey of 840 miles (1352 kilometres). All was well to Bulawayo, however, on the return journey, she had engine trouble. It was sunset. Not a good time to be beside the road.

"Oh, dear, what to do?" Joy thought to herself.

In the split-second that it took to think that thought, there came a rap at the window.

"Having a spot of bother, are we?"

A distinguished looking gentleman in full dress suit, a monocle glued to his right eye, was peering into the window and signalling to Joy to wind the window down.

"I said, are you having a spot of bother?" He repeated in his perfect Oxford English accent.

"So it would seem," she responded. "I have no idea what is wrong with her." "Let's take a look shall we? Pull up the bonnet."

Joy pulled the lever.

He tinkered around under the bonnet for quite some time. "Start her up."

Beroom, beroom...

"Ripping. You should be tickety-boo for Jo'burg." He closed the boot and came around to the open window.

---

[218] "Tokoloshe" in Zulu and "Tikoloshe" in Xhosa

"Might I suggest, my dear, that you have her looked at by someone who knows what they're doing as soon as possible after your arrival. *Maintenant!* [Now!] Wind up the window. Lock the doors. Keep to the speed limit and – Tally ho!" "Thank you so much."

Joy went to wave goodbye but there was nobody there. No man. No car. No dust on the road. "Where did he go? And how did he know I was going to Jo'burg?"she asked herself.

There are no answers to some things in life.

"Another 15 centuries under his belt, Lindrum leaves us today for the land of the Long White Cloud."

On this visit to New Zealand Horace had the enormous privilege of playing at Parliament House in Wellington. However, it was on his previous visit to New Zealand that the then Prime Minister the late Mr Fraser, and members of Parliament, had presented him with his leather cue case.

Mr Lindrum, it is with great pleasure that we present this cue case to you with our deepest gratitude for your wonderful work in nurturing good trade relations between Australia, New Zealand and the Mother Country[219]

Horace said he always felt at peace with the world in New Zealand. He believed there was, to quote: "A tranquillity in the heart of the people; a rare quality in this atomic-minded world."

In January 1953, the *Strathnaver*[220] docked at Port Melbourne. Despite the heat, hundreds of people had turned out to greet family and friends. Standing at the rail on the upper deck, Horace searched the sea of faces below, thinking to himself: "How nice it would be if someone from the family was here to say, 'Welcome Home'." Then Joy grabbed his arm and excitedly pointed to a figure dressed in a light grey suit. Horace knew instantly it was his uncle Walter. He knew by the hat. Walter always wore his fedora distinctively. June was with him. Horace had met June on a previous occasion and, despite the heat, she was still courting what had become her trademark fox stole.

Horace was looking forward to seeing Melbourne again. He was the proud owner of three small terraces, numbers 40, 54 and 56 Page Street, Albert Park. At least, he thought he was the proprietor of three houses in Page Street.

Melbourne was abuzz with news of Walter. His charity work was worthy of attention. The fundraising of other family members was equally impressive but, for whatever reason, there was an obsession with Walter's efforts. I think this was partly because of Walter's very strong connections at the top end of town and his position within the Masonic Temple. According to the reports he had raised £25,000, bringing his total to a little over £100,000, a lot of money then.

But although the press was interested in Walter's fundraising activities, reporters were more interested in his divorce proceedings and, to add spice to the story of Walter's divorce, *The Argus*, *The Herald Sun* and *The Sydney Morning Herald* dug up his past.

Walter Lindrum, who is playing in a tournament at Bristol, left for London at midnight, and was married at the Henrietta-street registry office at lunch time to Alice Hoskin, a 27-year-old Victorian. Clark and Gertrude McConachy and two

---

[219] Wool was big business in those days. It took five yards of finely spun wool to cover a billiard table
[220] Built by Vickers Armstrong in Barrow, Furness, United Kingdom, RMS *Strathnaver*, later S.S *Strathnaver*, was the first in the "Strath" class, comprising ships with better technology than their predecessors, including direction-finding equipment, echo sounding, gyrocompass and advanced turbo-electric equipment, enabling them to sail three knots faster than the earlier ships. Launched by the Peninsular and Oriental Steam Navigation Company on 5 February, 1931, *Strathnaver* was also the first of five sister ships which came to be known as the "The Beautiful White Sisters."

other friends were the only ones present. Lindrum will resume play in the tournament on Monday, dispensing with a honeymoon. He hopes to spend the summer in England to watch Larwood exploiting the leg theory. Though Lindrum has taught his bride to play billiards she prefers swimming and tennis.

TWENTY YEARS on and the honeymoon is OVER!

Walter Lindrum accuses Alice of adultery.

Alice (Pat) has counter-claimed on the grounds of desertion.

"Lipstick on his Collar" was the phrase that caught the public imagination. Truth or lemon juice and sugar crystals?

How would you ever know! History is full of stories.

Mr Justice Martin declared the content of the affidavits peculiar and told the parties:

"For the life of me, I have absolutely no idea what you two are going on about.

My advice is, stitch up the problem. Think of your reputations," he cautioned.

"Divorce is an unsavoury matter."

Walter dug his heels in.

So, too, did Alice.

The judgment made interesting reading.'

> However acute the petitioner is on the billiards table, in the witness box he showed he has a poor memory and very slow mental reactions. Notwithstanding, he satisfied me he was trying to be honest.

A relatively short time after the decree became absolute, Walter embarked on another sexual odyssey. The object of his affection this time was Beryl (June) Elaine Carr, a legal secretary in the employ at Freehill, Hollingdale & Page. Six years later, Walter was six feet under. Dead without a Will leaving the punters betting 100-1 on "Who Killed Walter Lindrum" and Hubert Opperman cycling Old Melbourne Town to raise money for a headstone.

Whether Opperman was commissioned by John Wren, I cannot say. What I can say is that Wren was the driving force behind the fundraising campaign.

To this day I can still hear my great-uncle's laughter.

"Top of the table all my life and what do they do when I'm dead? They put a bloody marble billiard table on top of me!"

Perhaps they wanted to keep him down!

Weeks prior to hearing the application for dissolution of Walter's marriage the judge bumped into the Prime Minister. Where they met is not clear. I seem to recall something about poached Scottish salmon and new potatoes at the Royal Automobile Club but I am not hundred-per-cent sure. After discussing the tawdry details of Walter's divorce, splattered across the front page, Sir Robert Menzies[221] returned to his office and picked up the telephone. Walter was in the billiard room when the call came in.

"It's for you, Walter. It's the Prime Minister."

Sir Robert asked Walter to attend at his offices. Walter thought a knighthood was in the offering. He was right except that it came with a condition. He had to withdraw his divorce

---

[221] Sir Robert Gordon Menzies (1894–1978). A liberal politician, Sir Robert became the 12th Prime Minister of Australia and remains Australia's longest serving Prime Minister (1949–1966)

petition. Walter was flabbergasted to learn that his friend would withhold the honour if he refused the request.

"I am sorry, sir, I can't do what you are asking of me. My private life is my private life."

Menzies lay his palms upon his desk and rose to his feet. He was a tall man who played a good game of billiards and he liked Walter; so what he was about to say and do would not sit comfortably. Walter had been good to him.

He had helped him to get the National Security bill passed through the Parliament by coercing a member of the Opposition to engage in a game of billiards. When the division bell rang, the member was so focused on the game that he simply did not hear it

"Very well, Walter. It is your decision. Good day to you."

Menzies waited for Walter to go then he sat down and thumped the desk with his iron fist. An hour later he picked up his pen and put a line through the planned honour, Knight Commander of the British Empire (KCB) became Order of the British Empire (OBE).

There is not much to report on our voyage back to the UK. Gulli Gulli man (magician) in Port Said...

We were home before you could say, Jack Robinson!

Photograph Horace, Janne and Joy returning to the UK at the end of the official tour

The boat train from Southampton pulled into Waterloo Station on 27 February 1954. Joy looked out the window. Heavy snow lay on the platform. I heard her sigh. It was a big sigh. A sigh tinged with melancholy. Squeezing her hand, Horace comforted Joy:

"There are plenty of good times ahead. Look forward, old girl, not backwards," he said.

I was excited to be home. I was looking forward to seeing my grandparents, my aunt and uncle and my cousins and to sleeping in my own bed. My grandparents could not believe how much I had grown. I guess that was because they were forever popping in and out of my life in those early years or, should I say, I was forever popping in and out of theirs. Naturally, they were overjoyed to see us and wanted to hear all about the tour.

It occurs to me that I have not told you very much about the official tour.

The reality is there is so much to tell it is impossible to tell it all. The following extracts will give you a feel for it.

Report of a speech by Mr V C Gopalaratnam

Indian Express

December 1952

"I have watched most of the world champions but I am absolutely certain that no one can claim to have the extraordinary charming personality of Lindrum and his almost magical wizardry of the cue in snooker. I do not think the piston of a first-class locomotive could be so correct as his cue when it moves forwards and back without the least bit wobbling."

"I think Lindrum is not only a fine billiards player but a great sportsman and a very delightful gentleman."

From the Australian High Commissioner in London 1952

"My mail has brought me a letter from Mr JC Bisset, the Chairman of the Billiards Association and Control Council, London, in which he quotes the eloquent tribute paid to you by the Chairman of the Billiards Association of India.

May I add my own felicitations to those of the Chairman on your outstanding success in the world's snooker championship.

So long as there is a Lindrum wielding a cue – and I hope there always will be – Australia's name will remain in the forefront of the world of billiards and snooker."

Four months after our return to the United Kingdom Horace received a letter from William Parker.

3 June 1954

Dear Horace,

Your mother is not well. She contemplates leaving Sydney on the *Himalaya*[222] on July 10 for the dual purpose of trying to regain her health and to see if it is at all possible to induce you and your family to return to Australia. She is prepared to give you a half share in the business and let your wife take an active part in its management.

If there are any points on which you would like further information, do not fail to let me know.

Kind regards,

William

---

[222] *SS Himalaya* was built by Vickers & Armstrong, Barrow in Furness, United Kingdom for the Peninsular and Oriental Steam Navigation Company, London. Launched 5 October 1948

Horace was surprised by the content of this letter. He had met up with his mother during the official tour and Clara had flatly refused to talk business. Twenty-four hours after her arrival in Britain, they met for afternoon tea at the Ritz. They talked of the boycott. They talked about highlights of the official tour. They discussed Lindrum's in Pitt Street, Sydney. Horace told his mother the business, in its present form, was no longer viable and that litigation with the landlord should be avoided.

Clara could not believe what she was hearing. She had fought long and hard all her life to keep the Lindrum name in lights. She never expected her son to tell her to walk away.

December 1956

Lindrum's in Pitt Street closed its doors but Clara refused to give up the fight. Embarking on a full-frontal attack against the gambling industry, she was featured in *The Sun-Herald* with a fist held high in defiance. Journalist Noel McDonald reported:

"New Boss of Billiards"

The First Lady of the Billiard Rooms, Clara Violet Lindrum, clenched her fists this week and got ready for a tough battle. Just back from London she has inherited sole control in Australia of the world's most traditional male sport. Billiards. And she intends to make same "respectable". To quote: "A game for nice gentlemen and nice ladies."

She told me: "I'm going to do some cleaning up around here."

In some of the billiard rooms of today, the game is played by roughs and hooligans. Actually, some of them are not billiards rooms, they are gambling dens. As a consequence, billiards in Australia is dying. Australia once had the greatest players in the world. Now that I am in charge players will have to shape up or ship out. And, as for those awful gambling machines, I just won't tolerate them."

Some of Sydney's billiard room owners (who incidentally denied the "DEN" accusation) said Miss Lindrum's organisation will be widely boycotted.

One city owner confided:

"Violet's a fanatic for strictness and it doesn't wash these days, but you have to give it to her, she's right in some ways. You hear police saying that billiard rooms are haunts for criminals."

A representative of the Billiard Control Union of New South Wales, with which most clubs are affiliated, told me:

"We'll probably go along with her. But she won't get us going over to her side. It will be a bloody battle if she tries."

This was not the first article featuring Clara with a fist held high in defiance.

The battle had been going on for a decade.

27 September 1947

The Sun

Journalist Jack Tier wrote:

> Dynamic, little auburn-haired billiards-room proprietress, Mrs Violet Lindrum, mother of snooker champion Horace Lindrum, has undertaken a task which would make most men quail.
>
> Love of a game which her family has dominated for the past 120 years is her sole motive for undertaking to put billiards and snooker back on a high place in New South Wales...
>
> An example of Mrs Lindrum's will and tenacity to accomplish any task she sets herself is the active role she played in securing recognition for her son's world-record snooker break of 141.

I imagine Clara making her way across Hyde Park, past the Archibald Fountain, down Elizabeth Street and into Martin Place. She is shaking like a leaf.

"This is not going to be easy," she is saying to herself.

"Horace will have a string of questions and I won't have the answers. I told him I would go down with the ship. What I didn't tell him is that – whether he liked it or not – he was going down with me. He's got to understand. At least, I've got to try to make him understand. I had to fight to the death. 'We' had to fight to the death."

Her mind is racing as she pushes her way through the revolving doors of the Hotel Australia. She finds Joy and Horace waiting for her at the reception desk. "My little sweethearts. I'm sorry to keep you waiting," she gushes.

Clara admires Joy's suit. Blue is definitely her colour. She also admires the magnificent cross she is wearing and asks whether it is Faberge. Joy tells her it is an original.

"Exquisite. You have good taste, my dear," she tells her.

Apart from Clara's marching into the kitchen with the Royal Albert teapot and telling the stunned kitchen staff they needed a lesson in how to make a pot of tea, the meeting was uneventful. Nothing was lost. Nothing was gained. There were no arguments. There were no tears. There were no answers. Horace read through the lines. His mother had exercised her power of attorney over his affairs and liquidated all of his assets to prop up the business. The houses in Page Street, the flats in Greenwich, his savings, Packard car – all gone. Poor woman had been fighting a losing battle. People no longer wanted to spend long hours bent over a billiard cue. Instead, they wanted to sit like couch potatoes pulling the handle of a Clubman poker machine.

The loss of his assets was a terrible shock to Horace who had worked 29 years for nothing. He forgave his mother. He loved her too much to do otherwise.

Two weeks after hearing the bad news, we were on our way back to Melbourne in a car Horace picked up at auction. We travelled through the night, as Horace and Joy wanted to see Tom Reece, who had been in Australia on holidays, before returning to the Mother Country. It was a good thing they made the effort, as it would be the last time they would see their friend. Reece was cremated at Golder's Green Crematorium on Tuesday 20 October.

After that, Horace was on the road for nine months of the year.

He took the call while on tour in South Africa. A big part of him was lost on the day that Clara died.

Back in London, Joy was busy typing articles, planning schedules, organising tours, writing letters and drafting promotional material. She was glued to the typewriter when the ambulance arrived to take her to Queen Charlotte's.

My sister Tammy was born on Tuesday 8 January 1957.

Horace came home for the birth of my sister then returned to Africa. We joined him a short time later. He recorded his 498th snooker century at the Norstel Royal Snooker Club against the champion from the Northern Transvaal. The manager at the German Club in Pretoria was so excited and so confident that the 500th century would be recorded in his club he told the press it was going to happen and telephoned Joy to tell her to come to the club.

Recording a century against Captain Steyn van Roogen was not going to be easy but Dame Fortune was with him. Away to a good start, Horace got the measure of the table and started building the break with a steady, consistent rhythm. This rhythm is much the same as the rhythm adopted by a golfer. The break stood at 98 and a strange quiet fell over the auditorium as if everyone had taken a deep breath and was holding that breath in a singular lung. When the green went down, the referee called the century. The final break was 138.

Horace was jumping out of his skin until he saw disappointment writ large on Joy's face. She had so wanted to see her husband record the 500th century but had not arrived in time. He vowed he would not make the next big milestone without her. A few months later *The Rand Daily Mail*[223] of Virginia, South Africa, reported:

> Horace Lindrum the most travelled sportsman of his era has recorded his 728th snooker century. On his return to the United Kingdom he will make his film debut in *The Counterfeit Plan* alongside Zachary Scott, Peggy Castle, Mervyn Johns, Sydney Tafler and Lee Patterson.

The Counterfeit Plan was released on 1 January, 1957

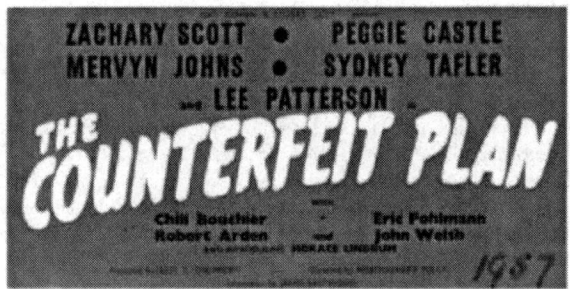

Promotional poster for the motion picture

Almost a year later, *The Music Man*[224] opened at the Majestic Theatre in New York.

---

[223] Founded in 1902 by Harry Cohen and based in Johannesburg, *The Rand Daily Mail* was purchased by mining magnate Abe Bailey. Journalists at the newspaper crusaded against racial segregation. Shrouded in controversy the newspaper closed in 1985 after adopting an outspoken anti-apartheid stance

After filming *The Counterfeit Plan*, Horace and Joy made the decision to live permanently in Australia. Reaching this decision was particularly tough for Joy. She was leaving her family, her beautiful home and her country. It was also a tough call for me. I confess to not wanting to leave Hillcrest, my grandparents, my aunt and uncle, my cousins and my school friends. Perfectly understandable. Composer Sir Charles Parry's uplifting hymn "Jerusalem" which resonated through the British nation was already embedded in my soul.

---

[224] *The Music Man* (1957), based on a story by Meredith Willson and Franklin Lacey, was a smash hit on Broadway, winning five Tony awards and running for 1375 performances. The success of the stage show on Broadway led to the motion picture adaptation directed by Morton DaCosta released on 19 June 1962 and starring Robert Preston

1959

Albert Park, Melbourne

Life changed for me the day we walked up the gangplank of the *SS Southern Cross*[225] Things would never be the same. Despite the fact that I had travelled all over the world for the first five years of my life, mixing in sophisticated worlds with important dignitaries, nothing could have prepared me for life in the Great South Land. The change was dramatically revealed to me the day I caught a glimpse of myself in the giant mirror that used to hang in the front room of the family home at Albert Park.

"Someone, please tell me that isn't me." A ridiculous muslin ribbon wound ever so tightly around my walnut, I looked like a giant fairy atop a Christmas tree. Reflecting on this memory, I realise that I was growing up, although I did not know it at the time. As I sit here, dragging the past into the present and telling myself, yet again, "Lindrum, don't get emotional", I relive those moments in time.

At any minute, any second, they will arrive. I know they will. While I am waiting, daydreams and wanderings. Grand voyages in tiny ships. A chat with Garibaldi[226]. A nod to Columbus[227]. All the time drinking in the light of the street lamps flooding the roadway.

A Rolls Royce Silver Cloud[228] swings into the kerb next to Auntie June's big shiny maroon Dodge and I push my nose to the glass. Feathers, graphics, motifs; the exquisite cut is unmistakably Chanel.[229] Silks, sensual satins, oceans of multi coloured tulle, Elizabethan velvets trimmed with brocade. A bow here, a button there, a string of sea pearls at the back. Gowns cut low across the breasts. Ermines and minks dripping off ivory shoulders. Imagine lying in a gondola in Venice listening to Pavarotti and you will find that moment of serenity before Michael Peck's *Archer*[230] takes his arrow to the bow.

Stomach filled with grasshoppers, I leap from the window seat and gyrate around the room singing "Diamonds are a girl's best friend". I am told to "stop it" and turn into Rodin's Thinker. "Don't let the wind change, you might stay like that" my mother tells me.

"Bell's going to ring. Bell's going to ring."

People, from all walks of life, were welcome at Lindrum's and the "our door is always open" policy saw plenty of comings and goings and turned the home into a stage of interesting characters.

Dogs are now yapping and Dolly (Irene May Dunn, my second cousin) is out the back with a popgun. She has already locked the cats up for the night. You have to lock the cats up otherwise they hide under the sofas, scratch the back of your legs and pounce on your chest in the early hours giving you one hell of a bloody fright. Enter the Spanish maid juggling a tray with a plated assortment of canapés and a punch bowl. Pimms and

---

[225] Built in 1955 by Harland & Wolff of Belfast, Northern Ireland for the UK-based Shaw, Savil & Albion Line, *SS Southern Cross* was launched 17 August 1954

[226] Guiseppe Garibaldi (1807–1882), Italian General, politician and nationalist he is credited with making the unification of Italy possible and, along with Camillo Cavour and Victor Emmauel II, is considered one of the "Fathers of the Fatherland". In 1849 he was appointed General of the Roman. He was also known as a "Hero of Two Worlds" because of his military enterprises in Brazil, Uruguay and Europe. Many Intellectuals of his time, including Victor Hugo, Alexandre Dumas and George Sand, held him in high regard. He is said to have sacrificed his liberal, republican principles for the sake of unification

[227] Christopher Columbus (1451–1506) was an explorer, navigator, coloniser and citizen of the Republic of Genoa. Under the auspices of the Catholic monarchs of Spain, he completed four voyages across the Atlantic Ocean. These voyages, and his efforts to establish a permanent settlement on the island of Hispaniola, initiated the Spanish colonisation of the New World, opening trade routes and leading to greater economic competition between nations

[228] Designed by J P Blatchley, the Rolls-Royce Silver Cloud was the core model from 1955 to 1966 when it was replaced by the Silver Dawn

[229] "Fashion fades, only style remains the same". This is a famous quote of Coco Chanel (1883– 1971), a groundbreaking fashion designer of the early 20th century whose legacy lives on. The Chanel label has been designed by Karl Lagerfeld since 1983. Chanel's life inspired the biopic *Coco before Chanel* (2009) starring Audrey Tatou

[230] Michael Peck's *The Archer* was a finalist in the Sir John Sulman prize (2014). The work, in the artist's words, "presents a figure pausing in a moment of contemplation. The boy, a hunter, stands very still. He is absorbed by his surroundings, aware of all his senses and place in the world"

Schweppes, half-a-dozen orange slices floating on the top, roughly cut; they look like dead goldfish.

Huddled in a corner of one room a small group of men looking at life with serious intensity. Behind the Chinese screen, a look-a-like Margaret Rutherford[231] peering into a crystal ball.

She produces a miniature tarot.

"Shuffle, darlink, and give me four piles."

In the centre of the room, a symphony of wild gesturing and facial grimace. Walt Kuhn's *Clown with a Drum*[232] sits on the sofa. Fat Sibyl stands in the shadows stuffing herself with Cadbury's Lucky Numbers. Tripping the light fantastic, eligible bachelors hanker for a gander at Betty Grable's[233] legs. "Forget your troubles, c'mon get happy"...[234]

The house literally shakes with excitement...

Sit down, sit down, my friend, have a drink of the best."

Do not ask me what a drink of the best was in those days because I have no idea whether it was a scotch on the rocks, a shandy or a mustick in vodka. All I know is the hospitality at Lindrums was enormous and enormously civilised. At the heart of the hospitality, June on the piano and Horace at the billiard table. I suddenly feel cold. I am haunted by the recollection. The clock on the wall is ticking. It is a Vienna regulator[235]...

"I've got a loverly bunch of coconuts"...[236]

Auntie June's bony fingers are banging on the keys, her body heaving under the framed myth hanging above her.

>My father came from Plymouth in 1838.
>
>Signed: Frederick William Lindrum II

There is no place in good history for fictitious mythologies. No matter how painful, you should always tell the truth about your heritage.

"Show me the way to go home..."[237]

---

[231] British character actress Dame Margaret Taylor Rutherford, DBE, who first came to prominence following World War II playing Madame Arcati in the film adaptation of Noel Coward's play *Blithe Spirit* and Miss Prism in the film adaptation of Oscar Wilde's play *The Importance of Being Earnest*.

[232] Painted by American artist Walt Kuhn in 1942 and featuring Kuhn's iconic and haunting portrayal of the solemn clown, Pierrot, a character from Italian theatre's Commedia Dell-Arte

[233] Born Elizabeth Ruth Grable (1916–1973, the American actress, dancer and singer Betty Grable got her big break in the industry when she replaced actress Alice Faye in the motion picture *Down Argentine Way* (1940). For the next decade she remained Fox's biggest box-office success. Throughout her career Grable was celebrated for her beautiful legs

[234] "Get Happy," composed by Ted Arlen, with lyrics by Ted Koehler. Released by Judy Garland (1950

[235] Unique handmade clocks from Vienna crafted from 1790 to 1910. During this period the design of Vienna regulators varied, so the versions are distinguished by first determining whether they belong to the early, middle or late period. In the early period, for example, the design known as "The Laterndluhr" resembled a coach lamp

[236] Novelty song composed in 1944 by "Fred Heatherton" a songwriting pseudonym for a collaboration of English songwriters Harold Elton Box, Desmond Cox and Lewis Ilda. The music and lyrics celebrate the coconut shy at fun fairs. The song was featured in Judy Garland's last film *I Could Go on Singing* (1963)

[237] Composed by English songwriting team James Campbell and Reginald Connelly under the pseudonym "Irving King" (1925).

Joy sings along and flits from guest to guest with a platter of cucumber sandwiches. She looks absolutely fabulous in her blue-and-white spotted cocktail frock.

> "Champagne Charlie is me name.
>
> Champagne drinking is me game…"[238]

Dolly appears. She looks sensational. She is wearing a low-cut, figure-hugging black satin number which catches the eye of an admirer. Before the night is out they will be caught pashing in the bushes out the back.

> "Put another nickel in, in the Nickolodeon,
>
> all I want is loving you and music, music, music"[239]
>
> Harriet the-Hard-as-nails is dead.
>
> The Ringmaster is dead.
>
> Clara, "The Entertainer" is dead.
>
> The Great White Hope is nearly dead from the drink.
>
> Morrell prowls like a wolf.

Me, I am sitting on the chaise longue, taking it all in. The goblins in my head recording every little detail. My great-uncle Walter has gone to bed. He is not one for parties. Social, when it suits him. Howard Hughes when it does not.

God knows how he manages to sleep through the racket.

> It was fascination I know
>
> And it might have ended right then at the start…"[240]

Down we go, across the sea of memory, all the way to Tin Pan Alley[241]. George M Cohan's "Yankee Doodle Dandy"[242] remains my favourite. Through my mind's eye I see my mother marking out the steps and trying to teach me to run up the wall like the great Cagney.[243]

> "Shine on shine on Harvest moon up in the sky,
>
> we won't have no lovin' till January, February, June or July."[244]

---

[238] A 19th century music hall song composed by Alfred Lee with lyrics by George Leybourne. The song was first performed and popularised by George Leybourne in a controversial performance in August, 1866 when Leybourne appeared on stage at the Princess' Concert Hall, Leeds, in a cut-down top hat, similar to that worn by the murderer Franz Muller (a German tailor who was hanged for the murder of Thomas Briggs – the first murder to take place on a British train). The song also inspired a motion picture of the same name featuring British stars of stage and screen Tommy Trinder and Stanley Holloway (1945

[239] Popular song composed by Stephen Weiss and Bernie Baum (1949). The most successful version of the song was recorded by Teresa Brewer and and the All-Stars on 20 December 1949 and released by London Records

[240] A waltz song, music by Fermo Dante Marchetti (1904) and lyrics by Maurice de Feraudy (1905 English lyrics by Dick Manning). The song first featured in the motion picture *The House on 56th Street* starring Kay Francis and has subsequently featured in a number of other motion films including the French black and white film version of *Gigi* (1949)

[241] Tin Pan Alley is the name given to a collective of music publishers and songwriters who dominated the popular music industry in the USA from 1880 to 1953; centred on West 28th Street and Fifth and Sixth Avenues, Manhattan. A commemorative plaque now marks the site on the sidewalk at 28th Street between Broadway and Sixth Avenue. London's West End also came to be known as Tin Pan Alley

[242] The Yankee Doodle Boy, "written by the man considered to be the father of American musical theatre' was composed in 1904 by George M Cohan for the musical *Little Johnny Jones*. Another famous hit from this musical was "Give my Regards to Broadway"

[243] American actor James Cagney played the role of George M Cohan in the motion picture "Yankee Doodle Dandy" (1942)

[244] "Shine on, Harvest Moon" was one of a series of Tin Pan Alley songs which debuted in the Ziegfeld Follies in 1908. The husband and-wife vaudeville team of Nora Bayes and Jack Norworth are credited with composing the song

So many happy hours spent singing around that piano.

'So be sure it's true when I say, I love you, 'cause it's a sin to tell a lie."[245]

June goes to a break, shucks a few oysters, drinks a few glasses of champagne, takes the last drag on a Sobranie sticking out of a diamante cigarette-holder. All very Mad Hatter's Tea Party and a whole lot Auntie Mame.[246] Guests to a Lindrum party came, saw and conquered. At least, that is what they thought they did. In reality, they slid like Alice into a world of sherry trifle and Guerlain.[247]

"Don't throw bouquets at me, don't."[248]

That was my mother's favourite song. I can still hear her singing it.

I have shed a few tears peering into the rear vision mirror. Here I go again: "Lindrum, for Pete's sake, don't get emotional."

It was 1960, Flinders Street Station, Melbourne. Walter and June travelled by train to the Gold Coast for a Magic Millions-style race meeting. Walter refused to fly.

"Even if they tie that ruddy contraption to a tree, I won't get in it."

According to family legend Walter stopped off at a pub on the way to the races to satisfy a craving for a steak-and-kidney pie. A short time after devouring the treat he fell ill. A doctor was called to the hotel. The diagnosis was food poisoning. As with Phar Lap, Walter was a creative, bankable and exploitable personality who had all the makings of a folk hero.

To say that he was a solitary hero, however, would not be the truth. To say that he was the only Australian sporting phenomenon to pass from view in suspicious circumstances would also not be the truth. Walter died, as Phar Lap died, of heart failure. I remember feeling terribly sad when told of the loss of my great-uncle Walter. I loved the man who wandered down the hallway at Christmas time, a barrel of Minties tucked under his arm, singing:

> He sent a note to Santa
>
> For some soldiers and a drum
>
> It broke his little heart when he found
>
> Santa hadn't come.[249]

---

[245] Popular song composed in 1936 by Billy Mayhew and originally introduced by Fats Waller

[246] Reference to runaway bestseller *Auntie Mame* by Patrick Dennis, inspired by his real-life eccentric aunt, Marion Tanner, whose life mirrored that of Mame. The novel inspired a Broadway production (1956-58) and a motion picture (1958) by the same name, starring Rosalind Russell in the lead role. Russell was nominated for an Academy Award and won a Golden Globe

[247] Founded in 1828 by Pierre Francois Pascal Guerlain at 42 rue de Rivoli in Paris, The House of Guerlain was managed by family members between 1828 and 1994. It was then acquired by LVMH Group, a multinational investment corporation specialising in luxury brands. Guerlain is among the oldest perfume houses in the world. My grandmother, Clara (Violet) always used Jicky by Guerlain. Jicky was launched in 1889

[248] "People will say we're in love", a song composed by Richard Rodgers with lyrics by Oscar Hammerstein for the musical *Oklahoma* (1943). A favourite song of Queen Elizabeth II and Prince Philip

[249] A song popularised by British actress, singer and songwriter Dame Vera Lynn (1917-). Dubbed "The Forces Sweetheart", she is famous for her renditions of "The White Cliffs of Dover", "There'll always be an England", "We'll Meet Again", "A Nightingale Sang in Berkeley Square" and "Land of Hope and Glory"

Janne, Walter and Minnie sitting on the step outside the billiard room

Walter had grown up with toys made from jam tins pulled together with pieces of wire. How the world had changed! He was born into one world and had come to inherit another.

30 July 1960

It's a sad day for sport with the passing of billiards legend Walter Lindrum. Walter Lindrum, the greatest freak in any sport, the man who said, "Billiards for women will come as sure as night follows day. The barriers are not strong enough to keep them out"...is dead.

Walter's body was flown home to Melbourne in a lead casket.

Three days later 2000 people packed St. Paul's Cathedral in Federation Square in Flinders Lane, Melbourne, for a State funeral. Men and women from all walks of life attended, including the President of the Royal Children's Hospital, Lady Murdoch. The card from Sir Robert Menzies and Dame Patti Menzies on the heart-shaped wreath at the doorway read:

In deepest sympathy, Patti and Bob

The Reverend Elliot from St Silas's Church in Albert Park delivered the eulogy.

> He did not call my great-uncle a saint but he came close:
>
> "Walter Lindrum's success in raising huge amounts of money for charity lay as much in the candour and simplicity of his character as in his consummate skill with the billiard cue.
>
> He walked with Kings yet never lost the common touch.
>
> He was a man who not only gave of himself but he gave of his substance."

They were all made of the same metal. My great-great-grandfather, my great-grandfather, my-great uncles, my father; they all knew what it meant to be glued to the one spot for eight hours a day. The leg cramps, the severe back and shoulder pain, the lactic acid build-up around the seventh cervical. It went with the territory. Service over, six burly rugby forwards heaved the casket onto their shoulders and, with the grace of Fonteyn, floated down the aisle to Mendelssohn's "Thanks be to God".[250] For those in the pews young enough to remember, it seemed like yesterday that Walter had taken a taxi up the Mall to Buckingham Palace to give an exhibition for King George VI.

I was not present at my great-uncle's funeral. I was sitting, on my own, in the cinema across the road from St Paul's watching Walt Disney's *Fantasia*[251]. In the fifties and early sixties it was considered taboo to take small children to funerals so you sent them to watch a mouse being tormented by an army of brooms and water buckets. But I was at the wake. Sitting on that same chaise longue. Taking it all in. After that I watched Horace complete the journey in the true spirit of "A Knight of the Cue".

But things were changing very rapidly. A new sporting model was progressively subverting the commandments of sport and radically altering perceptions of the sporting hero. This was largely attributable to the heavy influence of big business interests and the increased political influence that is inextricably linked to rabid nationalism.

The acceptable pre-requisites for the sporting hero – physical, social and moral excellence – were also being subverted and the "hero" label, which is a reflection of our divinity[252] or, to put it another way, a reflection of the state of a nation's soul, was taking on new meaning.

"The [true] hero..[was] running up against a [brutal] world that [was] in no way responsive to his/her spiritual needs'"[253] The kind of world foreseen by British author George Orwell as depicted in his novel *Nineteen Eighty-Four* (1949) and, in more recent times, by author Peter Carey in *The Chemistry of Tears* (2013):

> I began to read the newspapers again. I learned that the Americans have made a robot to teach autistic children. In many respects it is superior to a human being. That is, being a robot, it never becomes emotionally exhausted; it never loses patience; tears and rage do not press its buttons.
>
> The robot is called KayKay. I am not sure why. It does not attempt to hide its wiring and other innards. The report said that children swarmed it when it first appeared at a "facility" in Austin, Texas.

At the end of the first day, a boy with Asperger's syndrome yanked its arms off.

---

[250] Composed by Felix Mendelssohn, the Oratorio premiered in 1846 at the Birmingham Festival. The work was inspired by Kings I and II in the Old Testament and, more particularly, the life of the biblical prophet, Elijah. The German version premiered in Leipzig on 3 February 1848 (the composer's birthday), a few months after his death
[251] A ground breaking animated feature released by Disney in 1940, featuring animated film and classical music
[252] Campbell, Joseph, with Bill Moyers, *The Power of Myth*, Editor Betty Sue Flowers, (USA: Anchor Books, 1991), 159
[253] Campbell, Joseph, with Bill Moyers, *The Power of Myth*, Editor Betty Sue Flowers, (USA: Anchor Books, 1991), 159

The journalist seemed a little too happy about the arm-yanking, but the company said it was a "learning curve". By the next public exposure, which was reported in the *Guardian*, KayKay had its arms repaired. Now, when KayKay cried, the little Aspies did not "hurt" it any more. If the sobbing continued they then gave the thing a hug.....

> Who would not prefer the company of normal people?[254]

---

[254] Peter Carey, *The Chemistry of Tears* (Australia: Penguin Books, 2013), 164

1963

At the request of the Australian Association, Horace came out of retirement from competitive play to aid flagging interest in the sport in Australia. He competed in and won the Australian Open title that year[255]. That magnanimous gesture opened the doorway to the successful Pot Black series of televised snooker matches, which heralded the rise of champion Eddie Charlton's career.[256]

On the back of the Australian Open win, Horace was on the road again, doing what he had always loved to do, entertaining people; but he was then being sponsored – albeit for a very small amount – by tobacco companies. The tobacco industry had gained a stranglehold on sport, particularly snooker.

Celebrity smokers. through print, film and television, had been promoting the habit for some time. There were Leo Burnett's Marlboro Man and advertising campaigns suggesting that people smoke Craven A Virginia cigarettes[257] for their throat's sake ("will not hurt your throat"). Other ads proposed that smokers "Play it Safe with Philip Morris" and that "more doctors smoke Camels". All of these campaigns transported smoking to another level. It took more than 30 years before a select number of leaders started to listen to the voice of reason. By then, of course, the World War II soldiers who had become addicted to nicotine via the free cigarettes tucked into their C-rations were fathers of children and grandchildren, even great-grandchildren, who were smoking two packets of cigarettes a day.

During Horace's long absences, air letters flowed in and out like waves on a beach. Reading the "Dear Sweeties" says everything about my parents' deep affection for each other, but I confide that there were times when our mother was lonely. In the December of 1963, we travelled to meet Horace in London. I am extremely grateful for the memories of that trip; it was time with my mother that I would never have again. Of course, I did not know that at the time. I hold dear the memories of standing at the ship's rail with mum and my sister watching for landmarks to sail into view, preparing for the fancy dress party, rehearsing for the ship's concert, enjoying festive dinners of Veal Scaloppine, Marsala and Poisson a la Bretonne, dreaming of a future that was only a blink away.

Excerpt from Janne's diary

> In Colombo we were taken ashore in the pilot boat courtesy Sir Razeek Fareed. On the dock, a tall, handsome gentleman was waiting for us. His name was Mr. Huzair.
>
> "Good morning to you, Madam," Huzair said to my mother. "Welcome. We are now taking you to the billiard room." "Billiard room!"
>
> Ten minutes later, we pulled into the kerb in front of a big shed with a large crowd standing outside. As soon as they saw the car the crowd raced towards it.
>
> "My friends, I ask you to give Mrs Lindrum and the Misses Lindrum, your warmest welcome."

---

[255] It is a national disgrace that the trophy Horace donated to the New South Wales Amateur Association to commemorate his winning of the world professional snooker title in 1952 which was donated to nurture up-and-coming players; has been converted for use in the 'Bob Hawke Open' without any consultation with the family and, further, that engraved on that trophy is the name of the winner of the Amateur championship in 1963, thus giving the impression that the Amateur champion was the Open champion that year. Frank Harris was the winner of the Amateur championship in 1963

[256] The Australian professional association wanted refused Eddie Charlton's entry to the professional league. Horace Lindrum lodged an appeal on Eddie Charlton's behalf. The appeal was successful. Horace also provided Eddie with early coaching. These facts are not recorded in the history of Australian sport

[257] A brand of cigarettes owned by Rothmans, Benson & Hedges Inc (RBH) named after the Earl of Craven in 1860, manufactured in Canada, Jamaica, Vietnam and North Korea and, in recent times, associated with entertainment events like the "Just for Laughs" Canadian comedy tour. Craven A, a favourite brand during World War II, advertised: "Smoke Craven A for your throat's sake""and Craven A "will not hurt your throat

Huzair opened the door, bowed and extended his hand. Those unable to get into the room stood cheek-by-jowl outside, craning their necks through glassless windows.

Misreading my panic Huzair grabbed a cue from the rack and, grinning like a basket full of possum heads, offered it to me. "Do you have a sugar bag?" I asked him. He looked all puzzlement but accommodated the request. Placing the bag dead centre of the table with the opening facing one of the middle pockets, I set up the balls, red in front of white and took aim. Red ball into bag, bag turned over and the ball rolled into the pocket. Delighted, the crowd clapped and cheered and I bowed and put the cue back in the rack.

In the photograph above Mr Huzair in white shirt and trousers is to the left. My sister Tammy has her elbow on the cushion. I stand behind her. Our mother is to the right of me. She is wearing her trademark smile.

"Would you like a song?"

"My Favourite Things"[258] must have seemed so strange to them and a poor offering to a people who, I am sure, would have preferred to see the smiling, cheerful Horace. Notwithstanding, they were warm, hospitable and generous with their applause.

On the morning of 17 December, we docked in Aden. At 7.30 am, the temperature was 53 degrees. To say it was muggy would be an understatement. Dressed in our lightest clothes we travelled ashore in a small launch. Mum had arranged a tour and the Arabian driver and guide were waiting on the dock. Neither guide nor driver spoke very good English and their beat-up vehicle had seen better days.

"We go, we go. Asre'...Asre'..."

Past the airport. Past the palace of a thousand toys. Past leagues of tents and turbans. Past markets and bazaars crammed with hundreds of produce baskets overflowing with fragrant herbs and spices. Past make-do stands with ceramic pots and brass jugs dangling on long pieces of string strung from the sides. Past women shrouded in burqas carrying pitchers of water on their shoulders and curly-headed boys herding goats. My head out the window, the delicious smell of pancake and honey wafting up my nostrils.

Suddenly, the car came to a screeching halt and the driver announced with aplomb:

"The Oasis. May Allah be with you."

"May Allah be with you, alright!"

---

[258] Composed by Richard Rodgers for the Rodgers and Hammerstein musical *The Sound of Music* (1959). Based on the memoir of the family von Trapp, the motion picture of the same name (1965) was directed by Robert Wise and starred Julie Andrews and Christopher Plummer. It won five Academy Awards, including Best Picture and Best Director, and a year after its release, became the highest-grossing film of all time, overtaking *Gone with the Wind*. It held that distinction for five years

No lush palm trees. No flash tents. No dates. No pools of crystal clear water. A few boys riding donkeys and a funny, toothless old man with a wizened face, wearing a turban on his head and a nappy on his lower parts, sitting on a string bed, puffing on a long pipe and directing the bleating and banging that goes with driving a camel train.

At the time, I am not sure we appreciated the experience. On reflection, there was something bewitching and beguiling about those beggars of no importance; a poetry that cannot be found riding in glass and steel elevators.

Years later, the Black Poker confided she felt that the 1963 trip was the turning point. When I asked her what she meant, she replied: "Men no longer escorted women to the dance floor. They didn't even bother to offer their hand. I grew up in one world and you've come to inherit another."

Seven years later Horace was still on the road and he was still an important state commodity as verified by the Letter of Introduction duly executed by the Premier of New South Wales.

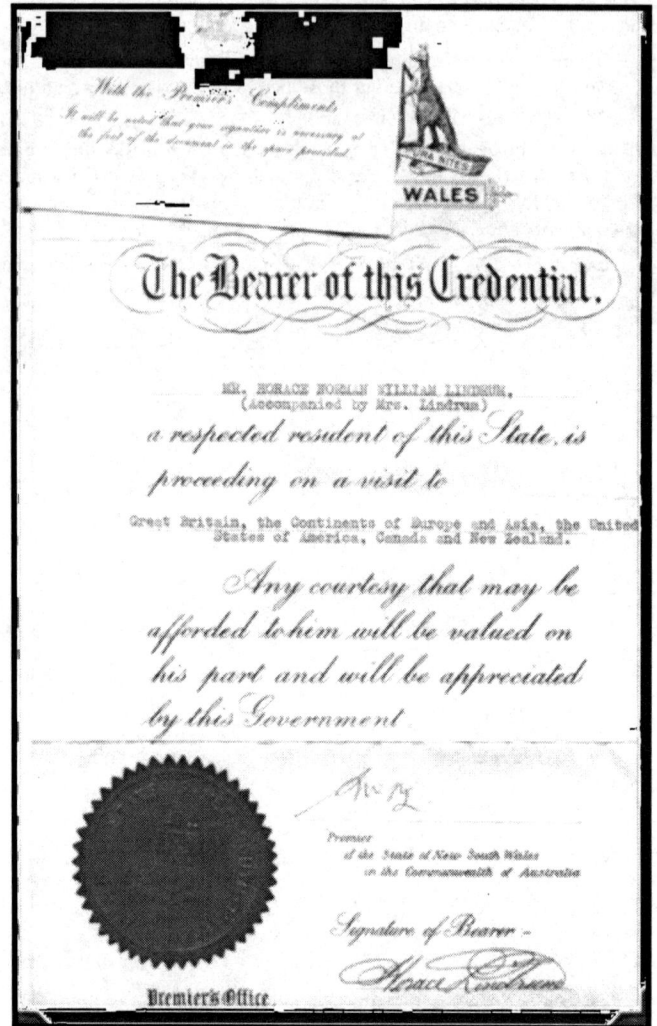

Horace recorded his 999th century in public performance early April, 1970 at Collaroy in Sydney and on 20 April of that year became the first snooker player in history to record 1000 snooker centuries in public performance. Many of those centuries had been recorded at world record speeds ranging from 6.0 minutes down to 2.5 and on tables and in conditions that were far from pristine.

Below Office Certificate issued by the Association on 20 April 1970, executed under seal by the Chairman of the Council, Jack Karnehm.

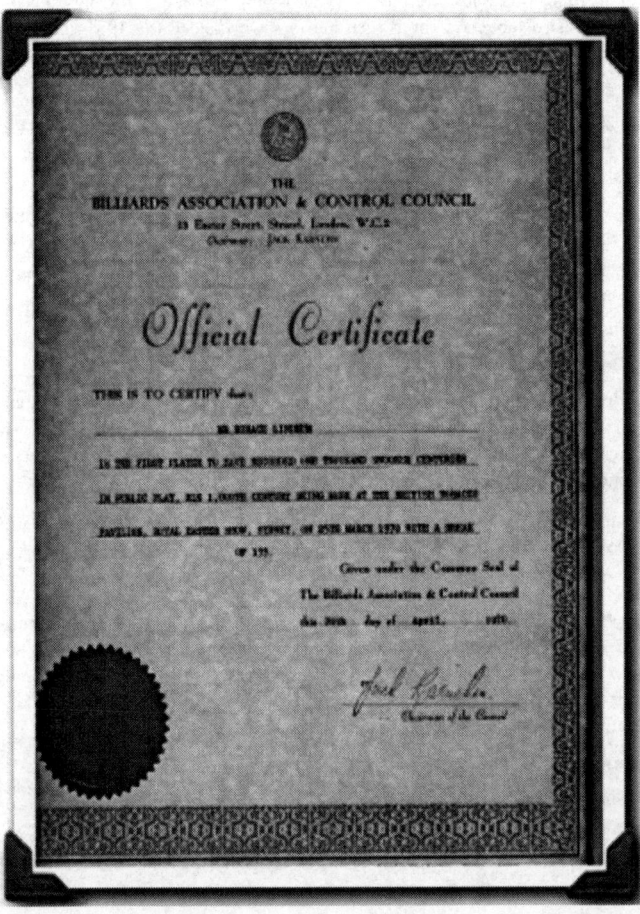

Yet, despite Horace's virtuosity with the cue and the sheer brilliance of his career, he continued to be plagued by the question: Is billiards the sign of a misspent youth? An idea which serves to highlight the schizophrenic nature of snooker and, indeed, the conflict, division and controversy that has dogged the sport of gentlemen for a long time.

Today, the controversy surrounding the boycott of the 1951–52 world professional snooker championship, for example, still rages; British players and their colleagues tell commentators on the BBC that: "If a championship was held like that today, it would be a non-event."

Quite an extraordinary statement when you take into account the short length of contemporary finals on tables with pockets that look more like ruddy big buckets than the pockets on a billiard table. As for British authors who allege the 1951–52 final was only one frame, **that is pure, unadulterated rubbish.**

On 5 May 2010, a BBC compere declared Australia's Neil Robertson – who stood before the cameras wrapped in the Australian flag – to be the first Australian to win the World Professional Snooker Title.

Robertson accepted the accolade with one qualification: "Horace Lindrum's name is on the Trophy."

In an article headed – "Only eye doctor knew: amazing secret of previous Australian to win world title"[259] – journalist Will Swanton penned the following response in *The Sydney Morning Herald*:

> We're talking here about a globe-trotting, generous, larger-than-life master of his craft from the golden age of snooker. Someone who put the prestige of a world title ahead of cash. Anyone discrediting Lindrum's 1952 world championship needs to indulge in a serious re-think. And consult the official record books.
>
> To put it into context – imagine during the Super League war that only two teams stayed true to the Australian Rugby League. All those two teams could do was play one epic series to decide the champion. That's how Horace Lindrum became world No. 1 in a marathon two-week play-off against New Zealand's Clark McConachy (McConachy was, at the time, the World Professional Billiards Champion). It wasn't his fault almost everyone else was consumed by Super League-style greed. Nowadays the British still try to discount the result but at the time the rebel players were branded 'The Bully Boys of Sport' by the British tabloids, who called Lindrum and McConachy heroes for respecting the traditions of the game.
>
> Lindrum is listed as the official 1952 champion.
>
> End of section!

---

[259] *The Sydney Morning Herald*, 5 May 2010, Sports Day, 22. www.willswanton-only-eye-doctor-knew-amazing-secret-of-previous-Australian-to-win-world-title.com.au

Epilogue

"I often see angels in my dreams and hear my mother call me." My sister and I burst out laughing. We had never heard our father speak like that before. Dad believed in a Supreme Being and had been known to enjoy a scotch at Christmas with Father Delaney and Father Grady but he was not a churchgoer.

The laughter triggered a discussion on the after-life and a pledge that the first of us to die would send those left behind a sign. A few weeks later mum and dad went for a chest X-ray in one of the mobile vans that used to travel around the countryside. Mum's card came back clear. Dad was asked to undergo a bronchoscopy.

Mum asked us not to tell dad the result but I can tell you, he knew.

Over the next few months we went to sleep every night preparing for the phone to ring but we were ill-prepared when it did.

20 June 1974, 2.30 am.

I knew before I picked up the receiver that it would be my mother's voice on the other end of the line.

I got dressed and drove along the Wakehurst Parkway, a dark and heavily wooded stretch of road between Balgowlah and the Collaroy Plateau on Sydney's northern beaches. On the journey I observed what appeared to be a bright triangle in the sky. When I reached the family home my mother asked me if I had seen the triangle.

We never did find out what it was.

According to psychiatrist, Carl Jung, symbols give meaning to the purpose of life. To mathematicians, a triangle is a three-sided object. To billiardists, it is a frame that organises the balls at the beginning of the game. To occultists, a triangle binds the earth with the heavens. To me, that triangle was the promised sign. My father was now on his way to that great billiard table in the sky.

A day later I visited my father's body in a chapel in Mona Vale. It was a strange experience. I remember thinking to myself, "That's not my father, that's a shell" but I felt that my father was watching me.

Dad's body was cremated at the Northern Suburbs Crematorium on 22 June. His mother had been buried in the Lane Cove cemetery across the road on June 22 1957. The number of years between the death of the mother and the son is 17. Whilst Horace made his debut into the professional league at 16, his professional career took flight a year later. My eldest son, Michael, was born exactly nine months to the day and hour after I last saw my father.

Interestingly, my second son, Robert, was born in 1988, 14 years after his grandfather's death; Horace was 14 when he won the Marbles Championship of New South Wales; my daughter, Samantha, was born 16 years after her grandfather's death; Horace was 16 when he made his debut into the professional league.

Pure coincidence?

We can never know the answer to that question.

Time is complex and no scientist has yet been able to master the concept. Perhaps Lewis Carroll's Mad Hatter was right. "You can't beat time." Certainly, there are some people who think time has beaten me.

My father lived so many years ago. "Who will remember him?" The important thing is, I remember him, and I have lived long enough to pay tribute to champion, father and man.

Horace's death not only sounded the death knell for the sport of gentlemen, but, ironically, just as Al Jolson's "Toot Toot Tootsie Goodbye" (1927) bid farewell to the silent movie era, Horace's death bid farewell to a snooker era the likes of which we will never see again.

Joy took up the torch and completed the marathon, publishing Horace's international bestseller *Snooker Billiards & Pool*, a book that marked him, as perhaps, the leading authority on the cue sports of the 20th century.

During Horace's lifetime, none of us could have foreseen the corrosive influence that gambling and business interests might have had upon his good name and reputation after his death. It is heinous that people waited for him to die before "rewriting" the story of his life; excluding him from the Lindrum family story, remaining conspicuously silent on his record of achievement, rendering his achievements out-of-context and referring to him on occasion as the "lesser" champion. (An act that led to a furious response from my mother)

The project of this book takes issue with false and injurious renderings of the lives of decent men and women, particularly when the deceased subject is unable to defend himself or herself.

The problem with rewriting a history is that the truth of that history always finds a way to bubble to the surface and, if you are a true Hercules, the legend of your strength will emerge no matter how hard people try to suppress it.

What would dad think of *The Uncrowned King*?

He would give the same answer he gave to my mother when she tried to persuade him to write his autobiography.

"My life [or any rendering of it] is for others to judge."

There were many admiring accounts of Horace's life and achievements after he died. Below are excerpts from a few. I am also including an excerpt from an article about Horace's skills on the cricket pitch

21 June 1974

HORACE LINDRUM,
giant of the billiards table, dies
SPORTS DESK By the Sporting Editor
The Manly Daily

International cricketers of the Bradman era can be thankful, in retrospect, that the late Horace Lindrum brought his talents to snooker, rather than to cricket.

Horace dearly loved to demonstrate his finger control of the balls on the billiard table.

This had to be seen to be believed.

Even having seen it, one might have felt an urge to dash away for an eyesight test.

With only the power imparted by his incredibly flexible fingers, Horace could make the balls do exactly as he intended, from the most delicate cannon to a complicated trick shot. Countless thousands of Sydney Royal Easter Show visitors over many years saw him do this as a variation of his snooker and billiards trick shots repertoire.

When his health unexpectedly failed during one of his performances at the last Easter Show, he found that he was not able to hold a cue firmly enough to carry on his normal programme. But, in the best showbiz tradition, Horace carried on with finger shots so deftly made that one would not have suspected his sudden inability to handle a cue.

Imagine the havoc he could have wrought among the world's best batsmen of his day had he applied to a cricket ball his prodigious power of spin and perfection of control.

Yet world-wide audiences his art enchanted throughout the greater part of his life will be ever grateful that he chose the green felt rather than the ticket pitch on which to practise his unique art.

20 June 1974

DEATH OF HORACE LINDRUM

The Daily Mirror

"Young Horace" made his [professional] debut in 1924 [professional debut was 1928 at age 16] and for many years was in the shadow of his uncle, the great Walter Lindrum. But he established himself in his own right and set records throughout the world. Horace became world champion in 1951 and held the title for six years. During his 50 years the wizard of the baize became the only man to make a century break 1000 times in public. In 1941 at the Penrith School of Arts he made the maximum possible break of 147, a feat he was to accomplish three more times during his career.

Horace literally played before all the crowned heads of Europe during his travels. He was particularly popular in India where the delighted maharajas used to reward his efforts with presents of jewels. One gave him a set of dress links made of platinum with onyx stones and 13 diamonds.

Admiring but beaten opponents used to say:

"Horace can make a snooker ball do anything but talk.'

21 June 1974

HORACE LINDRUM dies, aged 62
Journalist Les Wheeler
The Sydney Morning Herald (an excerpt)

Horace was Australia's only world professional snooker champion. He won the title in England in 1952 and held it until 1957, when he returned to Australia.

He came back to competitive snooker to assist the game's revival in Sydney in 1963, and, wearing contact lenses as well as spectacles, beat a top-class field to win the Australian open championship...

His trademarks were a mercurial style, a flashing smile, and a line of amusing banter as he swept from shot to shot. He was a popular performer in a sport known for the grim professionalism of its champions...

E J O'Donoghue, first to make the magic 147, had this to say:

> "Horace Lindrum was a gifted cueist. Any man who can make breaks of 1000 at billiards and score 1000 snooker centuries, has to be outstanding.

HORACE LINDRUM: A TWO-SPORTS SHINER Swan Hill (local) Newspaper Cricket season [1933–34]

Cricket enthusiasts gifted with a high sense of imagination have often, in the excess of their joy, picked teams consisting of footballers, billiardists and others, and tallied up the total score likely to be made by such a side, but they have little thought that one day their dreams, or part of them, would come true. The following is taken from the Swan Hill (Victoria) local newspaper:

"One of the most sensational matches ever played on the Mystic Park ground took place last weekend [season 1933–34]. The club captain called correctly and decided to bat, opening the innings with Dr Phillips and T Green. The latter started brilliantly, getting 4, 4, 2, 6, and was then taken in the slips by Cartwright – a beautiful one-handed catch.

On the arrival of Horace Lindrum, the Australian snooker champion, the

real fireworks started, as he hit the Mystic demon bowler for 3 consecutive sixes to the Kerang Road – a feat never before accomplished on the local ground.

Dr Phillips was keeping the other end going in his usual graceful, Kippax style. Lindrum treated all the bowlers alike, hitting fours and sixes to all parts of the ground. The gem of the lot was one through the window of the grain-shed. On reaching the century, Lindrum graciously retired, and was greeted with applause from the large crowd of spectators.

Dr Phillips remained unconquered with 80. The innings closed at 276, made in 150 minutes.

The opposition then went to bat, and made merry at the expense of the local bowlers. In desperation the captain threw the ball to Lindrum, who promptly finished off the remaining batsmen by securing 5 for 10, off 2 overs.

THE MAGICAL 147 (maximum break at snooker)

Horace recorded the maximum break of snooker at the Penrith School of Arts (NSW) in 1941. He was aged 29 years.

Horace's greatest adversary, British champion Joe Davis finally recorded the maximum break in 1955.

Horace and Joe were first to record the highest break at billiards under the new Baulk-line rules. Horace recorded a break of 1008 in Glasgow, Scotland. Joe recorded a break of 1008 in London.

Author's biography

Janne Clara Lindrum

Janne (Jan) was born into a family of British and Australian champions within the sound of Bow Bells London in 1950 and refers to herself as a Cockney/ Aussie. A proud wife, mother and grandmother, the early part of her career was spent working full-time in marketing and business development in the legal industry and teaching and directing dramatic art performances part-time. Graduating with a BA from Note Dame University Sydney in 2009, Jan completed an Honours year under the guidance of Professor Gerry Turcotte the following year. Losing Professor Turcotte to Canada was a terrible blow but Jan remembered what Professor Turcotte had told her: "Whatever you do in your life from here on, you must complete the story of *The Uncrowned King*." To this end, she completed a doctorate in the creative arts at the University of Wollongong under the supervision of Dr Siobhan McHugh and Professor Cathy Cole. Her degree was conferred in October 2015. Published for over a decade in *Who's Who of Australian Women*, *The Uncrowned King* is Jan's debut work.

Acknowledgements

I acknowledge the tremendous assistance I received during my candidature for my doctorate and the support and encouragement provided to me by the Faculty of Law, Humanities, and the Arts at the University of Wollongong, the University librarians and the University's Research Department.

My thanks especially go to my supervisors, Dr Siobhan McHugh and Professor Cathy Cole, who opened my mind to a world of new ideas. You are my heroes and I am deeply grateful for your inspiration, patience, competent direction and, above all else, belief in my capabilities.

We set sail on this journey in a tiny boat with a compass. We returned with boat intact towing an incredible booty.

Next I thank the truly wonderful people who helped and supported me through this pilgrimage.

Professor Gerry Turcotte, whose lectures inspired me and who encouraged me to write *The Uncrowned King*. Thank you so much for believing in me, Gerry. Your belief in me changed my life.

Janne (left) Professor Gerry Turcotte (right) on the occasion of Janne's graduation BA (Hons) First Class Notre Dame University Sydney 2010

Dr Deborah Pike, whose English lectures inspired me and reignited my passion for books.

Dr Peter Dean, who accepted me into Notre Dame University in 2006, reignited my love of history and taught me the value of working to uphold historical traditions.

Professor Hayden Ramsay and Dr Angus Brook, who instilled in me a love of philosophy.

Professor Edward J Blakely, who critiqued my thesis proposal and read and commented on my manuscript.

Robert Lynden-Bell, who read and re-read my manuscript and dissertation, an arduous and time-consuming task. I am deeply and profoundly grateful to Robert for his generosity of spirit, meticulous attention to detail and professional approach, and for his continuing support and belief in me.

Jane Marton read aloud some chapters of an early draft of my manuscript so that I could hear how it was reading.

Robyn Richardson provided insights into the evolution of cue sports after my father's death, shared stories of her life with snooker champion Eddie Charlton and provided an introduction to distinguished journalist Les Wheeler.

Les Wheeler kindly provided an oral interview, statement in support, cards and a photograph of my father shaking hands with British champion Joe Davis before the world professional snooker championship final in 1946 and shared beautiful memories of playing billiards with my father.

Army Officer Matthew Kitchen

Matthew pointed me to a photograph of my father presenting a trophy to the Armed Services during World War II and showed me the trophy that my father had donated in the war years for the armed services tournament.

Australian boxing champion Tommy Burns sent me a photo and a note on his friendship with my father.

Neil McCormack introduced me to the life story of Australia's first literary treasure Charlotte Atkinson.

Friends Keith McDonnell and Helen and Marty De Jong for many, many kindnesses extended to me when my mother went into full-time care and subsequently.

Friend Keith McDonnell for caring for my mother's beloved dog Rusky when she was moved into full-time care and for taking such good care of me during my visits to see my mother.

Friends Lee and Gayle Evans and Nancy and Bill Meehan for welcoming me into their community.

Friend Chloe Higgins for recommending the University of Wollongong when I lost my amazing supervisor, Professor Gerry Turcotte, to Canada.

Dr Georgine Clarsen from the University of Wollongong who told me to "Leave history to the historians. Go write your family story. I can't wait to read it."

I am also grateful to the librarians at the Mitchell, State and National libraries and librarians at the Universities of Wollongong, Sydney and Notre Dame.

I was greatly assisted by the staff at Office Works in Wollongong and Rutherglen.

The late Bryce Courtenay inspired me with his lecture on storytelling at the National Library in Canberra in 2011. His subsequent encouragement helped to foster my early storytelling instincts.

I thank the people at Sorrento in Smith Street, Wollongong, the community at St Francis Xavier Cathedral and the community at the Nan Tien Temple and Nan Tien Institute in Wollongong for their hospitality over my four-year stay in the Illawarra. I proudly remain a member of the ethics committee at the Nan Tien Institute.

I am especially grateful to the good people of Coffs Harbour who have welcomed me into their hearts, and to all of the people listed in the credits on my web site www.lindrum.com

To journalist Will Swanton who jumped swiftly to my father's defence; and To the great journalists, cameramen and documentary makers in Australia and across the globe who, over 109 years, recorded my family history:

THANK YOU. We are deeply, deeply grateful.

I struck gold! A brilliant wordsmith, my editor John Carrick gave *The Uncrowned King* that dose of oxygen a good book needs before it goes to final publication.

Finally, I would like to pay tribute to my grandmother, Clara (Violet) Lindrum. If my grandmother had aborted her baby, a great champion would never have been born and I would not have existed nor would Horace's children, grandchildren and great-grandchildren. That is a scary thought. We owe our grandmother, great-grandmother and great-great-grandmother a debt of gratitude. She is, unquestionably, the uncrowned queen mother

Did I find the myself along the way? I certainly found *The Uncrowned King* and I came to a better understanding of the little person who used to scoot around the pathways at *Hillcrest* on a tin horse.

I hope you enjoyed the story of *The Uncrowned King* as much as I enjoyed the privilege of writing the story for you; that privilege sustained me on my journey towards its publication.

Please let me know if you would like to be first in line for the "NEXT EPISODE" – www.lindrum